FRONT UP, RISE UP

www.transworldireland.ie

www.penguin.co.uk

Also by Gerry Thornley

Trevor Brennan: Heart and Soul
Ronan O'Gara: Unguarded
Pulling the Strings (with Peter Stringer)

FRONT UP, RISE UP

The Official Story of
Connacht Rugby

GERRY THORNLEY

TRANSWORLD IRELAND

TRANSWORLD IRELAND PUBLISHERS
28 Lower Leeson Street, Dublin 2, Ireland
www.transworldireland.ie

Transworld is part of the Penguin Random House group of companies
whose addresses can be found at global.penguinrandomhouse.com

Penguin
Random House
UK

First published in the UK and Ireland in 2016
by Transworld Ireland/Doubleday Ireland
an imprint of Transworld Publishers
Transworld Ireland paperback edition published 2017

A CIP catalogue record for this book
is available from the British Library.

ISBN
9781848272392

Typeset in 10/13pt Minion by Jouve (UK), Milton Keynes.
Printed and bound by Clays Ltd, Bungay, Suffolk.

Penguin Random House is committed to a sustainable
future for our business, our readers and our planet. This book
is made from Forest Stewardship Council® certified paper.

1 3 5 7 9 10 8 6 4 2

To Connacht
Its rugby
Its people

Contents

Prologue

Saturday, 21 May 2016 – Guinness Pro12 semi-final
71st minute: Connacht 16 Glasgow Warriors 11

Celebration time at the Sportsground. Entering the last ten minutes, leading 16–11, Connacht appear to have sealed their place in the Guinness Pro12 final. The inspired Bundee Aki now empties Duncan Weir in the tackle, Sean O'Brien pouncing on the loose ball to complete the turnover. John Cooney, Jake Heenan, Robbie Henshaw and Tiernan O'Halloran work the ball to Niyi Adeolokun, and their Nigerian-born winger finishes brilliantly for, it seems, his second try of the match, bursting through two tackles in the corner of the College Road Terrace. Those in the main stand salute him all the way back to his own half, and the Sportsground, heaving at the seams with a 7,800 capacity, goes wild. Connacht are 21–11 clear with a conversion to come.

Pat Lam thinks they are in the clear too and decides to take Aki off the field. On the previous Tuesday, Aki had hobbled from training on crutches to Adeolokun's car, with his left leg in a brace to protect a twisted knee, for a lift home. Aki couldn't train for the rest of the week, much less drive.

Standing in the coaches' box with nine minutes to go in the semi-final, Lam declares, 'Right, let's get Bundee off.' Aki is replaced by Peter Robb, their ex-Blackrock College 21-year-old academy player plucked from Leinster. He'd made his Connacht debut only the previous November on their infamous week-long European Challenge Cup trek to and from the freezing temperatures of Krasnoyarsk in Siberia.

But at this point, the Romanian-born Italian referee Marius Mitrea asks his television match official (TMO), Carlo Damasco, to check on the origins of the 'try'. After Aki had emptied Weir, Alan 'A. J.' MacGinty kicked the ball ahead, only for it to rebound off Aki in front of him. But for that, MacGinty would have had an easy touchdown under the posts himself. Technically, it was accidental offside. So Adeolokun's try was overruled.

'I thought, "Holy heck!" I couldn't believe the decision,' recalls Lam. 'It felt like a crucial moment, but then I said, "No, trust Peter. All right, Pete. It's time. Let's go! Just get in behind him [Robb], and he'll get the job done."'

But with his first touch, steaming on to MacGinty's pass, Robb knocks on! Worse follows. Within another two minutes, the Connacht replacement prop Rodney Ah You is sinbinned for a high one-armed tackle on the Scottish full-back Stuart Hogg. Now Connacht have to defend a one-score lead with 14 men.

It should never have come to this. In the 21st minute, Mitrea had gone to his TMO after Eoin McKeon had seemingly scored near the posts – following Tiernan O'Halloran's wonderful goosestep, break and pass. On that occasion, slow-motion replays had shown that Aki fumbled when pouncing on the original loose ball. Another try disallowed.

Connacht should have been out of sight. Instead, they faced the longest seven minutes and 47 seconds of their season.

Glasgow begin their slow, remorseless march downfield. Initially, they attack on the blindside from a line-out, but John Cooney tackles Glasgow's Fijian replacement Taqele Naiyaravoro into touch. The cheers soon subside when Mitrea penalizes Tom McCartney and Connacht for a delayed throw-in. Glasgow tap the penalty and go from inside their half. Robbie Henshaw pushes up and, helped by Robb, nails Weir. 'Great read!' exclaims Lam. But Cooney then fumbles an attempted intercept. Scrum to Glasgow on their own 10-metre line.

Connacht are forced to bring on replacement prop J. P. Cooney in the absence of Ah You, and sacrifice their Kiwi flanker Jake Heenan. Seventy-four minutes, 25 seconds. Connacht have five and a half minutes to defend.

Glasgow move the ball back and forth and straight for 17 interminable phases, probing Connacht's 14-man defence across the pitch. Their Fijian try-scorer and danger-man Leone Nakarawa towers above his Connacht tacklers, offloading one-handed as if the ball were a miniature toy.

But Connacht keep making their tackles – John Cooney, Sean O'Brien, MacGinty, Andrew Browne, Robb, Dave Heffernan, Browne again, Adeolokun, Cooney again, Robb again, Browne again, Cooney again, Aly Muldowney, O'Brien again, MacGinty again, Matt Healy, Browne again, J. P. Cooney this time, John Muldoon, O'Brien and J. P. Cooney in tandem, Heffernan again on Nakarawa, and Robb again. When the shimmying Hogg, another danger-man, shows and goes, McCartney slows him down with one hand and Henshaw stops him. Glasgow are the current champions, but they've been rocked by losing to Connacht here two weeks previously, and by Connacht's improved performance today. Their grasp on their title has loosened, and they've become a little frantic. The 10-12-13 axis of MacGinty, Robb and Henshaw never wobbles. Everyone keeps communicating. There's no hint of a dog leg or a chink of light in Connacht's green line. In Robb they trust.

'He brought energy, and he bought into the system,' says Lam. 'We want all the boys who come on to maintain that system. He made some good D [defence], some good tackles. He got the shape going, like Bundee does.'

John Cooney tracks Grayson Hart's snipe and offload to Mark Bennett, tackles the Scottish centre and forces a knock-on. From the ruck, Cooney box-kicks, the ball just eluding the chasing Henshaw to bounce wickedly over the touchline. The crowd takes a deep breath. Line-out to Glasgow 30 metres from their line. Some of the crowd attempt 'The Fields Of Athenry' one more time. But most are too busy biting their knuckles or just roaring their encouragement to join in. The clock hits 78 minutes.

Muldowney hauls down Ryan Wilson at the line-out, O'Brien makes another tackle and when Glasgow go wide to their right, Healy comes in off his wing to read Hogg's delayed pass and clatters Bennett, forcing another spillage.

'Knock-on white. Knock-on white,' Nigel Owens informs Mitrea from the touchline. Connacht scrum. Now the crowd can belt out 'The Fields'.

After a re-set scrum, the clock passes 79 minutes. Muldoon picks up at the base and, with 35 seconds remaining, is tackled, Henshaw rushing in to ensure there's no turnover. Glasgow players counter-ruck desperately. John Cooney excavates the ball and passes to O'Brien. One pass will do. Nothing fancy required. Browne rucks over him to secure possession, helped by O'Halloran and J. P. Cooney.

As if pulled by a magnet, the game's final throes have even been brought towards the Clan Terrace, which joyously gives the countdown: 'Five. Four. Three. Two. One!'

Cooney passes to MacGinty, who hoofs the ball over the Clan Terrace, clearing the roof with plenty to spare. Mitrea's full-time whistle signals the end. Muldoon, sitting on the turf at the end of his 213th League match, seems in shock. He's lifted to his feet and embraced by Dave Heffernan, and then the captain sets about hugging every teammate.

Heenan runs on to the pitch to make a dancing and screaming foursome with the back three – O'Halloran, Adeolokun and Healy. Some of the crowd begin to invade the pitch as the two teams shake hands. Weir, Glasgow's replacement out-half, is in tears. He's not the only one.

Having finished second in the 22-game campaign to earn a home semi-final, Connacht will be in the 2016 Guinness Pro12 final against Leinster a week later at Murrayfield.

Connacht's finishing positions in the League for the previous 11 seasons had been somewhat different.

Tenth of 11.

Tenth of 11.

Tenth of 11.

Tenth of 10.
Tenth of 10.
Tenth of 10.
Ninth of 12.
Eighth of 12.
Eighth of 12.
Tenth of 12.
Seventh of 12.

Despite a gradual upward curve, it's not exactly the stuff of finalists, much less champions. But here they were – the 50/1 outsiders to win the League at the start of the season – in the final. They had defied expectations, including their own at the outset, by finishing second. They'd edged out Glasgow from the top two a fortnight beforehand by dint of beating them 14–7 at a rainswept Sportsground. Although wins such as this in the Wild Wild West were generally treated as trademark one-off Connacht ambushes, their victory had earned them a home semi-final against Gregor Townsend's well-oiled, offloading champions.

Within the camp, Connacht had decided that the Glasgow game of a fortnight previously would make or break their campaign, according to captain John Muldoon: 'We had treated that last home game against Glasgow as a quarter-final. We didn't say it publicly, or as a group, but in one-on-one conversations we agreed that you don't lose at home to Glasgow and then beat them in an away semi-final. No one had won an away semi-final. Ever. So if we beat Glasgow at home, then we had a semi-final at home. And getting Glasgow to the Sportsground for the semi-finals was huge for us. I don't think we'd have reached the final otherwise.'

A fortnight before, Connacht had duly won a torrid, rain-sodden affair, which had hinged on the sending-off of the Glasgow prop Sila Puafisi, with the score at 7–7, after he floored Kieran Marmion with his head. That left Glasgow reduced to 14 men for the final half hour.

Muldoon recounts, 'They probably thought, "We got a man sent-off and they only just beat us." But we chucked away so many tries that day. I think that was a big learning curve for us. We became a little afraid to play because of the pressure that came with them being down a man. Everyone in the ground expected us to win from that point on.

'When we watched the video on the Monday morning, everyone was thinking, "Oh, what was I doing there? Why didn't I pass that? Why didn't I . . . ?" So it was probably a good experience for us – to learn how to play under pressure and not be afraid. There were a few big days in the season but none bigger than beating Glasgow at home in that "quarter-final".'

The semi-final came with headaches, chief amongst them the scarcity of tickets, even for the players. Muldoon himself was entitled to only two match-day tickets, with the option to buy two more, the same as any other player. Hence, despite demand now way exceeding supply, even with an enhanced 7,800 capacity, Muldoon couldn't hope to cope with the requests.

'I'm not a huge fan of autobiographies, but you read one like Roy Keane's and he said he doesn't even remember the FA Cup final because all he was worried about was his family not having tickets. I remember him writing: "I gave my brother five grand just to get everyone into the game." For the Glasgow semi-final, Jaysus, trying to get tickets and organize stuff was unlike anything I've ever known. The fans had been queuing from 8.30 a.m. on the Monday. I was inundated with requests, so I just texted a couple of the groups that I'm on and said: "Don't even bother asking me, because this is mental."'

Despite securing a home semi-final, and although no team had ever lost a semi-final at home, Connacht were still 6/1 outsiders behind Leinster, Glasgow and Ulster going into the knockout stages. Underdogs as ever.

'A lot of people didn't expect us to beat Glasgow a second time,' says Ronan Loughney, a ten-season Connacht veteran from Galway. 'We'd beaten them in wet weather, but we'd done that in the past. Even that week I received loads of texts saying: "Regardless of what happens on Saturday, you've done us proud." It was kind of like: "That's grand. Well done."'

Connacht should actually have won the semi-final more comfortably. For his part, Loughney lasted 66 minutes. 'The semi-final was a bruising game,' he recalls. 'The ground was hard, and it was great to be able to play our fast-paced game, but I cramped up pretty badly. Everybody was wrecked after it. The pitch was mobbed as soon as the whistle went, and we didn't get a chance to clap the Glasgow players off. We came back to the dressing-room in dribs and drabs.'

When they'd all eventually made it back through the throngs, Lam, as is the custom, spoke first. 'Well done. We're extremely proud of you,' he began, as ever starting on a positive note. 'We beat the defending champions two weeks ago, and don't underestimate what we've just done by beating them back-to-back. That's another lesson about preparing for international rugby – when you've got to play a second test and do the job again.'

Then, as usual, he underlined his mantra about the 'process'. 'We come back on Monday. It's going to be a big week. There are going to be a lot of distractions, but we make sure we go through our process. What did we do well? What could we do better? We'll go through the review, but everyone should go through their own personal review. Tick the boxes off. Winning starts on Monday.'

Muldoon then spoke. 'Lads, it's great winning a semi-final, but if we don't win the final it will be forgotten fairly quickly. If we really do want to make history, it's about winning it now. Is anybody afraid of going over and playing Leinster? We should be confident of playing them. We've nothing to be afraid of.'

Another post-match custom is to sing 'The Fields Of Athenry'. If they win! 'We earn the right to sing "The Fields Of Athenry",' according to Lam, and this was the 14th time in 15 home matches this season that Connacht had earned that right.

They sang and spirits were high. Earlier that season, Lam had asked Aki, his fellow Aucklander of Samoan parentage, to close all the training sessions with a Samoan chant, and towards the end of the campaign it became more of a post-match ritual as well.

'*Mili, Mili, Mili*,' Aki begins, rubbing his hands together, which is the signal for everyone else to rub their hands together simultaneously.

According to Lam: 'It's a Samoan tradition. If he then says "*Pati*", it's a way of clapping, and if he says "*Po*", it's another way of clapping. If he puts a Samoan number on it, like "*Lua Pati*", that's two claps. Or "*Lua Po*", it's a different two claps. The same with "*Pati, Pati, Po.*" He's speaking in Samoan, and the boys respond to his chant by clapping in rhythm with him.

'He'll then throw in an animal call. If he says "Tiger", the boys will roar. If he says "Cow", they go "Moo". He might want to have a laugh and say "Pussycat", and the boys will all go "Miaow". Or he might say "Snake", and everyone hisses. Then he'll call for a clap again. You just listen to him and follow.'

'I don't have a clue what's going on half the time,' admits Loughney, 'but we were all laughing away anyway, because it usually means we've won.'

This was almost an hour after the whistle. Lam, Muldoon and selected players left for media duties. Lam then returned to the coaches' room for a meeting with his assistants. At the end of it, he was asked, 'What's the schedule?'

'Give me five minutes.'

So Lam made the short walk from the home dressing-room to his office. He opened his computer, logged in and looked over the file from the semi-final week.

'The only difference for the final was the kick-off time, 5.30 instead of 6.30, and the venue, Edinburgh instead of Galway. I asked Tim Allnutt, our manager, "Tim, what's our flight? When are we going?" I put in the travel arrangements and had a look through the whole week. Sorted. Nothing else to change. The media time on Tuesday was the same.'

Louise Creedon, the Connacht press officer, knocked on Lam's door to tell him, 'There's a lot of requests and stuff that need to be looked at.'

Lam said, 'No. Same routine as before. Nothing extra. Just the normal exceptions for one-on-one interviews. Nothing changes.'

Lam recalls, 'I sent the group email of the schedule to everybody within ten minutes of leaving the dressing-room.'

After the bigger home games, Lam and Allnutt usually divvy up two post-match gatherings of supporters – either in the Connacht Hotel on the Old Dublin Road, or in the marquee in the Sportsground. Lam went to the former and Allnutt to the latter.

Loughney also went to the marquee to meet his fiancée Finn, whom he was to marry in exactly two weeks' time, the Saturday after the Pro12 final. His future father- and mother-in-law, Fergus and Jackie Dillon, were also there, as were Peter and Rose Ott, neighbours and best friends of Loughney's parents, of whom he says, 'They're hardcore Connacht.'

His sister Sheena, home from London, was also there. Earlier on that morning of the semi-final, Loughney had attended the christening of his brother's little girl, Isla, before dashing off to the Sportsground.

'They'd been trying to pick a date,' recalls Loughney, 'but I couldn't name one in advance. The week of the final didn't suit our sister, so my brother said, "I'll have to book the week of the semi-final and hopefully you can make it." So I made the christening. It was a strange one. Everybody was asking me about the game. I have a routine on match-day, and Finn usually heads off and lets me do my own thing. I don't like veering from it but maybe it was no harm, as I was more nervous about that semi-final than any game I'd played before. So I went, took a few photos and headed to the Sportsground.

'The priest had asked me if I knew the dates of my christening or my baptism. Of course I didn't. No one knows them. But I'll always remember Isla's christening.'

Meanwhile, Lam had left the Sportsground and stopped off at the Connacht Hotel for some food before driving home to review the semi-final. This review normally keeps him up until 1 a.m. or 2 a.m., and this time was no different. But Sunday is a day off. Lam and his wife Stephanie have five children, all but one of whom live in Galway.

'Sunday is family time, a meal at home and just time together, and maybe some trampolining with the little one [Bethany] and her friends. It's cool, because I can hang out with the older ones, and maybe have a drink in the pub.'

That said, Lam did put aside an hour for Connacht. 'I like to assemble all my footage and movies and planning for the week so that I'm ready for our first meeting at 8 a.m.'

Winning starts on Monday.

1

'How Many Balls
Do You Have?'

Thursday, 29 August 1996

Billy Glynn picked up his phone at about 5.30 p.m. in Galway and rang Warren Gatland at his home in Hamilton, New Zealand, where it was about 4.30 a.m.

'Hello, Warren, it's Billy Glynn here.'

Gatland and Glynn had come to know each other well during Gatland's four years as player-coach at Glynn's club, Galwegians, from 1989 to '93. Gatland immediately presumed it must be bad news, perhaps concerning one of his friends from that time in Galway.

After exchanging pleasantries, Glynn cut to the chase.

'Our coach at Connacht has resigned. I'm just ringing you to see if you'd be interested in coaching us?'

Gatland thought about it for a few seconds. 'Yeah, I would be interested,' he said. 'When do you need to know?'

'Yesterday,' said Glynn. 'The squad are travelling to Sweden for pre-season tomorrow.'

'Damn. OK, I have to speak to Trudi and the school principal,' said Gatland, in reference to his PE teaching job at St Paul's Collegiate School in Hamilton. 'Ring me back tonight my time.'

He told his wife, Trudi, about the phone call from Glynn. She said, 'Just go. You might never get an opportunity like this again.'

Gatland then spoke to his school principal, Steve Cole, son-in-law of the former All Black John Graham.

He told Cole, 'I've got the chance to do some coaching in Ireland for 12 weeks.'

'Go for it,' said Cole.

Gatland flew from Auckland the next day, arriving in Stockholm on the Monday morning to meet the players, who were based not far from the Swedish capital.

Gatland, then 32, was coaching a club side, Taupiri, and had been assistant coach of Thames Valley for a couple of years. 'I'd already been player-coaching at that stage,' he recalls. 'I had retired from playing two years before. I just thought it was a great opportunity. There were just three Interpros and the European Challenge Cup left, so it was only for three months. And I'd never been to Sweden!'

Eddie O'Sullivan had been due to coach Connacht again in 1996–97, the second season of professionalism. He had done so since 1993, in succession to George Hook, but earlier on that fateful Thursday, 29 August, he had called in to see Glynn, then the chairman of selectors and de facto team manager at Connacht, at his offices, W. B. Glynn and Co. solicitors in Augustine Court in Galway.

'Eddie had been on a five-year sabbatical from teaching, which was coming to an end that September. He had worked as a development officer with the IRFU [Irish Rugby Football Union] and then coached Connacht as well, and in the summer of 1996 had been in protracted negotiations with the IRFU, conducted by Bobby Deacy as the honorary treasurer of the union. We had nothing whatsoever to do with those negotiations. Eddie was being offered only a one-year contract and needed more security if he was to give up his job as a teacher. In fairness to Eddie, it was perfectly understandable.

'At 11.30, he called into my offices and said, "Billy, I have resigned as Connacht coach." He explained that he hadn't reached a satisfactory conclusion to his negotiations with the union. I asked if there was anything I could do to resolve the matter, and he said no.

'It was a short conversation,' recalls Glynn. With the squad due to fly out to Stockholm the next morning, Glynn was at a loss to think of a replacement as head coach at such short notice. He walked down St Augustine Street to the Scottish Provident Insurance Company offices and called in to Joe Healy, a former Galwegians and Connacht number 8 and lock who was then coaching the Connemara All Blacks.

'I've no coach of Connacht, and the squad are off to Stockholm tomorrow. The union couldn't agree terms with Eddie.'

'Wow!' exclaimed Healy.

Looking over the upper rim of his specs at Healy, Glynn said, 'I don't suppose you'd do it?'

Looking back, Healy laughs and says, 'I think he was just being polite.'

Glynn added, 'Well, what am I going to do?'

After giving it some thought, Healy said, 'I know of a Kiwi, whom you also know, and who might be interested,' in reference to Gatland, his teammate and coach at Galwegians from 1989 to 1993, and with whom he had become good friends.

'Jeeze,' said Glynn. 'I never thought of him. Yes, of course. Do you have a number for him?'

'Yeah, I have his number at home. I'll bring it in after lunch.'

After phoning Gatland, that evening Glynn drove to the Skylon Hotel in Dublin, where the Connacht squad had assembled before their flight to Stockholm the next morning. He informed the players that O'Sullivan had resigned.

O'Sullivan had requested the opportunity to address the players and explain his decision, which he did and wished them well. Glynn then informed the players that he was in negotiations with a replacement and that there was a reasonable chance this coach would accept the position.

'All I can say is you will be thrilled when you hear his name,' recalls Glynn. 'But I won't announce it until I get final confirmation from him, and I'll tell you at 10 a.m. in Dublin airport tomorrow. Some of you know him very well.' He left it at that, and the next morning rang Gatland again in New Zealand.

'Yes, I'll come,' said Gatland.

'OK, you better pack your bags and get to Stockholm.'

'Fine, I will.'

The night before, Glynn had also telephoned the Connacht treasurer, Eamonn Feely, to agree a figure for Gatland's salary, which Gatland accepted, and to arrange his flights from New Zealand to Stockholm.

Seven years previously, Gatland had been one of the All Blacks hookers in their squad which toured Wales and Ireland in 1989, and played one of his 17 uncapped representative matches for New Zealand in their 40–6 win over Connacht at the Sportsground that November. It had been his misfortune to understudy the indestructible Sean Fitzpatrick in the days before tactical replacements, and thus he never won a test cap for the All Blacks.

What happened next would have repercussions to this day and beyond, for the events that followed changed Gatland's life and perhaps rugby in Galwegians, Connacht, Ireland, Wasps and Wales, where he would go on to coach.

Mickey Heaslip, and a few other Galwegians stalwarts, had been chatting in the clubhouse bar one day with the club treasurer, Pat Holland, after a home defeat to Longford. Galwegians were at a low ebb, so bad that Holland said to Heaslip, 'We have to do something about this.'

Holland, an accountant, had recently returned from working in New Zealand and suggested, 'We need a new coach. Why don't we try and get one of the All Blacks to stay back as our player-coach?' They concluded that a prop who could combine the roles of player and coach would be the best fit.

After the All Blacks beat Connacht at the Sportsground on Tuesday, 14 November, their squad travelled to Dublin for the test against Ireland at Lansdowne Road the following Saturday. Accounts of what happened next vary, but according to Holland, 'Mickey, who was like the "patron saint" of Galwegians for 40 years, took it upon himself to travel to Dublin.' He had bumped into their loose-head prop Steve McDowell and introduced himself some time before, and now he called into the Berkeley Court Hotel to find McDowell and ask him if he was interested in being the Galwegians' player-coach.

McDowell declined the offer but suggested Gatland. The next day Heaslip and the Galwegians captain Enda Guerin met Gatland in the All Blacks' team hotel. They confirmed they were looking for a prop to become their player-coach and asked him if he could play at prop. 'I said, "Yeah, I can do that", although I'd never played prop in my life,' Gatland recalls.

He agreed to become their player-coach after the tour concluded against the Barbarians in London the following Saturday. On Sunday, 26 November, as is customary, Gatland and one or two other players who were staying on in Europe rather than returning with the rest of the squad to New Zealand had to perform the haka as a parting gesture.

The next day, Gatland took a train to Luton, from where he flew to Waterford for a connecting Aer Arann flight to Galway airport, where he was met by Shane O'Mahony, the Galwegians club president from the previous year and then treasurer of the Connacht Branch.

At the age of 26, it was Gatland's first player-coach role.

They went for a coffee in Heaslip's bar, and Gatland's first question to O'Mahony was, 'How many players do you have at training?'

Putting together the firsts, seconds and thirds, O'Mahony estimated around 30 on a good night.

'How many balls do you have?'

'About five,' guessed O'Mahony, which might even have been stretching the truth.

'I need 15,' said Gatland. In other words, one ball for every two players. In the event, over 30 turned up at his first session. There had only been six the previous week.

With that, team manager Peter Crowley was sent shopping in the Great Outdoors and Staunton's, to buy up as many balls as he could find.

O'Mahony recalls Gatland introducing high-speed skills drills, in which some were more adept than others. Galwegians won their first 11 games under his watch.

'Gatty turned it around,' says Healy. 'He revolutionized the place. He brought a bag of balls where before we were looking around for one, and he insisted that everyone train with their own rugby ball so as to become more comfortable in their handling skills. And he wasn't such a disciplinarian that we weren't able to have a few pints and a bit of craic after games. He was one of the lads very quickly, which was great.'

In 1990–91, Galwegians missed out on qualifying for the second division of the inaugural All-Ireland League (AIL) in the round-robin play-offs between the four provincial league winners. This happened again in 1991–92, but they won promotion to the AIL a year later. Gatland played and coached for another season, 1992–93, then returned to New Zealand and his career as a PE teacher while also playing one more year for Waikato prior to retiring.

In 1996, he arrived in Stockholm having answered Glynn's SOS to replace O'Sullivan.

'At the time, I didn't know it was Eddie I was replacing,' recalls Gatland. Helpfully, he did know some of the Connacht players from his time at Galwegians, and had played against Michael Cosgrave, his assistant coach, in the All Blacks' game against Connacht in 1989, although didn't know him. On that first Monday evening, Gatland and Cosgrave joined the Connacht committee members who had organized a boat cruise through Stockholm, and they began getting to know each other.

Connacht trained for almost two weeks in Stockholm and had a couple of practice matches against the Swedish national side and a regional team. According to Gatland, 'The weather was lovely and probably the most memorable thing was that boat cruise through the city. I also remember how incredibly expensive it was.

'I detected a fair bit of apprehension about me coming in as their new coach. Cozzie [Cosgrave] and I didn't really know each other, but we became great mates. We had some good laughs. Even though the game had gone professional, no one in the squad at the time was pro-fessional. Most of the players had taken time off work to go on pre-season. In those days, we trained on Tuesday and Thursday nights in Athlone, because seven or eight of the guys were coming from Dublin, and then met up on Friday night in Galway for a team run, played on the Saturday and then dispersed until the Tuesday.'

When Gatland arrived, Connacht were in their customary place: at the bottom of the Irish Interprovincial heap. Since the advent of the Interprovincial Championship, Connacht had only managed to share the title on three occasions in 1956, '57 and '65. There had been a revival under Hook and O'Sullivan, but in the inaugural season of professionalism, 1995–96, they had lost to Ulster (27–9), Leinster (41–9), Munster (46–11) and the Exiles (28–22), before beating the touring Fijians (27–5).

The 1995–96 season also marked the inaugural European Cup, featuring teams from France, Italy, Wales and Romania, along with three from Ireland. Needless to say, those three were Leinster, Munster and Ulster, with Connacht not invited to participate. The following season, Gatland's first, saw the advent of a secondary European competition, the European Challenge Cup, in which Connacht competed, while the big three again took part in what was now called the Heineken Cup.

Prior to the European competitions, the Interpros were run off over three weeks in September and October, and Connacht were immediately much more competitive. They lost 45–28 to Munster in Temple Hill in Cork, and by 32–27 to Ulster in Ravenhill, before maintaining their biennial habit of scalping Leinster at the Sportsground, 22–13.

'I knew that Leinster weren't up for it when I saw Neil Francis go off injured in the first half,' recalls Gatland of a typically wild, wet day in the west, the wind whipping in off the Atlantic to make the goalposts slant.

'We were pretty competitive. For me, it was about putting some structures in place for guys who hadn't really had much coaching before. We changed the way we defended and brought in that aggressive blitz defence. In those days, there was no real video analysis. You were catching teams cold, and they weren't expecting you to do those things. I remember we had a pretty good scrum, and we tried to play to our strengths. We weren't the most athletic team, but we were pretty physical and got in people's faces.

'The thing I liked about the Connacht boys was that everybody knew we were up against it, but, man, when they put that jersey on, they gave everything for it. We adopted the "To Hell or to Connacht" slogan then [in reference to the infamous quote by Oliver Cromwell], and we had a really good balance. We worked hard, trained hard and then enjoyed ourselves.

'We had players coming out of club rugby playing against teams with internationals, and that's when we struggled a little bit – due to the greater quality of players we were up against.'

In theory, the Interpros were also the qualifying mechanism for the following season's Heineken Cup; that is, the top three in the table would qualify. Connacht finished level with Leinster and Ulster on a win apiece but ended up in last place due to a points difference of -13 compared to Ulster's -8 and Leinster's -4.

In the first Challenge Cup, Connacht began their campaign with a 34–12 win over Petrarca of Italy at the Sportsground, before losing 26–9 away to Dunvant in Wales the following Wednesday. 'That night in Dunvant was a terrible night in Wales,' recalls Gatland. 'We went there fancying our chances, but everything just stuck for them. We didn't play well, but they were amazing that night and scored a couple of incredible tries.'

Three days later, Connacht were beaten 31–11 at home by a Northampton side laden with five prospective Lions for the 1997 tour to South Africa: Tim Rodber, Matt Dawson, Gregor Townsend, Nick Beal and Paul Grayson. 'Against a team of that quality, we just struggled, really.'

Connacht then lost 44–10 away to Toulon. 'Toulon were just too big and physical for us,' said Gatland, of a game that was stopped for over ten minutes due to a scary injury for Mick Devine.

Gatland was a popular coach amongst the players, according to Cosgrave. 'Not even the subs could find a bad word to say about him. He was innovative but also very inclusive, and was open to ideas from myself or the players. There was plenty of card-playing in those seasons, and Gatty was part of it. He didn't treat the players like kids. But once or twice he cracked the whip, and after everybody went out on the night of that Toulon game, the following morning at 9 a.m. he called a training session and had all the players running up a big hill next to our hotel.'

A week later, they beat Orrell 30–18 at home and thus finished fourth in their pool of six. 'Orrell were struggling at the time and we played pretty well that day, and we came away from that season thinking we'd done all right,' says Gatland. 'We'd beaten Leinster and were competitive in Europe, winning two out of five. We didn't disgrace ourselves and had done pretty well.'

Connacht probably saved their best until last, extending Australia to a 37–20 win at the Sportsground, one of 12 wins out of 12 by the Wallabies on their tour of Italy, Scotland, Ireland and Wales. They went on to beat Ulster (39–26), Ireland (22–12) and Munster (55–19).

Gatland slipped into the crowd to watch the Wallabies train at Corinthian Park. 'A couple of the players recognized me, and I got kicked out of the training session.

'It was Stephen Larkham's first game for Australia,' adds Gatland. 'He played 10 in the first half and he was so poor they moved him to full-back in the second half.'

But with that, Connacht's season was over in mid November. Gatland hung around until Christmas before returning to New Zealand to play with Waikato and teach. Before he left, he was interviewed by the then IRFU Director of Rugby, Ray Southam, and offered a full-time role as Connacht head coach for the next season.

For Gatland and Trudi, the timing was right. 'Our kids were really young. My daughter, Gabby, was three and my son, Bryn, was just learning to talk. They both developed a really strong Irish accent. Gabby did Irish dancing and they both started school in Ireland.'

2

Daring to Believe

In Gatland's second season, 1997–98, Connacht's pre-season camp was held in the Oratory School in Reading, a red-brick, olde worlde, fee-paying school founded by Cardinal John Henry Newman in 1859 as a Catholic alternative to Eton College.

Aside from its sumptuous, tree-lined rugby pitches, the Oratory is noted for its rowing on the nearby Thames and for being one of only three schools in England with 'real tennis' courts. Connacht were moving up in the world, and Brian Ashton, then coach of Ireland, attended a couple of their training sessions.

'The boys trained very hard, and we put a lot of effort into our fitness. At the time, we still didn't have any full-time professionals. In those days, most guys considered their jobs as pensionable for life. People generally stayed in the same job for their whole working life. That's the way it was in Ireland. When I first arrived in Galway, unemployment was 20-odd per cent and interest rates on houses were 20-odd per cent.'

Gatland also brought over lock Mark McConnell and flanker Junior Charlie from Taupiri. 'At that stage, we were allowed to bring in two overseas players, and I thought they'd bring a Kiwi mentality and attitude, that a couple of forwards would be good for us. And they were great.'

McConnell masterminded an exceptional line-out, while for his part Charlie became a totemic figure with his big carries and big hits.

Gatland recalls an interview before the season started with the Galway-based, New Zealand-born *Galway Advertiser* rugby writer Linley MacKenzie. As well as the three Interpros, only one of which was at home, their six pool games in the Challenge Cup were against Northampton, again, and two top-flight French championship sides, Bordeaux-Bègles and Nice.

'Given your draw in Europe, what games are you targeting to win?' she asked him.

'I can't tell you which game we're going to win, but I promise you we will win a game.'

'Which one is that going to be?' she asked.

'I don't know yet,' said Gatland. 'But we will win a game.'

True to his word, despite 29–9 and 23–6 defeats at home to Munster and away to Leinster, in between Connacht beat Ulster 27–12 at the Sportsground. To put this in perspective, it was Connacht's first win over Ulster since 1983, which had been their sole win over the northern province since 1964.

'I said to Gatty, "Why not throw on Merv [Murphy]?"' remembers Cosgrave. 'Merv worked a dummy and broke clean through for the try, which sealed it.'

'We played really well that day and matched them up front,' says Gatland. 'And if you're going to compete in the Irish Interpros, you have to match them up front.'

But they were again edged out of third place in the Interpro table on points difference to Ulster. The word on the Connacht grapevine was that had they finished above any of their provincial rivals, the IRFU would have shifted the goalposts to maintain the status quo in the Heineken Cup. But the rumour was never put to the test.

'That's why we desperately wanted to finish above them,' says Gatland, 'just to see what would have happened. At that time, we were probably catching sides a little bit cold. They weren't expecting Connacht to be up to much, and yet it was tough coming to the Sportsground with the dog track and howling gales. We kind of made the most of that and tried to make it as difficult as we possibly could for anyone coming there.'

Connacht's first game in the Challenge Cup was at home to Northampton, who had beaten them 31–11 in the Sportsground eleven months previously. The game had originally been scheduled for Saturday, 6 September, but this was also the day of Princess Diana's funeral in Westminster Abbey, and as a mark of respect no English team played in either of the European competitions that day.

Most postponed games were rearranged for the Sunday, but Northampton travelled to Galway on the Tuesday. On that opening weekend, Leinster had lost 34–25 at home to Toulouse, Munster had lost 48–40 away to Harlequins, and Ulster had been beaten 18–12 at home by Glasgow.

Ian McGeechan left out several of his five-strong Lions' contingent who had been part of the series-winning tour to South Africa the previous summer and only brought on Nick Beal and Gregor Townsend in the second half. Even so, few held out much hope of Connacht providing Ireland's first win in Europe that season. But on a glorious, sun-drenched day at the Sportsground in front of a small Tuesday-afternoon crowd, Connacht beat Northampton 43–13.

'It was a beautiful day, and we were just on fire; they just didn't know how to handle it,' says Gatland. 'It was pretty special.'

Elwood created the first try for the Australian centre of Irish extraction, Pat Duignan, who had arrived at the start of the season, and Shane McEntee added the second as Connacht raced into a 20–0 lead by the 28th minute. Late breakaway tries by full-back Willie Ruane, who had been plucked from Ballina, and Nigel Carolan completed the rout.

Of Ruane, Gatland says, 'He was good, a big strong runner, a good full-back with a good boot on him. Just a really, really solid rugby player.' While of Carolan, he comments, 'The thing with Nigel is that you always got 100 per cent out of him. He gave you everything he had. He lacked that out-and-out pace of an international winger, but he worked hard and he was a good team man.'

Elwood, then 29, kicked 18 points that day in what was a vintage season for him. 'You probably couldn't get a more passionate rugby player,' says Gatland. 'Sometimes that was to his detriment. He was so focused on performing well, and emotionally that would get to him occasionally. He was a very proud Connacht man, and moving to Lansdowne from Galwegians had been good for his rugby, to give him the confidence and self-belief that he was good enough at that level.'

Elwood and Mervyn Murphy, now a video analyst with the Irish team, were effective in employing Gatland's more aggressive defence. 'Merv won't mind me saying he was a little bit limited as a rugby player. He had a bit of a dummy, but jeepers he could get up in defence. He was ideal for that defensive system.'

As for Conor McGuinness, who was to make his Irish debut against the All Blacks in November of that season and would become first-choice Irish scrum-half for two seasons, Gatland says, 'He was a youngster who came to us from St Mary's and was a little bit under-rated as a 9. We never really got to see the best of him, but he was very quick, and technically he was really good.'

The team was captained by flanker Rory Rogers. 'He came down from the North and was an antique dealer, a bit of a wheeler and dealer,' says Gatland. 'What I liked about him was that he was a little bit like a southern hemisphere 7 – really good on the ball.

'So we had a pretty good balance of a strong set-piece pack, a good 9 and 10, players working really hard, and we took our opportunities. That was the key.'

When Townsend's restart at 33–3 failed to go ten metres, a wag in the sparsely populated terracing across from the main stand shouted, 'Hey, Gregor, didn't I see you on the TV this summer?' It was quite a comedown for Townsend, and the laughter could be heard on both sides of the ground.

There had been an IRFU committee meeting scheduled for the afternoon of the Northampton game, so none of the committee members were in attendance, and after the game the call came from Lansdowne Road to the main landline in the Sportsground asking for the result.

'It was 43–13.'

'That's not too bad. Sounds like Connacht put up a good fight?'

'Eh, actually it was 43–13 to Connacht.'

'Are you sure it wasn't the other way around?'

'No. Connacht won 43–13.'

'Oh!'

Next up were back-to-back games away to Nice the following Sunday and Bordeaux-Bègles six days later, and, as it was cheaper than making two treks, Connacht opted for a week-long stay in the south of France. 'It was brilliant, because it meant we were in camp for a week,' says Gatland.

However, they lost to Nice 20–16 due to a late penalty try for the home side, awarded by English referee John Pearson. According to Gatland, 'It was an unbelievable penalty try. In my opinion, it was probably one of the worst decisions I've ever seen. The referee penalized us about three times inside our own 22, and then he just ran under the posts and gave them a penalty try. We had been leading 16–13, and I remember they [Nice] were embarrassed by it. They were even more confused than we were.

'And he had penalized us earlier when we had kicked the ball out for our forwards being in front of the kicker. I said to him, "The ball was out. Once the ball is dead, you can do whatever you like." But he penalized us after Eric had kicked the ball out. And then there was the penalty try.'

Six days later, Elwood kicked five penalties as Connacht won 15–9 in Bègles to become the first Irish side to win on French soil. 'We really muscled up in a tight game, and we just strangled them,' says Gatland. 'There was a big crowd, and it was a pretty emotional day for us. We were so disappointed by the Nice result, so after beating Bordeaux-Bègles we thought, "We've got a chance here." From that point on, we dared to believe.'

Back at the Sportsground on the following Saturday, Connacht extracted revenge over Nice 28–25, Elwood augmenting tries by Murphy and Graham Heaslip, older brother of Jamie, with six penalties. Moving into October, a week later they beat Bordeaux-Bègles 22–15 at home, with Elwood kicking five penalties and converting a try by Nicky Barry. Barry was a once-capped Irish out-half now playing on the wing and also known as 'The Prince'.

'I had a lot of time for Nicky,' says Gatland. 'He did a great job for us and was such a good team man. He believed in his own ability and that was good for the other players. He was still pretty quick and had some great skills.'

Connacht were not a team of all the talents but made the most of what they had, with some well-honed scoring manoeuvres. Most famously, there was the 13-man line-out, whereby the forwards lined up to the front to set up a maul, and the entire back division bar the scrum-half joined in to forge an often unstoppable drive.

That one had been introduced in the first season against Australia. 'We scored off it, and they were all bitching and moaning, complaining it was illegal,' remembers Gatland. 'But the referee said, "No, no, that's fine." I was always looking at the rules and seeing how you could use them to your best advantage and catch teams unaware. At that stage, you could have a 13-man scrum as well if you wanted to. There was no limit to the number an attacking team could put in the line-out. As a defending team, you couldn't have more than the opposition.

'We called it "psycho", on the basis that you had to be crazy to do it,' says Gatland.

When he first suggested it at a training session in Athlone, many of the players looked at him as if he were indeed insane, one of them asking, 'What happens if we lose it?'

Gatland answered, 'Well, that would be fun, wouldn't it? That would be even more exciting than if we scored from it.'

But that never happened, and the move was well in credit over Gatland's two seasons.

There was also the 'scoop ball', designed to maximize the pace of McGuinness if there was a sufficiently spacious blindside channel to the right of the Connacht scrum. 'It was just something a little bit different, trying to use his pace so he could get outside the opposition loose forwards,' says Gatland.

From a quick strike off the scrum-half's put-in, the number 8 (usually Barry Gavin) would take his trailing right foot off the ball to leave it for McGuinness to gather, or scoop, left-handed, on the run and then be clear of the opposition blindside flanker before he'd barely lifted his head. And more often than not, that's what happened.

Then there was 'the flipper', the move which had Elwood flipping the ball, blind and right-handed, behind his back for the left-winger to ghost through the gap created by Elwood's angled run infield and the use of decoy runners, with Carolan, now Connacht's highly regarded academy director, the beneficiary. With the move having been honed repeatedly on the training ground, Elwood and Carolan rarely got their timing wrong.

'They were awesome,' recalls Gatland of that play. 'I tried to use that move with Wales a few times, and other sides, but they couldn't do it. Nigel's timing was always perfect. The idea of it was that the number 8 picked up from a scrum and took out a loose forward, and then from the recycle Eric would run infield at a 45-degree angle with the blindside left-winger trailing him. Very often a lock would fill in that inside space for the defending team, and sometimes he'd stop chasing in order to do so. Eric would just leave the ball in the air behind his back, step out to the right, and Nigel would run into the hole from where Eric had engaged their 10. The midfield also did a switch to keep the opposition midfield honest.'

Those three successive wins set up a pool decider away to Northampton in their Franklin's Gardens lair. This time, McGeechan's Saints were also locked and fully loaded, with their Lions – Dawson, Townsend and Beal – all starting alongside Martin Bayfield, Budge Pountney and Ben Cohen. They also had the Ulster and Irish centre Jonny Bell on the bench.

Gatland's 'To Hell or to Connacht' phrase had been adopted with chip-on-the-shoulder gusto by the squad and those close to them. 'It was playing the underdog, going back to the old Cromwell days – everyone writing us off. We were a bit of a thorn in the side of the IRFU too. You sensed they were hoping we would go away.'

The squad also adopted a song, 'Red Is The Rose', introduced by the Buccaneers prop Martin Cahill. 'He used to sing it, and then we adopted it in the changing-room afterwards,' says Gatland.

Sensing a twitchiness amongst the players in the team hotel before making the coach journey to Franklin's Gardens, instead of a team talk Gatland asked them to sing 'Red Is The Rose'. 'We didn't have to say anything after that,' according to Gatland, 'and just hopped on the bus. The boys were in tears. It was incredible.'

Connacht's first try by prop John Maher was the product of their 13-man line-out. Elwood set up Junior Charlie for the second with a sweet break. After a burst by tight-head prop Mick Finlay, who had a huge game, Murphy worked a dummy pass with Duignan for Ruane to make ground and put Carolan over.

That gave Connacht a 20–10 lead to defend in a frantic final quarter, which they needed after Townsend had created a try for Bell. Gatland recalls, 'They should have scored a try late in the game, but Nicky Barry made an unbelievable tackle, probably one of the best tackles I've ever seen. He came flying up his wing and smashed Gregor Townsend, I think it was, before he passed the ball. They had a four-man overlap, and it probably won the game for us. That's a guy who played at a high level and made an unbelievable read and backed his decision. Most players would have held his position, and they would have romped in.'

The *Irish Times* match report noted: 'One Northampton blazer, having been informed that this Connacht team costs the IRFU about £300,000 (no pool bonus was even discussed), responded: "Heck, we could shoot our lot, hire you guys, and save £2 million."'

As the Northampton players formed a tunnel off the pitch, some of them became impatient with Connacht's celebrations and motioned towards the entrance to the dressing-room. 'No, let them have their moment,' said Dawson, insisting the players wait to clap Connacht off the pitch.

Whereas Leinster, Munster and Ulster had all fallen well short in their Heineken Cup pools, finishing third, fourth and fourth in their groups of four, the win earned Connacht an away quarter-final against Agen. Unhelpfully, that match was four weeks later, and, unlike their opponents, Connacht had no games to keep themselves ticking over. The Agen pack featured the French internationals Jean-Jacques Crenca, Marc Dal Maso, Philippe Benetton and their iconic captain Abdelatif

Benazzi, who, prior to the match, had been quoted as asking, 'Connacht, where's that?'

In seven European games that season, Connacht started only 17 players, and for this quarter-final Gatland selected an unchanged side for the fifth game in a row. Again, they irreverently took the lead through their 13-man line-out, courtesy of Maher once more, thus putting Agen behind for the first time in seven Challenge Cup matches. The ensuing cheers from the noisy knot of Connacht supporters were drowned out by the derisory whistling and jeering from the 7,000 home crowd.

Leading 10–6 approaching half-time, Elwood's pass out of the tackle put Murphy through, but faced by Agen full-back Vincent Thomas he opted for a long skip-pass which went to ground rather than going for the line himself. Agen responded with a sustained 60-metre drive, which culminated in a try by Dal Maso. A lead of 17–6 rather than a deficit of 13–10 might have been interesting.

'If we had scored just before half-time, we might have won,' said Gatland. 'In fairness, they were such a big side, and Benazzi was unstoppable. But it was a great game.'

After Elwood levelled the sides early in the second half, Agen's power game was too much, and two tries apiece by Benazzi and winger Laurent Loubère made it 40–13. Defiantly, Connacht and Elwood worked their flipper for replacement winger Russell Southam to score. This was executed with such precise choreography, and ensuing high-fives, that it even drew appreciative applause from the home crowd.

A week before his Ireland debut, McGuinness was again outstanding, and he had the final say, scoring untouched from 50 metres off the scoop ball. He left Benetton and Benazzi for dead, swerving first past out-half Guillaume Bouic and then past full-back Vincent Thomas for a stunning solo try.

Back in the away dressing-room, they linked in a circle for one last time and belted out 'Red Is The Rose'. 'Let them hear it,' beseeched Elwood, 'open the door.'

Good times. Good memories.

Looking back, Gatland says, 'It was like the old days, sort of semi-pro cum amateur. The boys trained hard, played hard and partied hard as well. You couldn't have had any more fun than we had as a team. We were just living the dream really, and every week was a bonus. At the start of the season, we were being asked what game were we going to win, and we ended up doing what we did.'

Gatland subsequently came to Dublin to help out at Ireland training sessions under Brian Ashton. Later, in February of the 1997–98 season, Ashton would summarily resign in the first season of a six-year contract as Irish head coach after the opening Five Nations' defeat at home to Scotland.

'The next day, Pat Whelan [Irish team manager] rang me up and asked me if I'd like to coach the team for the rest of the season.' Gatland, at 34, became head coach of Ireland.

Glynn recalls meeting the then IRFU president, Noel Murphy, in Cork while the selection process was ongoing.

'Billy, I've bad news for you.'

'What is it, Noel?'

'The IRFU have decided that Warren should be the national coach.'

'You're making a terrible mistake,' said Glynn.

'Why?'

'The man needs more time. He's not ready to coach a national side yet.'

'Ah well, that's the decision we've made,' said Murphy.

Glynn now says, 'Warren was a great coach. He'd revolutionized Connacht, and he had players playing way out of their skin. But I thought it was too soon for him, and I'd have liked to have seen him stay on with Connacht for another year or two. He'd only coached us for 19 games. That's all he had under his belt apart from club coaching. It was too soon.'

Gatland was left with a sense of unfinished business at Connacht, but as he puts it, 'When you get offered an opportunity like that [coaching Ireland], you don't turn it down. Connacht's season was over as well. There was no Celtic League or anything like that. True, there was no security in the job. This was 1998, and I think I was the sixth Irish coach in the 1990s. There was no longevity in being Irish coach then,' he says with a chuckle.

Sure enough, Gatland's time with Ireland was ended by the IRFU in November 2001 after a 40–29 defeat to New Zealand, even though it was only their second defeat in eight tests that year.

'I would love to have gone with Ireland to the 2003 World Cup and finished then,' he admits. But it wasn't to be. He was replaced by his assistant, O'Sullivan, from whom he had previously taken over at Connacht.

After telephoning Trudi, the next person he called was Glynn.

'Billy, I'm here at the IRFU. I've just come out from a meeting. I've been fired. They're not renewing my contract.'

'You're not serious?'

'Yes,' he said.

'You're not serious?' Glynn repeated.

'Yes,' Gatland repeated. 'They've advised me to get a solicitor. I told them you're my solicitor.'

'Look, as I'm on the IRFU, I'll need their consent.'

The union consented. 'I was furious,' recounts Glynn. 'I took the thing personally, because I had brought him back to Ireland. I felt a responsibility for him. He was my friend more than my client.'

Glynn travelled to Dublin to represent Gatland when negotiating his severance deal with the union. The union had a committee meeting at 6 p.m., at which they wanted to reveal their decision prior to publicly announcing it the next day. After some bartering, just before 6 p.m. Glynn and the union came to an agreement.

It was, at least, a good deal.

3

The Sword of Damocles, 1998–2003

The legacy from those two seasons under Warren Gatland lingers on. On any given Saturday at the Sportsground, up to seven players from the Connacht squad of the late 1990s and early 2000s will be part of the province's working fabric on match-day – be it Willie Ruane as CEO, the academy manager Nigel Carolan, team manager Tim Allnutt, forwards coach Jimmy Duffy, Conor McGuinness and Barry Gavin (both members of the Rugby Advisory Board – RAB) and, of course, Eric Elwood, now the domestic game manager. Even Mervyn Murphy, video analyst for the Irish team since 2001, is usually based at the Sportsground.

'That's actually something that I've said to people who can't understand what Connacht are about,' says Eric Elwood. 'What they can't understand is that those who are working for Connacht now are from Connacht because it means something to them! Even Tim, as a Kiwi, is the manager because he's played here. I've played, Nige has played, Willie, Jimmy, Conor and Barry have all played here, and I'm a firm believer that being from somewhere means more to you, and you'll care more and you'll give it more.'

The passion and work ethic in the building are palpable, as evidenced by Connacht's strategic five-year plan, 'From Grassroots to Green Shirts'. It is championed by everyone from Ruane down. 'Willie is a natural leader,' says Elwood. 'I'm here a long time and that strategic document is fabulous. It required a lot of time and effort, but now that we know where we're going, it gives us a sense of direction in simple plain language that everyone can understand. There's no silly speak, as I call it. I firmly believe in the motto "Keep It Simple, Stupid", so that everyone can understand and then you get buy-in.

'We're currently going through a governance review internally, which is about putting the right people in the right seats; in that way everybody will be responsible and accountable not only in Connacht but also in the clubs and schools.

'The phrase I hear all the time which I hate is "What are you doing in the branch?" Or "What are the branch doing about this?" and "What are the IRFU doing?" We're all part of the branch. That's why I say back to them, "Lads, you are the branch as much as I am. I happen to be paid by the IRFU and work for Connacht Rugby, but I can't do my job without the assistance of you and the school, or you and the club, you as a volunteer, you as whatever." We are all part of the branch, ideally aiming for the same thing.

'That governance review will examine how we run our business, how we will liaise with our clubs' and schools' volunteers and committees. We are all in the rugby business, and we're relationship-building as well. So that's what it's about, engaging with people face to face whenever we can. I think interacting is so important: keeping the lights on in clubs, getting your hands dirty and your boots mucky, working with the people. They appreciate that.

'They talk about my role and time here, and I get a little bit embarrassed at times. There were people here before me. There was Steph Nel [2000–03], there was Brads [Michael Bradley, 2003–10] and there was me [2010–13]. Yeah, I got a bit deeper into it [than coaching]. I wanted to change the landscape; I wanted to get more respect within the League. We wanted to fight with the IRFU for what we believe is right internally.'

Specifically, he wanted the four provinces to be treated equally. 'The four-legged stool is much more stable than the three-legged stool. We just wanted to play our part, and I felt that there are good people and good young players here, and we needed to harness that talent.'

On the pitch, though, Gatland proved a tough act to follow. After Gatland took over Ireland during the 1998 Five Nations, and partly at his recommendation, another Kiwi, Glenn Ross, succeeded him as head coach from 1998 but resigned after two seasons.

During Ross's time, Connacht failed to progress from the pool stages of the Challenge Cup, winning three from six in the first season to finish fifth of seven in their pool. The following season they beat Steaua București and Toulon at home but lost their other four games, including home and away to Ebbw Vale, as well as an embarrassing defeat in Romania.

Nel took over for three seasons, Connacht finishing bottom of a pool including Béziers, Montferrand and Neath in 2000–01. They lost their opening five matches, including 45–0 and 58–21 defeats away to Neath and Montferrand, and had two narrow losses to Béziers before beating Neath 13–11 at home in their final match. In 2001–02, Connacht beat Roma home and away and Narbonne at home to finish second behind Sale Sharks, and a year later they overcame Mont de Marsan and Narbonne in two-legged ties before losing to Pontypridd in the quarter-finals.

Nel's second season, 2001–02, also coincided with the inaugural Celtic League, in which they reached the quarter-finals before losing to Glasgow. They reached the same stage a year later before Nel stepped down on 26 April.

Connacht had won their first five Celtic League games that season, including a dramatic 26–23 win over Leinster at Donnybrook thanks to an 83rd-minute drop goal by Mark McHugh. It was their first win over Leinster in Dublin for 17 years and ended the home team's 17-match unbeaten run in Donnybrook. But heavy defeats against Pontypridd and Glasgow condemned them to an away quarter-final in November against Munster, which they lost 33–3.

After the ensuing European campaign, and the quarter-final defeat to Pontypridd, Nel had probably had enough, not so much on the pitch as off it. For the drama of his departure was as nothing compared to the off-field battle that had preceded it.

Thursday, 30 January 2003

Sporadic one-off wins against the odds such as that one against Leinster in September 2002 had punctuated Connacht's history. It's doubtful, however, that they've ever had a bigger one than in the rooms of the IRFU on a fateful night in late January 2003. That evening, the union's officers agreed to relent on their plans to disband Connacht's professional squad from the 2003–04 season onwards.

This stay of execution completed what was, almost certainly, the most tumultuous few weeks in the province's history. The saga began earlier that month when a passing remark by a leading IRFU figure to the then *Irish Independent* rugby correspondent Tony Ward implied that, as a cost-cutting measure, the union were considering the option of disbanding Connacht as a professional entity. Ward duly reported this, and Connacht were up in arms.

The union had been readying themselves for a €4 million loss on the financial year, with a further projected loss of €7 million for the following season. Disbanding Connacht appeared to be both a favoured option and a fait accompli. Following that leak, the province's future was left hanging in the balance after a stormy but inconclusive four-and-a-half hour IRFU committee meeting in Dublin's Berkeley Court Hotel on the Thursday evening of 9 January.

A statement from the union confirmed 'no decision had been taken' regarding Connacht's future, beyond holding another specially convened committee meeting in a fortnight's time, at which a vote on the province's existence as a professional entity would most probably be taken.

It was felt that a majority of the 22-man committee would support proposals from a four-man subcommittee of the IRFU, comprising the union's chief executive Philip Browne, director of rugby Eddie Wigglesworth, honorary treasurer John Lyons and director of finance Conor O'Brien, to cease funding Connacht as a professional entity while preserving the branch's administrative staff and amateur status. Only the three Connacht delegates on the committee, IRFU president Don Crowley, Billy Glynn and Jeff Smith, as well as the

Exiles' Phelim McLoughlin, seemed likely to oppose Connacht's proposed extinction.

The committee's impending decision would then be referred to a full IRFU council meeting – most likely in early February – as requested by Connacht Branch officials. The council, which encompassed the committee, about a dozen past presidents of the IRFU and ten delegates from each branch, was the ultimate decision-making arm of the union.

The committee meeting of 9 January took place less than 48 hours ahead of Connacht's European Challenge Cup quarter-final first leg against Pontypridd at Dubarry Park in Athlone. This was a 5,500 sell-out, and, needless to say, the union's proposal sent shockwaves through a Connacht squad that was facing the stark possibility of imminent unemployment.

'It's extremely worrying,' admitted the then Connacht CEO Gerry Kelly. 'As the person who interlinks between the players and management, and the union, it makes life very difficult.'

A statement issued on behalf of the players described the timing as 'appalling' and added:

For the past number of years we have operated on less resources than the other three provinces, yet the progress made in that time has always been on an upward curve, reaching the quarter-finals of the Celtic League in the two years since the competition started. In tandem with the success of the flagship team, there have been tremendous developments at youth and schools level in the province. Is this now to be lost because of the decisions that are being considered by the IRFU? Where will the young players in the province go to in the future?

Just before Christmas nine Connacht players featured in the Irish development squad which played Argentina, clearly indicating just how bright the future is for Connacht players. More young players are taking up the game in Connacht, more people are following rugby than ever before and massive money has been spent on the redevelopment of the Sportsground. The future has never

been as bright for rugby in Connacht before. It just does not make
sense to cut it off at this stage.

Support began to mobilize around Connacht's cause, and reaction
west of the Shannon came not just from the rugby world but from
other sporting disciplines and beyond.

The hastily created Friends of Connacht called a public meeting
for Wednesday, 15 January in Galway's Radisson Hotel, which 600
attended. The mood was defeatist but also defiant.

When collecting the Liam MacCarthy Cup in 1980 on behalf of
Galway, Joe Connolly was reckoned to have given one of the best
acceptance speeches of its kind at Croke Park. When he took to the
rostrum at the rally in the Radisson Hotel, he was in vintage form.

'There's talk about the struggle that's facing Connacht rugby, sure
what's new about Connacht and a struggle?' he said. 'Hasn't that been
the make-up of Connacht in all walks of life? Where in Ireland has
been cursed more with emigration than Connacht?'

He then invoked the book *Nineteen Acres* by John Healy 'that
famous journalist from Charlestown. One woman's fight to keep her
19 acres to keep her identity,' he said. 'It was Connacht that was deci-
mated in the forties, fifties, sixties and again in the eighties by
emigration.'

Connolly recounted the beginnings of Monivea, and how, lacking
any floodlighting system, they'd connected their lights to the home of
an elderly bachelor living nearby. When the ESB man called to his
door, he readily believed the man couldn't have run up such a massive
electricity bill, so went on his way without collecting.

'That's the struggle that Ulster, Munster and Leinster can't understand. That's what it's been like for Connacht rugby over the years,'
said Connolly. 'Rugby isn't in competition with the GAA or with soccer. We're all in this together. The competition is drink and drugs, as
if the figures aren't bad enough already,' he said, referring to the estimated 90,000 underage alcoholics in the country at the time. All
sports were weapons in this fight, he said, concluding, 'Ultimately, it's
all about youngsters.'

The IRFU's prevailing attitudes then, long established through-out their history but now completely changed, are illustrated by an excerpt from an article in the *Irish Times* on Saturday, 18 January 2003.

At the annual general meeting of the IRFU, six members of the 22-man committee are elected by ballot. It is an open, fair, demo-cratic vote. Two delegates are nominated from Leinster, Ulster and Munster, and one from Connacht. In other words, six out of seven. And the last time they elected a Connacht delegate was in 1980. Even that was only because politically incorrect remarks by one of the Munster nominations had given the Ulster delegates no option but to break ranks with the cartel. Otherwise, the Ulster, Leinster and Munster delegates could nominate a couple of tailor's dum-mies for all the difference it would make. They will always be elected.

But just for the heck of it, last year Connacht decided to put up two nominations. When the two names were read out, along with the proposers and seconders, this so bemused one Leinster man that he asked where they were from. 'They're from Connacht,' he was informed from the top table, which prompted objections from one of the Connacht delegates. But it had clarified the equation. The non-Connacht half dozen were duly elected. Quite why the IRFU bothers with such an archaic and bigoted ritual is a moot point.

However, this pretence at democracy served to demonstrate Con-nacht's standing within the IRFU hierarchy.

A week after the rally in the Radisson, a Connacht Branch delega-tion sought to meet all the TDs in the province, and others from neighbouring counties, at Buswells Hotel on Wednesday, 22 January. A former Mayo East TD and one-time Connacht player Séan Cal-leary, from the Ballina rugby club, was one of the branch's delegation at that meeting. 'We need to show that there is political support for us as well. This is just pure discrimination.'

The Fianna Fáil TD Frank Fahey told RTÉ Radio that in the event of Connacht's being jettisoned, he would actively lobby government ministers to withhold any financial aid to the IRFU, for game or ground development.

The Irish Rugby Union Players' Association (IRUPA), just recently formed, took a dim view of a proposal that would make over 20 per cent of its 116-strong membership unemployed, and threatened a players' strike. Its then chairman, the Leinster flanker Liam Toland, said, 'The union might be surprised by the depth of feeling amongst the players. I don't think the IRFU realize how seriously we take these proposals, and they may not realize how far the players are willing to take this.'

With the four provinces still engaged in European competitions, it had been difficult to organize a group meeting, but IRUPA representatives had briefed the Connacht, Munster and Ulster squads, while Toland had addressed his Leinster teammates. They were, he said, 'disgusted' by the union's proposals and unanimously agreed they would explore what action was required to prevent Connacht's disbandment.

'The vast majority of the players are concerned by the move to lose one of the four professional teams. The players have displayed their commitment, consistently and excellently, towards the contracts they have signed – in many cases they have gone above and beyond what was expected of them when competing in Europe. All four of them have reached the quarter-finals or better of the European competitions, and Connacht were the first province to do so.'

Toland cited the example of Eric Elwood. 'In 13 or 14 years with Connacht, he has consistently ignored money and success abroad. Is this how the IRFU are going to reward him and his team, by retiring them before their time? If Munster don't qualify for the knockout stages and lose €250,000, are they the next team to go?' asked Toland rhetorically.

He then praised the IRFU for creating 'a template which is the envy of the world. We as players would hope to maintain the success that both the IRFU and the players have created.'

But, he observed, 'Amateuristic committee men have failed to maximize the resources. In seven years, they haven't constructed one corporate box in the whole of Ireland. One of the most successful aspects of the game has been the professional players and teams, yet we're the ones expected to carry the cost and sacrifice one-quarter of our members.'

The threat to Connacht's IRUPA members was very real. In light of their financial losses, the IRFU blueprint for the Irish game incorporated a reduction in the professional playing pool from 120 to 90. An IRFU spokesperson explained: 'The issue of Connacht is part of a wide, sweeping series of savings from top to bottom of every single aspect of the union's affairs, encompassing the club game, professional rugby and general overheads.' But clearly the favoured option to meet this end was to disband Connacht.

The threat to Connacht's very existence also came at a time when Galway was booming and the underage scene in the province had never been better.

Few towns or clubs epitomized this growth more than the hurling stronghold of Portumna. About 40 kids from Portumna Community School had travelled to Athlone to support Connacht against Pontypridd. The following Wednesday, a squad of about 30 Under-13s were going through their paces and overall they had five teams from the Under-13s up – about 170 boys all told in a school where the game had been introduced in 1986 by then PE teacher Daithi Frawley. Frawley was born literally across the road from the school. Based for six years in Donegal as a teacher, he returned to his roots in Portumna and played rugby with Galwegians.

John Muldoon was a particular source of pride, having become the first product of the school to come through the IRFU academy, and speaking on that Wednesday afternoon in January 2003, Frawley said, 'If you look at it from my perspective, I'm 62 years of age. The two greatest pleasures I have had from the game were winning the Junior Cup and the second was Johnny Muldoon becoming a fully fledged Connacht substitute [in a European game] last Saturday against Pontypridd. That's what makes it all worthwhile.

Everything is relative. Down here, getting on a Connacht team is all you aspire to.'

Rugby would never have grown in the school without the coaching assistance of Connacht players such as Elwood. 'I couldn't have done it without them,' said Frawley, who was the incoming Connacht Branch president for the 2003–04 season.

'I'm a Connacht man first and foremost,' added Frawley. 'I think it's absolute nonsense. It is unthinkable. What about the hundreds like me who've given all their life to the game? I've been 50 years either playing or coaching without a break. If this happens, and the IRFU do away with the Connacht senior team, I will never coach again.'

The Connacht Youths team had won two out of three for the previous two seasons, contributing more than a quarter of the Irish Youths team; the Connacht Under-21s had won a provincial grand slam two seasons previously, and in 2002–03 had won three out of five, despite four of the games being away.

'The huge input into the development of players in the province is only starting to bear fruit now,' said Gerry Kelly, stressing that the best years were yet to come if they were allowed to continue.

Eamonn Feely, an accountant for whom the position of honorary treasurer of the Connacht Branch was a labour of love, had been one of those who had formally received an IRFU delegation at their Sportsground offices the previous December. What galled him more than anything else was his contention that Connacht had been operating with the tightest budget of the four provinces. Of the estimated €1.8 million set aside for Connacht (compared to roughly €4 million each for the other three provinces), Feely oversaw a budget of just €500,000 for what he described as the 'provincial management account', i.e. the entire annual administration of the Connacht team.

Leaving aside the salaries of the Connacht players and then coach Steph Nel, this €500,000 covered all hotel, food and travel costs, as well as wages and fees for management and assistant coaches. Through sponsorship deals with O2, Bank of Ireland and the Radisson Hotel, the Connacht professional team had helped to generate almost

€100,000 (it was €96,553 for the 2001–02 season) towards the running of the underage and amateur provincial teams.

Speaking from his office in the Sportsground, Feely said, 'For example, we sent our Under-18s on a tour of England without any help from the IRFU. We depend on the Connacht senior team to generate significant funds, otherwise the game in my opinion will die. They may say they're going to keep the amateur game running down here, but who's going to run it for them? What's an amateur senior Connacht side going to do? Who's it going to play? We'll never get a sponsor again. So the Connacht senior team is vital to the Connacht Branch.'

Feely had asked the IRFU delegation if they had conducted an impact study into the consequences of disbanding Team Connacht. The answer, of course, was that they hadn't. 'Most of all, the psyche in the province will become totally negative, and people will just walk away from the game,' said Feely. 'In a nutshell, I can't see the game surviving. But you wouldn't be involved in Connacht rugby for 25 years if you weren't an optimist. It just doesn't make sense, having invested so much money in the province, to then have no return on that investment. I hope that sense will prevail.'

At the same time, the Welsh RFU were in an even more penurious financial position. Having decided to trim their professional entities in both the Celtic League and European competitions from nine clubs to four regions at the end of that 2002–03 season, their committee members had sanctioned proposals aimed at reducing their overheads by disbanding the Welsh A team. They also agreed to curb their own Six Nations' trips to away games from two or three matches to one per committee member; something the IRFU had not proposed to do.

Two of the Connacht Branch delegates on the committee, Jeff Smith and Billy Glynn, put together a list of possible cost-cutting measures along with one of potential additional revenue sources to present to the IRFU committee meeting of Thursday, 23 January.

The Friends of Connacht hired a train from Galway to allow them to join a planned march by supporters in Dublin from Baggot Street to Lansdowne Road in advance of that committee meeting. The meeting had been moved from the Berkeley Court Hotel to the committee room under the West Stand at Lansdowne Road. As one Connacht representative observed, 'perhaps because it has more exits'.

Ahead of the proposed committee meeting, Glynn outlined his stance. 'I want to seek an assurance that we're not going to be faced with the touting of our players by other provinces, something that has already happened, and secondly that the union won't go down the avenue of cutting our money to the extent that we're not able to compete, and that we die a slow and painful death. What I want to happen at Thursday's meeting is that the committee establish the principle that there must be four provinces. I want that principle established. It's what the people want. It's an issue way beyond money. For me it's an issue not only of importance to Connacht but for the whole of the island.'

But on Monday, 20 January, the IRFU cancelled their committee meeting for the following Thursday. Regardless, The Friends of Connacht went ahead with their proposed march.

Danno Heaslip, one of the organizers, explained at the time: 'Out of courtesy, I notified the IRFU last week that we would be handing in a letter on Thursday, at some time before 5 p.m., and I have requested that Philip Browne accommodate us by briefly accepting the letter.'

Assembling from 3.30 p.m. outside Searson's and the Waterloo Pub on Upper Baggot Street, an estimated crowd of 2,000 marched to 62 Lansdowne Road from about 4.15, arriving at the union's offices at 5 p.m.

The *Irish Times* of Friday, 24 January, reported:

Car horns tooted in support, with one driver waving a Lansdowne scarf. Banners fluttered on behalf of Garbally College, Sligo RFC, Connacht Fans, Ballinasloe, Portumna Community School, Blackrock, a 'Gaillimh' flag with the GAA crest, the Connemara All Blacks and Ginger Supports Connacht. The now Wales-based Ginger McLoughlin was joined by other former internationals Robbie

McGrath, Mick Quinn, Phil O'Callaghan and Noel Mannion, and senator Jim Glennon.

A placard from Clifden asked 'Underage Connemara RFC – Future Asylum Seekers?', while a leaflet doing the rounds 'cordially' invited the IRFU to a 'Connacht Rugby Club on any Saturday to observe the future of rugby in Ireland. No presents, please, just yours will do. RSVP'.

Their numbers were swelled by the majority of the current Connacht squad, out to try to save their careers and their livelihoods, and by Alec Blayney, a past Connacht president now in his mid 80s, who also walked the walk. The petition was handed in by two of the elected Friends of Connacht representatives, Danno Heaslip and Tommy Conlon, as well as three mini-rugby players from Galwegians: twins Daniel and Cassie Deegan, and Michael Fallon. Philip Browne, the chief executive of the IRFU, along with the union's honorary treasurer, John Lyons, bravely accepted the petition at the front door – surely more than Browne's 'job spec' had outlined. 'The first thing it shows is the passion in Irish sport, which is such a fundamental part of our achievements on the pitch,' said Browne. 'Secondly, it shows that there is genuine concern out there, and we've got to take that on board.' More concern than the IRFU had bargained for perhaps.

The letter called on the IRFU 'to discontinue the process they are currently engaged in, which is designed to lead to the expulsion of Connacht from professional provincial rugby', adding: 'This process is divisive, damaging to the future of the game and could threaten the security of the institutions of the Irish Rugby Football Union.'

'We didn't say too much,' admitted Heaslip after emerging from the IRFU headquarters. 'It's being said outside on the road. The Friends of Connacht only started a week ago. I'm absolutely astonished at the turn-out.'

Heaslip also commented, 'If Irish rugby is being run at a loss, it is not the fault of Connacht. Those at the top in Irish rugby need to take a look at who got us into this mess and get the answers from these people.'

The Galway Bay FM rugby commentator and Connacht rugby historian Ralph O'Gorman then introduced a succession of speakers beginning with Glennon, who commented, 'The day that the demise of Connacht rugby arrives on the scene is the day that Irish rugby begins to disintegrate.'

The then Fianna Fáil senator and former minister Mary O'Rourke demanded 'justice and rights for our province'.

The Fine Gael leader Enda Kenny said, 'This is much bigger than just Connacht. We stand for inclusion in Irish sport, and sport is part of Irish society. I will not stand for the segregation of one-quarter of our country in any sport. It's just not on.' While commending the IRFU for the 'great job they've done over the years', Kenny concluded, 'Any child has the legitimate right to aspire to play for his province and his country.'

Amongst the other politicians in attendance were Jim Higgins, Terry Leyden, Denis Naughten, Paul Connaughton, Paddy McHugh and senator Geraldine Feeney from Sligo. In conclusion, O'Gorman referred to the final paragraph of the letter handed in to 62 Lansdowne Road: 'The demonstration which accompanies the delivery of this letter is not the culmination of our protest but merely the beginning.'

After that march, however, the IRFU line began to soften. Two evenings before the march, John Hussey had presented the union's case to a Leinster Branch committee meeting. Hussey was chairman of the strategic review committee that produced the first IRFU strategic plan for the period 2003 to 2007, and as part of this process Hussey became the first chairman of the union's management committee, serving two three-year terms (2003–09) in that capacity.

The vast majority of the delegates present reputedly supported the under-fire province. The feeling was summed up by one committee member, who was also on the IRFU 22-man committee, in his comment: 'When you amputate one of your limbs, you don't get to put it back on again.'

At this juncture, an IRFU spokesperson admitted there was no guarantee a vote would be taken at the planned committee meeting of 7 February. Both the Connacht Branch and the Irish Rugby Union Players' Association had been asked to make their submissions by 1 February, while the union would do likewise.

'There will be a lot of presentations to discuss and debate, and whether the committee will then make a decision or not I don't know,' said Browne. 'That depends on the dynamics of the meeting.'

Connacht would also be required to provide some good solutions and ideas of their own, given that the union's coffers were not a bottomless pit. Then again, as one of the Connacht lobbyists remarked, were the other three, more spendthrift, provinces, being obliged to come up with submissions as well? Or, as he put it: 'Since when did Connacht suddenly have a monopoly on ideas?'

After a meeting of union officers on Thursday, 30 January, the IRFU announced that they would not disband Connacht's professional team. The union issued a statement confirming that they would, after all, be contracting players in all four provinces:

> The Irish Rugby Football Union commenced a strategic planning process in August 2002, which has yet to be completed. The IRFU officers will be recommending to the union committee that on the completion of this process a draft strategic plan will be produced and there will be consultation with all the stakeholders of Irish rugby.
>
> Following this, decisions will be taken as to the future structure of domestic club rugby and professional rugby in Ireland, and in the meantime the process of contracting players will continue as heretofore in all four provinces.

In response, the Connacht Branch called off its request for a special meeting of the full IRFU Council, which would have been empowered to overturn any decision by the committee to disband Connacht. Had that come to pass, it might have made the positions of the IRFU officers and committee members untenable.

On hearing of the IRFU's volte-face, IRUPA's chief executive, Niall Woods, welcomed the union's rethink: 'We're just delighted. It's definitely common sense and we're glad to see that the strategic process is continuing and that we are recognized as a part of that strategic process. This news is great for rugby in the country and great for rugby in the west particularly, giving a chance for the game to develop further in Connacht.'

Leo Galvin, outgoing president of the Connacht Branch, also welcomed the decision. 'We look forward to playing our full part in the ongoing strategic review and to our continued participation in the Celtic League and Parker Pen Challenge Cup.'

Endangered species they may have been, but Connacht would not become extinct after all.

Looking back now, Connacht CEO Willie Ruane admits, 'It was a big moment.' He adds, 'My view is that I think the IRFU misjudged the passion there was for Connacht actually, because I'd say that most of the people that marched weren't rugby heads. It was a passion for where we were from, and I'd say the IRFU misjudged that badly.

'But there was some context to why they felt they needed to do it, and I think that might have been an awakening for Connacht rugby as to why we needed to get our act together. The IRFU then needed to back it with funding, because there's no point in just keeping us alive just for the sake of it. That came slowly, but once it came then it had a positive effect, so overall I would view that period as being positive as well as negative.'

It also proved to be a pivotal point in Connacht's often troubled history, and, over time, attitudes within the IRFU changed considerably. During the 2013–14 season, when the branch had no CEO following the departure of Tom Sears, the IRFU's chief operating officer Kevin Potts oversaw the running of Connacht. This afforded the union an opportunity to closely examine the operation, and after Ruane became the Connacht CEO, Finbarr Crowley, chairman of the IRFU's management committee, the IRFU treasurer Tom Grace and Browne recommended and oversaw a sea change in the union's funding of Connacht. The province's budget reputedly increased significantly, to bring it in line with the other provinces. Accordingly, Connacht were able to recruit the likes of Mils Muliaina and in turn Bundee Aki. 'In my time here,' says Ruane, 'I can't say enough for Philip, Tom, Finbarr and the union.'

All has changed, changed utterly.

However, Elwood accepts that Connacht had brought much of their woes upon themselves.

'Yeah, absolutely, and that's the beauty of what we're doing now with Willie [Ruane]! It's about changing the landscape and getting people to buy in and believe. It's about having that credibility so that people can trust us. If we say we're going to do something, then do it! If we ask for money, we must deliver on the promise. Too often a Connacht solution to a Connacht problem over the years was: "Can I have some more, sir?" That's not right either; I appreciate that 100 per cent. Gerry [Kelly] fought for years, to be fair to him, and now Willie, young and enthusiastic, is trying to put the right people in the right seats.'

Connacht is in better shape, for sure, nowadays than before, and Elwood admits he can walk around Galway with his head held a little higher.

'It's great when you can walk around town without keeping your head down. I used to say to Eamonn McGuffin [a long-serving Connacht Branch administrator] that I'd be afraid to walk around town sometimes. "Shoot, did we pay him?" or "Did we pay for that bus?" Our credibility was poor, but now people can again build trust and relationships with us, and thankfully that's what's been happening of late.'

Finally, they are dining at the top table. It had taken them only 127 years or so to take their seat.

4

Baby Steps: The Michael Bradley Years, 2003–2010

Two days after the announcement of Steph Nel's departure in April 2003, it was confirmed that Michael Bradley would be his successor for the following season. This was largely welcomed west of the Shannon, for although he was a Munsterman and an IRFU appointment – as an IRFU employee Bradley had been coaching the Irish Under-21s – it suggested the union had more of a vested interest in Connacht.

Coming after that turbulent January, though, these were decidedly tricky times, to say the least, for Connacht, even if that wasn't the way Bradley saw it, initially at any rate. 'I was actually quite excited, because it was a full pro side. I only ever saw it as an opportunity, and I would have approached it that way. I met Gerry Kelly in the IRFU headquarters just before the interview with Eddie Wigglesworth, and he expressed his desire to have me there. It was an opportunity for me as a coach, albeit on the understanding that Connacht were in a precarious position within the long-term plans of the IRFU, and you couldn't necessarily control that with rugby alone. It was also a financial and political struggle.'

Despite a turnover in players, Bradley's first season was encouraging. Eric Elwood, Darren Yapp and Tim Allnutt remained the backbones of the back-line, so to speak, and the former Australian Under-21 and Queensland lock Andrew Farley was an important signing. He would play over one hundred League games and over fifty Challenge Cup matches in the first six seasons of Bradley's reign, appearing as captain for three seasons. He earned an Irish A cap before moving on to Grenoble in 2009, and finished his playing career in 2014, becoming Grenoble's team manager. He was recently inducted into the Connacht Hall of Fame.

'As a player, and a person, he made a fabulous contribution,' says Bradley, 'and embraced what Connacht was and still is now: a family first, where the sum of the parts was bigger than the individuals. The thing about Andrew was his enthusiasm. He was a "hundred per-center". He felt the losses and enjoyed the victories. He was such a good, consistently reliable player and person.'

In the League that season, Connacht had some notable wins at home to Leinster and Ulster, while suffering the first of two 3–0 defeats to Munster: one in Athlone, and then again the following season at the Sportsground, on days you wouldn't have put the cat out. 'Oh God, they were horrible days,' says Bradley.

To put the 31–20 win over Ulster (Mark McHugh kicking seven from seven) into perspective, the northern province, then League leaders under Alan Solomons, were only denied a Celtic Cup and League double on the last day of the season in a title shoot-out away to the Llanelli Scarlets.

Connacht also did the double over the Ospreys and finished ninth, above the three Scottish sides and within four and seven points of Leinster and Munster. 'The boys played with plenty of freedom,' recalls Bradley. 'But purely from a rugby point of view, they were baby steps. The reality is that our League position thereafter was near the bottom. It reflected where we were in terms of the ability of the coaches, players and organization to be as consistent as we needed to be.'

Under Bradley, Connacht performed better in Europe. They reached the semi-finals of both the Challenge Cup and Celtic Cup in that first season, losing to Edinburgh by a point in the latter.

In the Challenge Cup, they lost out narrowly over two legs against Harlequins to a 69th-minute try by English World Cup-winning centre Will Greenwood at the Sportsground when leading 23–10 and 45–41 on aggregate. Paul Burke, a former Connacht Under-20 player, added an 80th-minute penalty, before Quins withstood ten minutes of injury-time pressure. The home-grown Gavin Duffy, in the first season of a three-year sabbatical with the London club, was in tears after the game. Nonetheless, he received a winners' medal four weeks later when Quins went on to beat Montferrand in a thrilling final in Reading.

The attendance of 6,000 for that semi-final demonstrates that sell-outs at the Sportsground are not new. For this reason and more, Bradley made a point of targeting the latter stages of the Challenge Cup, reaching three semi-finals and two quarter-finals in his time there. 'We needed to keep visibility within the rugby calendar,' he says, with one eye on the media and another on the IRFU. 'The Challenge Cup helped keep our heads above water.

'It's also important to recognize that at that time there was that interest amongst the Connacht supporters, if the event was big enough. Those attendances gave a huge boost to the organization, and politically with the IRFU.' More baby steps.

'Those first couple of years were all about survival. We lived year to year, but I would feel for the IRFU. They had to pay for four provincial sides, and that was a huge commitment financially. As an accounting exercise, it made sense to trim that down to three teams, but as a rugby exercise it didn't. So we had to fortify the rugby argument, because we were losing the financial one.

'Connacht weren't good at fundraising, and the package for supporters wasn't great either. There were days when, as a supporter, you could not be in a more miserable place. To me, those who stood by us in those years and before were the real heroes.

'First of all there were no lights, so all the kick-offs had to be on Saturday afternoons; perversely, if it was a nice day you mightn't get too many supporters either. A dull day was the best.'

In Bradley's second season, Connacht won seven and drew one of 20 games to finish tenth of 11 in the League above the Borders (the Celtic Warriors having been disbanded). Connacht reached the semi-finals again in the Challenge Cup, losing both legs of their semi-final to Sale Sharks, the first by 25–18 at home and the second leg by 59–9 at Edgeley Park. Philippe Saint-André had taken over at Sale as head coach from Jim Mallinder and had signed French internationals Sébastien Bruno and Sébastien Chabal to buttress a squad that already included Jason Robinson, Mark Cueto, Charlie Hodgson, Bryan Redpath, Andrew Sheridan and Ignacio Fernández Lobbe. Sale hammered Pau in the final and won their sole Premiership title the following season.

That last game against Sale also marked the end of Eric Elwood's playing career, whereupon he became Bradley's assistant coach for the next five seasons. 'We were good friends going back to when we played together for Ireland, and we remain good friends today. I think Eric and I have the same value structure, in the sense that we would both value hard work and honesty. Eric was a natural coach anyway from my point of view. He commands the respect of the players, and particularly in Connacht.'

A year later, following his retirement, Dan McFarland was also co-opted to the backroom ticket as forwards coach. 'Like Eric, Dan is a very good coach. Their methodology is slightly different, but both are very good coaches. I could see that, in the way they approached playing, coaching would not be an issue for them. They were easy decisions.'

A few fallow years followed. In 2005–06, Connacht won six of 20 games and again finished tenth of 11, above Glasgow, while losing away to Newcastle 23–3 in the Challenge Cup quarter-finals. The following season was worse, Connacht winning just four of 20 League games to finish tenth of 11 once more, above the Borders, while winning just one of six European pool games at home to Montpellier.

In the pre-season of 2007–08, Connacht hosted Jake White's South Africa, who won 18–3 as part of their warm-up preparations for the 2007 World Cup, which they won in France. Bearing that, and Harlequins and Sale in mind, Bradley quips, 'We must have been a lucky charm for opposition teams. We put them on the right road, but it was a good game and again a huge crowd.'

In that 2007–08 season, Connacht posted five wins – four against the Welsh regions – but lost all six Interpro derbies to finish tenth of ten (the Borders also having been disbanded). They finished third in their Challenge Cup pool, completing a double over Spanish side El Salvador and beating Newcastle at home.

'That was Carl Hayman's first game,' recalls Bradley of the All Blacks tight-head's debut for Newcastle. 'I had the misfortune to walk down the narrow hallway into the dressing-room to the physio's room as he was leaving the Newcastle dressing-room, and I had to get out of his way he was so big.' It would be interesting to know how much of Connacht's annual budget Hayman's salary might have accounted for at the time. 'Maybe all of it,' jokes Bradley.

'We limped along in those years, without a whole lot of extra finance coming in our direction,' reflects Bradley. 'If you look at, say, Munster in 2006 and 2008, when they were winning the Heineken Cup, they would have had more current internationals on their bench than we would have had A internationals. Ulster were gaining momentum, and Leinster were young but coming on strongly, as well as making good signings. We could take them in the Sportsground if we got them on a good day for us, but no matter what side Munster put out, they were extremely strong at that time.'

Significantly, though, Connacht re-signed two prodigal sons, Duffy in the summer of 2006 from Harlequins, and Johnny O'Connor from Wasps in 2007: both indigenous internationals.

'It was at least a strong statement to the IRFU, because it bene-fited the national side that they came back,' says Bradley. 'And it was a huge boost to us, because they are from the province. They were also hugely positive in the dressing-room in that they'd gone away, been successful and had come home.'

Helped by Elwood and McFarland, then also coaching the Irish Under-21s, Connacht were also able to sign Ian Keatley, Sean Cronin and Fionn Carr in 2008. Lock Mike McCarthy and prop Robbie Morris had also joined from Newcastle in 2007 (McCarthy rejoining, having played for Connacht in Bradley's first season), following on from the Samoan flanker Ray Ofisa who went on to spend five seasons at Connacht.

'A wonderful player, that fella [Ofisa],' says Bradley. 'Hard as nails. For me, when he was injury-free, pound for pound he was as good as any of the overseas signings. Just fantastic to coach, because you'd ask him to do things and he did them.'

In his last two seasons, beginning in 2008–09, Bradley targeted home games, often making wholesale changes for away games, so the team suffered some heavy defeats on their travels. 'You just couldn't back it up,' he explains. 'It wasn't possible. In fairness to those lads who played away from home, they would have done so in a difficult situation. That's just the way we were, and everyone knew that.

'If you were a Connacht player, as opposed to being with Leinster, Munster or Ulster, you had the hardest job of professional rugby players in Ireland. You were not playing with many stars of the game. Your contribution, and your work ethic, had to be stronger. Whereas if you were the same player with one of the other provinces, you played with 10, 12, 14 internationals, or 22 if you went to Leinster. And in a way it's easier to play there. The environment at Connacht is one of working hard. It's not one of going out and "dollying" around the place and getting away with it because you're playing with better players.

'We had to place a huge value on culture and environment, before we put a value on results, and the players had to be on board. They have to want to do it. I'll give you an example from a while back, when SportsCode [the computer software] first appeared on the scene. We had just two or three computers, but we needed a lot more, and we had no analysts. We had discussions with wholesalers who sold Apple computers, and the boys coughed up money to get 22 individual computers with SportsCode. The boys paid for them. We had a room for all these computers but no money.

'John Muldoon has a bank of this knowledge, emotion and connection with Connacht, and he can draw on that. He's seen the darker days, and the darker days are important, not by design but because it gives you the desire to earn and then savour the good days.'

A week after losing 58–0 away to Cardiff, they beat Leinster 19–18 at home. After losing 53–13 away to Ulster, in their next game

Connacht beat Munster 12–6 at the Sportsground during the festive period in front of a crowd of 5,000 – their first win over Munster in the League.

'Ian Keatley kicked four penalties,' remembers Bradley. 'That was huge. It was a watershed in terms of making a statement for the Connacht supporters, who were still being soaked. There was no Clan Terrace yet.'

Connacht also felt they were receiving a bum rap in Interpros from Irish referees, and McFarland produced the stats to support their paranoia. 'We had our knuckles rapped for saying it, but the stats were there. Dan produced them for us. This is where the battles were.'

There were other battles, and Bradley also singles out Kevin Craddock, the then Connacht fitness adviser, and Des Ryan, their strength and conditioning coach for their contribution. 'Their enthusiasm helped build a gym which was the best in the country. It cost €1 million and was on-site, something no one else had. We were totally enclosed in the Sportsground itself.'

Connacht reached the quarter-finals of the Challenge Cup again, losing to Northampton. But going into his seventh season, 2009–10, Bradley decided it would be his last. 'There were other things happening. There was more pressure financially on Connacht at that stage, and any potential funding for recruits was being swallowed up by the domestic game. The union needed to make a decision as to whether they were going to support Connacht more or not, and they weren't going to do it that year anyway.

'Gerry was my CEO throughout my time there, and we remain very good friends today. Gerry wasn't going to tell me to move on, so the conversation was more along the lines of: "Do you think I can do any more here? Do you think you need a change?" By mutual consent, really, we agreed to see if someone else could bring Connacht on to the next stage.'

Bradley's decision to step down was announced in November of his final season. His policy of targeting home games reaped a bigger dividend in that campaign, as Connacht won five and drew one of their nine League games at the Sportsground – only the Ospreys, Ulster and Munster left with a win.

In Europe, Connacht won all six pool matches, completing home and away wins over Montpellier, Worcester and Olympus Madrid to earn a home quarter-final against Bourgoin. Two of Connacht's true stalwarts, Michael Swift and Muldoon, scored the tries that earned a 14–10 interval lead.

Then trailing 20–14 in the final quarter of the game, Connacht were indebted to two penalties and a 78th-minute drop goal by Miah Nikora, their former New Zealand Under-20 out-half who spent six seasons at Connacht.

Bradley says, 'John Muldoon is, to me, like Eric. He's reached that sort of status now. He's given everything to Connacht rugby. I signed him from Under-20 rugby. John could have gone to Ulster but stayed and committed his life's work to Connacht, as did Eric.'

No less than Muldoon, Swift's work-rate over 15 seasons and 269 games was savage. 'Swiftie is a legend as well. An ever-present, always enthusiastic, and he was the most awkward man in the world on the pitch. He's the Paddy Johns of Connacht rugby. His parents came over to all our home games and then moved here before his dad passed away sadly in 2015.'

Like his English compatriot, Dan McFarland, Swift came from Richmond, but as Bradley says, 'You don't have to be from Connacht to feel part of Connacht. That's the beauty of it. It is very welcoming, and there is a sense of belonging.'

In this, Bradley singles out Mick Grealish, and Johnny Holland, two long-standing volunteers. Grealish is a former Connacht Branch president, while Holland's father and then his son, David, have ensured the Sportsground pitch has been tended to by three generations of the same family. 'Mick and Johnny have been best buddies for 65–70 years and are next-door neighbours not far from the Sportsground, working underneath the radar. When a club has people like them, they have a chance,' says Bradley.

Back in the Challenge Cup semi-finals for the third time under Bradley's watch, a crowd of 7,000 packed the Sportsground when Connacht hosted a Toulon side featuring Jonny Wilkinson. With Wayne Barnes as referee, Toulon had seven 5-metre scrums on the Connacht line approaching half-time, earning four penalties, before Mafi Kefu barged over in the ninth minute of overtime to give the French outfit a 19–9 interval lead. Keatley soon trimmed that to 12–19, and, with the wind behind them, Connacht huffed and puffed – Cronin and Frank Murphy each coming close to scoring – but couldn't blow down Toulon's house.

'If you went back seven years, to have that sort of crowd even there, and to have that level of performance, was a huge difference from where we started,' says Bradley. 'That was a good memory, and that was a rugby statement.'

Reflecting on his time with Connacht, Bradley says, 'I'll always be very positive about those seven years. First of all I was made very welcome. I still have fantastic friends from that time. Gerry Kelly was very supportive, as was Tim Allnutt. Again, he's worked a little bit under the radar. He'd have signed the likes of Ray Ofisa.'

Although Connacht did not always win the fights on the pitch or financially off it, Bradley also hails the way Billy Glynn and Leo Galvin led the political fight. 'Billy put himself out on a limb when he took part in the march to Lansdowne Road in 2003. He alienated himself [from other IRFU members] but worked his way back in there. He's been an ever-present through the good and the bad days, and his heart is in Connacht 100 per cent.'

Galvin was a driving force behind Buccaneers, which was a merger of Athlone and Ballinasloe, and former president of the Connacht Branch. 'Leo is a good political operator, and where Connacht needed most to improve was not on the pitch, nor even financially, but politically, within the IRFU.

'If you were with the union, I'm sure you could become quite frustrated with Connacht, but the union were ultimately wise, because they put enough pressure on Connacht to knock them into a professional organization; they are now reaping the rewards for retaining all four provinces.'

Bradley also stresses that Eddie Wigglesworth, the IRFU's

director of rugby, became a Connacht ally within the corridors of 62 Lansdowne Road, even though he had been one of the four-man sub-committee that explored the possibility of dismantling Connacht's professional set-up in 2003.

'He got his hands dirty with us and helped us on the recruitment side. People would have seen Eddie as an obstacle to Connacht, but he often donned a Connacht hat at meetings when the other provinces had more representatives. On the rugby side in particular, Eddie was our go-to guy and was very capable in terms of getting an end result and keeping it politically correct.'

In particular, Bradley looks back fondly on the pre-season of 2008, when he and the rest of the management staff, along with Muldoon, Duffy and Swift, devised a motto that would define Connacht: 'With pride in our hearts, the strength in our limbs, the commitment to the promise, we will fight.'

Bradley says, 'The promise being Connacht rugby, the supporters, the backers and sponsors. To play for Connacht wasn't only about winning. Winning is a by-product of doing all the other things right as well as you can.'

So in 2010, Bradley passed the baton on to Elwood.

5

Eric Elwood

Eric Elwood has been coming to the Sportsground for as long as he can remember. As a kid, he sold match programmes at Inter-provincials in the late 1970s and early '80s, when Connacht were competing against the odds as well as the other three provinces.

This was the era of Ulster dominance, when they won or shared seven titles in the 1970s, and then ten in a row from 1985. At the time, Elwood was playing underage rugby in Galwegians.

'My abiding boyhood memories would be of the Sportsground, selling programmes, watching matches and thinking "What if" and "If only" and "I'd love to be playing". They were big days – only one or two home games a year and maybe a warm-up game against the Army. Then when I started playing, I'd be thinking, "Pleeeease, don't pick me against the Army", because they would kick lumps out of you!'

Playing for the Galwegians Under-8s simply entailed jumping over the wall from his home in Mervue into their grounds in Glenina. Mervue football club was also nearby and his school, St Michael's, as well as the GAA club of the same name, was directly across the road from home.

'I was within throwing distance of it all. But that's the type of community Mervue was: the same boys played the soccer and the Gaelic. Not many of us jumped the wall, but those who did, did quite well! I ended up going to the Jes – Coláiste Iognáid [secondary

58

school] – on the other side of town where, because there was rugby, I became more involved in it than any of my pals. That's where I got the *grá*,' says Elwood, meaning the love for rugby.

In a further irony, not only was there no rugby in the family tree but 'no sport at all in our house,' admits Elwood. 'There's two Elwood families in Galway. My dad's family home is literally across the road from the cemetery. You can see it from here in the Sportsground,' he says, nodding towards the house from the Sportsground's main con-ference room, the windows of which provide a panoramic view of the surrounding suburbs.

'The other Elwood family played Gaelic football with [Father] Griffins and hurling with Liam Mellows, and rugby with OLBC [Our Lady's Boys Club],' says Elwood.

Elwood's dad, Eamonn, worked for P&T (Posts and Telegraph) as it was then called, before becoming first Telecom Éireann, then Eir-com and now Eir. He is now retired. Elwood's mum Margaret (née Egan) was a waitress who hails originally from Clarinbridge. 'So a "townie" married a country girl,' as Elwood puts it.

Elwood is the oldest of five. His sister Elaine is married and living in Boston. Nicola and her husband and three kids live in Athenry. Enda lives in Knocknacarra, with his wife and their three kids. His youngest brother, Emmett, is engaged and lives in Galway with his kids. Both brothers played rugby, Enda giving it up when he moved to America, and Emmett packing it in because of a curvature of the spine.

There was never much chance that the eldest would pack it in. 'I just loved it. I vividly remember that wall. Actually, at first there was no wall back in the day, but then they put up the wall. There was a gate in the wall, and then they closed the gate. Then they put glass on top of the wall. So we had a lot of obstacles to get to the other side of that wall.' Perhaps it would serve as a metaphor for his career.

In any event, no obstacle ever prevented him from scaling that wall into Galwegians. 'I never went in the front gate once in my life. Well, until I got a car. Even on match days I jumped the wall.'

One of his earliest coaches was George Parkinson, whose son has recently been coaching the Galwegians Under-10s along with Elwood. George was 'a great man', says Elwood, adding, 'We had great people who looked after us. There was also Mick Casserley and the great Billy Quinn, God rest him.

'They would all have taken me under their wing. There was real camaraderie there, and I suppose unlike the soccer and the football at the time, rugby had a clubhouse. Galwegians also had a bar, not that I was thinking of a bar as a ten year old; it was a place to meet after your rugby. And we had our own little room where we used to watch anything on a Saturday morning, with a bag of crisps and a drink. And then there was your annual trip to Lansdowne Road to the south terrace for a test match. We didn't call them test matches then; we called them internationals.' For the Connacht youngsters and for many others, this pilgrimage always included stopovers in Harry's of Kinnegad.

'Once in Dublin, we'd drive our coaches nuts,' Elwood recalls. 'We'd try to get lost in the south terrace, while they'd try to corral us in. It was just the journey. The day trip. The road trip. Watch the match. It was brilliant! Now I go up with my son to all the matches.'

Utterly hooked from the off, Elwood brought two kitbags into school, one for training with the Jes, and then another for when he was 'legging it' to more rugby training with 'Wegians, or soccer with Mervue United, or Gaelic football with Mervue. He continued to combine all three through school until he was 18.

'We had a great Gaelic team which went from junior B to junior A to intermediate in four years, and so achieved senior status. And then I was on the county team in '88 for a season. So I was playing inter-county football for the Galway senior team and I was also playing soccer, and I really loved soccer with Mervue. We actually played in the FAI Cup one year. But I had to make a call, and I just went with rugby.'

Why rugby?

'Because I just wanted to play for Ireland. It was always my dream. Another good friend of mine, Paddy Barrett, lived three or four doors from me, and we used to call in to each other's houses. Well, it was more that I used to call in to his house, where we watched Five Nations matches, and my heroes Ollie [Campbell] and Tony [Ward]. I could see, on the TV, where I wanted to get to: Lansdowne Road and the crowd. I also loved our day trips with 'Wegians from Under-10s on. So that's where I wanted to be. How I'd get there was the next challenge.'

To this end, it helped that Elwood was part of a Galwegians under-age generation that was also successful, staying together through the Under-16, -18 and -20 cycles, before graduating to the adult sides, be it firsts, seconds or thirds.

In addition to Casserley, Quinn and Parkinson, he mentions Mickey Heaslip, Frank Kinneen and Mike Deasy. 'Real club men – great "sky blues" – and brilliant mentors to me. Mickey gave me my first job in the Lions Tower pub in Galway and, with Frank and Mike, always supported me throughout my career.

'Back then everybody wanted to play for the club. There were no academies or sub-academies. It was all about playing for 'Wegians and in the AIL,' says Elwood, of a competition that started in 1990–91, just as his adult career was taking off.

In fact, by then he had made his Galwegians debut at 18 and was given his Connacht debut at 19, against the Scottish Districts in 1988, by Declan McDermott – still heavily involved in Corinthians and a Connacht season-ticket holder. The following year, George Hook was coach when Elwood played against the All Blacks in November 1989.

'The mighty All Blacks were the team that everyone looked up to, and they were coming to the Sportsground! It was a foggy, dewy kind of day, and they say there were over 10,000 people here. Not much health and safety back in those days. If you're not cheating, you're not trying! So they crammed them in. That was some experience, although it gave George the material for a story he always tells about me.'

Elwood had purchased new Adidas boots, which the match referee, Les Peard of Wales, inspected along with everybody else's in the Connacht dressing-room beforehand.

'Adidas had brought out this new range, and the studs went in like a plug; you had to turn them not screw them in. Do you think I could get those new sets of studs in Galway? Do you think I could? I tried every sports shop in Galway. They were new boots. New boots!'

Instead, Elwood tried to play with the old plastic studs, and on examining the boots Peard called Hook over.

Hook, furious, commented, 'Biggest game of your life, Elwood, and you've no f***ing studs!'

Peard said, 'He can't play.'

'What?' said an incredulous Elwood.

'You can't play in those!'

'I can't f***ing play? Les, you must be joking.'

A defiant Elwood played in his plastic studs. 'Les was a far more senior man than I was. He was OK with it, but it was a wake-up call! Ever since then – boots in order, socks in order! Tools of the trade in order! George tells that story all the time.'

Peard is a referee's assessor nowadays, and to this day whenever he runs into Elwood, he says, 'Show us your boots, Elwood!'

Elwood's early years with the Galwegians seniors also coincided with Warren Gatland's arrival at the club in the 1989–90 season. 'Gatty was the biggest influence on my career,' he says of the man who would subsequently coach him at Connacht and resurrect his international career when he became Irish head coach.

'Gatty just transformed how we played and how we thought of the game at Galwegians. Then he asked me to go to New Zealand.'

Elwood took up the offer and went out with his long-time girl-friend and wife-to-be Tara to play for most of 1990 in the same Taupiri team as Gatland.

'Gary Catley was the main man behind Taupiri, which is a country club, and he enticed city boys out there. I went out there to play rugby for a year. That was my university so to speak.

'They were beautiful people. To this day I think my name is on a board of honour there because I played for the club and went on to play for Ireland. Even now they're in touch with Tara through Face-book. I don't do Facebook or that stuff.

'That Taupiri team included about seven or eight of the Waikato team. We had serious players and played in a good competition in the

Waikato district, often coming up against All Blacks like Graham Purvis, Richard Loe, John Mitchell and Brent Anderson.

'That is where I decided "This is what I want to do". When I returned to Galway, we lost out narrowly in the round robin [in 1991] and I said, "Right, I gotta go to Dublin."'

Galwegians missed out on the first two seasons of the All-Ireland League, which consisted of two divisions of eight teams, via the round-robin play-offs for the provincial league winners. So Elwood decided to move to Lansdowne. It was them or St Mary's, two teams with strong Connacht connections. But his parting from Galwegians did not go well, for several reasons.

'We were playing Dolphin in Temple Hill. Trying to go long with a quick drop out, I kicked it out on the full to give them a scrum underneath the sticks. Mick Kiernan kicked the drop goal to win the match. The following season I joined Lansdowne, so in 'Wegians they said, "Not only did you make a mistake, Elwood, that lost us the game, then you feck off to Lansdowne."'

'But if I was to get where I wanted to be, I needed AIL football, and at the time Lansdowne had just been relegated. So in my second year we were in Div 2 and we won that. We had a good team that included Gussy [Irish scrum-half Fergus Aherne], [winger] Johnny Sexton, Clincher [Paul Clinch], Pete Purcell, Mano [Ryan], Charlie Quinn, and Willie Burns was captain, and two other Connacht men, Tom Clancy and Noel "Fly" Mannion, were there too.'

Elwood spent six seasons at Lansdowne before returning to Galwegians in 1997. 'Tara and I moved up to Dublin, and we had a fabulous time. We lived on Pembroke Road. It couldn't have been better.'

He had transferred from Irish Distillers in Galway to Irish Distillers in Leinster, before being offered a job in their Dublin base while he was playing with Lansdowne. His move also helped his rugby ambitions, as he made his Irish debut against Wales at Cardiff Arms Park. 'The sixth of March 1993,' he recalls immediately.

Two weeks beforehand, Ireland had suffered a 21–6 defeat at home to France – their 11th defeat in a row. Elwood was one of only two changes for the ensuing trip to Cardiff, when partnering Michael Bradley at half-back.

'That was my theatre of dreams. For me there was always something special about Cardiff. To hear the Welsh sing their national anthem in the old Cardiff Arms Park was amazing. Gerry Murphy was our coach, Noel Murphy our manager and Willie Anderson coached the forwards. So that was special. Your first cap, in Cardiff Arms, away from home, to break the duck with a win, kick a couple of goals – fantastic!'

Elwood had an immediate galvanizing effect on the team, kicking 11 points that day, and Ireland backed that up with a 17–3 win at home to England a fortnight later, with Elwood kicking a couple of drop goals as well as two penalties.

'I'll always remember that month, my debut in Wales, our win over England two weeks later, and then that Monday I went to Hong Kong. Hong Kong! Like what? Ten of us went to Hong Kong. Later that year, we were beaten in the semi-final of the inaugural World Cup Sevens in extra time against Australia at Murrayfield. So that was a fantastic month.

'The stand-out highlight has to be the World Cup in South Africa in '95! The Mandela story and the buzz in that country at the time, and then they eventually won it, with Mandela presenting the trophy to Francois Pienaar. With all that history and all the political issues, to be a part of that World Cup with your country was a privilege. I was fortunate enough to play in two World Cups, but for that particular one, just to say I was there was amazing.'

Ireland had lost in the quarter-finals to France by 36–12 in Durban, when Elwood kicked all Ireland's points. 'Jeeze, we let that go.' His appearances became more sporadic until he was restored as Ireland's first-choice out-half in the 1997–98 season.

He was, however, effectively back-up to David Humphreys in the 1999 World Cup, which would be an anticlimactic swansong to his test career; he watched from the bench in Lens when Ireland infamously lost their quarter-final play-off to Argentina.

'That was horrible, watching us pummelling their line at

the end. That was hard to take, but then it [the World Cup] seems to be a mental block for all Irish teams – even with the best players of our generation we've struggled a bit. We can't get beyond the quarter-final.'

Regrets, he has a few. 'I had a great time – two World Cups, 35 caps, Hong Kong Sevens. Rugby was so good to me, and I travelled the world, but I'd be nitpicking at myself more than anything. I didn't like the way it ended after the World Cup in '99, and there's been something nagging at me since. That maybe I could have gone on a bit longer or done a bit extra. And that's down to me. Could I have done more myself? It's certainly not a reflection on playing with Connacht. I wouldn't have dreamed of going anywhere else. I made my bed, and I lay in it.'

Elwood played 168 times in a 17-year career with Connacht from 1988 until his retirement in 2005, which remained a record until his tally was overtaken by Michael Swift in 2009. Given he played only four seasons in the Celtic League, heaven knows what his total might have been had that competition been around earlier. But on staying put with Connacht, no regrets.

'I do things for a reason. It's gotta mean something to me, and I like the challenge, and I like the fight, and I do what I believe is right. Connacht is my team.

'I used to have my annual free lunch in the Burlington with Jim Glennon and Deano [Paul Dean].

' "Are you going to play for Leinster?"

' "No, lads, I'm not, but thanks for the lunch."

'I was happy to travel up and down in the years I played with Lansdowne. Under Gatty, we'd meet halfway in Athlone or use the Tullamore facility, and I got to know fine people down there. It's what I wanted to do.

'People have told me I should have moved away, or "What about that time you could have gone to France?" I don't have regrets about that, because Connacht is my team.'

On another occasion, the Llanelli coach Gareth Jenkins asked him to join the Welsh club. But again he declined.

In 1996, he and Peter Clohessy had become the first Irish players to sign professional contracts with the IRFU. Elwood had initially been offered a one-year contract, hardly enough to tempt him away from a pensionable job with Irish Distillers but he changed his mind after the union upped it to three years, and with some persuasion from Noel Murphy, the then Irish team manager.

Alas for Connacht, Gatland, after his two seasons at the helm, was then whisked away by the union to coach Ireland.

'I remember talking to Johnny O'Connor about this recently, and we agreed that when we thought we had something, or a nucleus or a spine, people moved on. Johnny went to Wasps. Reddser [Eoin Reddan] went. Fla [Jerry Flannery] went. You'd always lose two or three. The good players left then because they felt they had to, and that's what we are trying to change, 15, 20 years later.

'But this is where I'm from. This is who I always wanted to play for. I played with some great people, and had some good days and bad days. Connacht is my team; I wasn't going to play for Leinster or anybody else.'

His last game for Connacht was on 24 April 2005, as a replacement in the European Challenge Cup semi-final second leg away to Sale in Edgeley Park, which Sale won 59–9. (Elwood had kicked eight points when starting the home semi-final defeat three weeks previously.) The expensively assembled Sale squad was studded with internationals – Jason Robinson, Charlie Hodgson, Bryan Redpath, Ignacio Fernández Lobbe, Sébastien Chabal and more.

'The last thing I remember was a cover tackle to try to stop a try in the corner. I think it was a nice sunny day. They beat us well. They were good back then. They had a wealthy owner [Brian] Kennedy, who was pumping money into them.'

Elwood went straight from playing into coaching, becoming Bradley's assistant at Connacht. 'I felt I might have had a *grá* for it. It was just a natural progression. I was doing the [coaching] badges, and I thought I might have a go at this. "Sure if it doesn't work out at least I'll have something to give back at club level."'

Soon after, he also became coach to the Irish Under-20s, guiding them to a Grand Slam in 2007 and coaching them in the 2008 World Cup in Wales. 'I lived on a roundabout in the Holiday Inn for three and a half weeks, with the joy of going over to Asda for a walk around and a McDonald's.'

In 2010, Bradley resigned at Connacht, and Elwood became head coach. Under Elwood, Connacht's League form improved, finishing ninth of 12 in his first season, then eighth of 12 in the next two. In the 2010–11 Challenge Cup, they were knocked out in the pool stages, finishing second in their group behind the eventual winners, Harlequins. At the end of the campaign, out-half Ian Keatley and hooker Sean Cronin moved on to Munster and Leinster respectively in order to improve their career prospects: a reminder of Connacht's status in the provincial pecking order.

Despite the team's improvement in form, if you ask Elwood to talk about his promotion, the first word which comes to him is 'challenging'.

He thought he'd been busy looking after the backs and Connacht's attack game. He'd do his working day, have a chat with his 'good pal' Bradley and then go home, relatively free of any more responsibilities. They were a two-man operation until Dan McFarland became forwards coach in 2006, a position he maintained when Elwood took over in 2010.

'I respect Dan as a player and a coach. When he first came over from Richmond, he completely embraced Galwegians and Connacht. We played together or coached together, at Irish Under-20s and Connacht, for 15 years. He was a great ally. He was strong-minded in his views. We had our disagreements, but the one thing I can say is that Dan's heart and soul, and his commitment to Connacht, was total. All he ever wanted was to see Connacht do well.'

It was only when Elwood assumed the role of head coach that he realized what came with it.

'Suddenly everyone is turning to you. I brought in Mike Forshaw from England as our defensive coach, which was a first for Connacht, and after him Billy Millard from Australia. So now we had these different departments, but they were all looking to me. It wasn't just a case of coaching the team. Then there was the matter of playing rugby, allocating time for one-on-ones, and that was only the coaching staff!

'I also had to deal with all our senior players, and our academy and sub academy. I had a brilliant working relationship with Nigel [Carolan], as we know each other very well from our playing days, and he has been doing a fantastic job with our academy. I was working closely with our manager Tim [Allnutt]. He's as Connacht to the core as any of us; he's always been a good people person, knows his rugby, and is ideal for any coach to lean on. And then I brought Conor McPhillips down from Dublin to do the analysis. Conor has a good rugby brain and he had a *grá* for the AIL game too, which was important to us at the time. We weren't shopping for players in Brown Thomas at the time. We were shopping in Aldi and Lidl, so we were looking for little gems.

'Then there was dealing with contracts and Gerry [Kelly, CEO] and Tim upstairs, as well as the media. I've known Gerry since I was a schoolboy in the Jes. He's been there for my whole rugby life. He gave me my first job as an assistant coach and then as a head coach. He's been a great servant to Connacht rugby, as a schoolboys' selector, Connacht president and Connacht CEO. Like Tim, Gerry was always there to lean on, and I'll always be deeply grateful to him for all his help and guidance throughout my career with Connacht.

'In the meantime, you're trying to get a lifestyle balance at home with three kids. It was daunting. I had an idea of what I was getting into, but no one prepared me for the job as head coach, with all its different facets.'

Elwood was also leading a campaign to improve Connacht's training, playing and spectator facilities, the resistance to which became frustrating.

'I got myself in hot water upstairs with Gerry numerous times. He was very understanding, but his hands were tied. So I used to vent that frustration in Dublin when I got the opportunity. I took exception to us being called a development province [by the union]. I had my disagreements, but I was only fighting for what I believed was right. Again, I use my four-legged stool analogy. I said [to key figures in the IRFU], "I'm not a development coach. I'm here to do a job to the best of my abilities, as are the other three coaches. We're not a developing province, and please don't say that again. We're here to do the best we can and raise the bar. We're here to improve our own indigenous players and to provide players at all different levels for Irish rugby. Yes, it's a challenge, but why can't I aspire, why can't I dream?" So I got in a bit of hot water with the IRFU and their committees and Eddie [Wigglesworth, the union's director of rugby]. We had heated discussions or debates, but I was only fighting for what I believe in and for the best interests of Connacht rugby. That's all I was doing.

'The reason I took the job was to make a difference. I wanted to add value, and I wanted to see could I do it my way. The pleasing thing for me was that during three years we gave starts to 18 indigenous players, and many have come through.

'That was important to me. If you want Connacht people to support the Connacht team, you need indigenous Connacht players, and that was my mantra: "We really want to promote our own." If our own were good enough, they would get a fair crack, or an even fairer crack than somebody else.'

In Elwood's first season, Connacht's season-ticket sales topped the 3,000 mark for the first time in their history. Their average attendance in home League matches climbed to 4,653 in the 2011–12 season, increasing further to 5,154 for 2012–13. (For the record, it was the Celtic League from 2001–02 to 2006-07, then became the Magners League until 2011–12, then the Rabo Direct League until 2014–15, and since then the Pro12.)

'I know it might sound clichéd, but that's what it's been, a journey,' says Elwood. 'Everybody tries to raise the bar and Brads [Michael Bradley] was terrific here. Brads introduced the concept of roadshows around the province. Brads was very committed for his seven years here, and he put good structures in place. I just tried to bring it on to another level.'

In Elwood's second season as head coach, 2011–12, Connacht made their first appearance in the Heineken Cup, due to a change in the rules that had seen Leinster earn Ireland a fourth place in the tournament by dint of winning the 2011 final.

Yet at no time in his tenure was the toll greater than during a 14-match losing sequence from September to January in that second season at the helm. This had featured five pool defeats in their inaugural Heineken Cup campaign, but the run finally ended with a 9–8 win over Conor O'Shea's Harlequins.

'It was a shocking day,' recalls Elwood of that horrid, rain-swept, mucky night in Galway. 'It was awful, but it was getting the win, our first win in the Heineken Cup on our first journey. That's probably the standout.'

The frustrations of that 14-match losing sequence, and the unbridled joy and relief of the win over Harlequins, were brilliantly captured by the televised documentary *The West's Awake*, for which cameras had followed Connacht for that season, and in which Elwood was the central figure.

'It only happened because the PGB [Professional Games Board] told me to do it. I didn't want to do it, because it's very intrusive. Yes, it was brilliant TV, but it didn't portray us in the professional light I felt we deserved. It was all about the "ra-ra-ra", but there wasn't the analytical stuff. There wasn't the meetings and the hard work that was done behind the scenes.

'I know it was driven for TV, but I lost a hell of a lot of credibility on the school run with my use of language in it. I had to show it to my own kids too, because they were mad to see it, but that's the world we're in,' Elwood says of rugby.

'We're in a man's world of high testosterone, and that's just some of the colourful language that's used. That's why I was nervous doing it. I get why they did it, I get why they showed what they did, because that's good TV. Personally, it wasn't my cup of tea, but I know it was a tough journey for me and for all the guys. The 14-match losing streak hurt me more, because I was the coach. I had to face people in the morning after we lost. I took it home with me. I couldn't walk down town without being afraid to make eye contact. I took it very personally, but it's all worthwhile. Eventually, it was going to break, but to break it against Harlequins in Europe and then to have all that in a movie with a happy ending, you kind of say, "Yeah, I suppose it was worth it." A part of me says that, although not a big part.'

That debut Heineken Cup campaign had extra poignancy for Elwood because his son Callum, who was then five years old and had never seen his dad play, had been the Connacht mascot for the first game at home to Toulouse, and so was led on to the pitch by Gavin Duffy, and the entire family were in the Clan Terrace. 'That's why there were all those tears in the [coaches'] box,' explains Elwood.

After qualifying again for the 2012–13 Heineken Cup through Leinster winning the trophy in 2012 and thus an additional place for Ireland, the experienced Scottish out-half Dan Parks was a marquee signing. Connacht won three of six pool matches, beating Zebre at home and away and Biarritz at home.

But by October of that third season at the helm, Elwood had decided he wanted his life and family back. In October 2012, he announced his decision to step down at the end of the 2012–13 season. He was letting the job consume him.

'I wasn't afraid of the hard work, or the fight. I was in here first thing every morning before seven and last to leave. But it is in my DNA, unfortunately, to take things too personally, and I let it get to me.'

Laura was then 13, Rachel 8 and Callum six. 'At home, the girls were starting to play hockey and their sports. I'll always remember something Callum said one day; it's always stuck with me. I would never make excuses or false promises to him. If I said I was going to be there, I always made sure I was there. There were times I had to say, "I'm sorry, guys, I can't be there . . . Rachel, I can't, Laura, I can't, I have a meeting in Dublin." Whatever it was. But coming up to Callum's birthday, I was being the good dad, saying, "What do you want for your birthday?" as I picked him up. And he goes, "Dad, can you be at my birthday?" And Tara looked across at me. Tara has always been understanding.'

Indeed. Neighbourhood friends in Mervue, they began going out as teenagers, and Tara has moved home and changed her various jobs with the Irish Film centre and Temple Bar Properties to wherever Elwood's career took them, be it New Zealand, Dublin or Galway.

'She was always minding the kids when I was away, but when Tara looked across at me, I said, "OK, love, leave it with me." When my kids started asking me to be at birthdays, when excuses had just run dry, I looked at myself. "What am I doing here? I'm on a treadmill that's getting faster. I don't know if the light coming at me is getting closer or is it a steam train. Am I enjoying it? I'm gone at seven o'clock in the morning and I'm home when they're in bed, kissing them goodnight when they are already asleep. So I'm not seeing them when they get up. I'm not bringing them to school. I'm missing all the important events in the house." I'm thinking, "I'm just passing in the night here."

'I sat down with Tara and said, "That's it." And she goes, "What are you talking about?" And I said, "That's it. I'm going to call it a day." She said, "Don't be stupid." But I went through the chain of events, and she said, "Not at all, we'll manage. We'll be grand. The kids are grand." But I said, "No, I'm not doing this again. I can't look them in the eye." She answered, "Whatever you want, I'll support you."

'"I know you will but I want to make sure you're happy with it."

'"OK then, we'll sleep on it and talk again another night."'

A few nights later, Elwood reaffirmed his decision to his wife. They sat the kids down and told them that their daddy would stop coaching Connacht. Whereupon Mum and Dad were hit with a barrage of questions.

'How are we going to get tickets?'

'Can we still go to games?'

'Will you still be allowed in?'

'Can we still get some kit?'

'Can I still stand there?'

Having addressed all these concerns, they were able to assure them their dad would be able to join them for longer on their annual holidays in Connemara, watch them play their sports and could watch the Connacht games with them.

When Tara and the kids headed to Connemara for two months,

Elwood's own treks there had shrunk in his time as head coach. 'I was planning for next season. It was my own fault. I was always trying to be ahead of the game, to do something different. I always said to Dan McFarland, "We've got to do it our way, the Connacht way. We gotta do something different. We are unique. Everything is different about us." So, yeah, it was overkill, and I suffered. Not that I didn't enjoy it. I enjoyed the challenge, but when one game was over you're on to the next one. That's the nature of the job. I never took the time to really stop and enjoy it.'

By dint of deciding in October, Elwood could actually enjoy the remainder of the 2012–13 season a little more. It also afforded Connacht more time to locate a replacement. After Pat Lam's appointment in January 2013, Elwood happily facilitated Lam's desire to assume a watching brief from early May in the latter stages of that season. So began the start of a beautiful friendship.

Elwood thought it would be unfair to Lam, and not beneficial to Connacht, for the new man to arrive in June or July. Elwood recounts the hoary old tale about the prop from London Irish who was about to join Connacht and when he arrived at Dublin airport, jumped into a cab and said, 'Take me to Connacht.'

Lam vowed not to interfere or go anywhere he might be in the way, but Elwood gave him carte blanche. 'It was simply my duty as an outgoing coach to give the next guy every chance, and it is still "our" team. I shared everything with him.

'I had too much respect for Pat, for Connacht, for the people here and for the players [to do anything other than welcome him]. We needed to give this man every chance, and anybody willing to come over months in advance showed that he cares. Pat wanted to get to know the area, the people, and if there was an opportunity for him and Steph to drive around the province and understand where Mayo or Sligo was, they took it. He could have easily said, "I'll pop over in July", but, no, he came early, and that's a credit to him.'

For the next two years, Elwood never missed a home game, whether en famille if the girls didn't have a hockey match or with Callum if they did, and enjoyed being a match-day supporter, 'looking through the lens of a supporter, listening to some great comments in the Clan Terrace. I'm going, "Jeeze, did they say that about me?" They're all passionate, but they all have their own ways. It's just hilarious. It was enjoyable though – family time. I didn't go to the marquee. I just brought the kids. Watched the match. We had our pizza on the way home. Did our own thing.

'I have a way of watching. I might pick an individual or the shape, whereas others just shout at the referee, but it's interesting. I was privy early on to the type of game Pat wanted, and it just evolved, evolved, evolved into what we have now.'

He didn't converse much with Lam or any of those on the inside. 'I was gone. It's Pat's team. I didn't want to be lingering around or loitering with intent. It's not my way.'

He thought that would be his lot with Connacht. Whereupon, out of the blue, Elwood saw an opportunity was coming up in Connacht as the domestic rugby manager.

Elwood had got a job as a medical rep with Omega Pharma after leaving Connacht. He was happy in his job. He was his own boss, in charge of the pharmaceutical company's operation in the west of Ireland. Omega Pharma were sponsoring a professional cycling team and bringing out a new sports nutritional supplement in which Elwood was to be centrally involved. But he thought the Connacht job would be a good fit. He researched it some more, submitted his application, went through the interview and the rest is history.

Elwood started his new job in January 2015. He's been taken aback by how much is included in his remit: the clubs and schools games, underage boys' and girls' rugby, the various competitions and meetings. He'd like to be doing more actual coaching. 'But we'll get a handle on it, and we think we know where we're going.'

He is combining this with his underage coaching of Callum's team in Galwegians, doing some kicking practice with the age-grade players, and working with the Connacht domestic staff around the province.

'It is good to be back, and it's really encouraging when you see what Willie [Ruane] has been doing. He's been brilliant. He's so level-headed and he's so driven and he knows what he wants. Hopefully we're doing him justice, because we're only as good as the people we work with.

'Everything seems to have a purpose in the journey, and I'm a firm believer in faith – that everything happens for a reason. I might be back here for a reason and maybe add another bit of value at this level.'

Elwood is back where his rugby heart belongs, and somehow you know he'll leave a legacy. Again.

6

Willie Ruane

Willie Ruane was a full-back with Ballina, playing in the Connacht Senior League, when Warren Gatland, in his second season as Connacht coach, brought him into the Connacht squad. For two seasons, Ruane was an ever-present in the number 15 jersey. Whereupon, though still only 25, he handed in his contract.

'To be honest I thought the whole thing was going to come crashing down around our ears. I just thought the idea that we got paid to play rugby was mad, so I took up a job with Bank of Ireland, who at the time were our sponsors.'

A week before the start of the 2000–01 season, both Tom Keating and Simon Allnutt damaged their cruciate ligaments, and Steph Nel prevailed upon Ruane to temporarily fill the void. But that was his lot with Connacht, as thereafter he confined his rugby-playing days to Galwegians and Ballina.

'When we went pro, we had no sense whatsoever as to what we could or couldn't achieve, and we went into it with a naivety. And for some reason or another it seemed to work. In that first early period with Gatty, all of a sudden we were doing stuff that probably no one thought we could do.'

From the outside looking in over the intervening years until returning as CEO for the 2014–15 season, Ruane reckons, 'We went from that state of early naivety and exuberance to realizing this is actually a business. Then, maybe, other problems arose, such as us not knuckling down in the way that we should have. I would say we had no sense as to what was needed.'

It was left to individuals to 'carry the cross', as Ruane puts it, be it the coaches, most notably Michael Bradley and especially Eric Elwood, who had also done so as a player. Ditto John Muldoon and others, who could have walked away but stayed.

When Ruane came into the Connacht squad, virtually all the players were on part-time contracts. 'There were only about five or six full-time contracted players, and the rest were all initially on part-time contracts. But Gatty was not your typical coach in the way he thought about the game. He was teaching us things that we didn't even know. It wasn't just that they were new; you just didn't know they existed, really.

'I was playing full-back at the time, and he was teaching me things about full-back play that no one had ever opened my eyes to, and he was a hooker! He was meant to have his head stuck in a scrum, and yet he was telling me how to attack off a scrum and line-out; he was great like that.

'He was hard to figure out as well, though. You wouldn't get two words out of him.'

That may be hard to tally with the current Gatland, never averse to some pre-match gamesmanship or provocative suggestions, but he was then only 34. The pity for Connacht was that the Irish job came his way within two seasons. He helped give Connacht a glimpse of what might be possible.

'Oh, if he'd stayed longer I think we could have embedded a lot of the good stuff, and it proved a difficult challenge for the coaches coming in after him. Then again, the bar was high with Gatty.'

Gatland had also recruited cleverly in Mark McConnell and Junior Charlie, both of whom stayed for five seasons until 2002, although not all subsequent signings were of that ilk. Curiously, of the southern-hemisphere recruits, Kiwis have traditionally settled in best with Connacht. 'People in the west of Ireland are pretty laid-back, which suits many Kiwi guys,' admits Ruane.

Standout wins included the 42–13 result against Northampton on

9 September 1997, with Ruane a try-scorer in the handsome opening victory at the Sportsground. 'I got an intercept, in our 22, and ran the length of the pitch. And I remember they had a big hefty Samoan fella at number 8 [Shem Tatupu] who nearly caught me as I fell over the line, absolutely knackered. Dick O'Hanlon, who was the bagman at the time, said, "Well done, but you need to sort yourself out. That fella nearly caught you there." Here was I thinking I did great! But anyway.'

Another highlight for Ruane was the ensuing week-long escapade to the south of France for the back-to-back games against Nice and Bordeaux-Bègles. 'It was funny, we were getting calls telling us what was being written about us back home – that no Irish team had ever won in France. None of us knew that. We hadn't a clue. I didn't have a clue anyway. But I would say that whole week gelled that team and gave us a bit of belief for the season.'

The 1998–99 season was different. 'Glenn Ross just struggled, in fairness, to capture that mood again, and even at club level we struggled. A lot of that team were playing with 'Wegians, and we were relegated. That just shows you that mentally we'd gone from a high and weren't able to reproduce it the following year. We just weren't used to it.'

During that season, Ruane and Jimmy Duffy were called up to play for the Barbarians as part of the Remembrance Day celebrations. 'About two months later, I'd say, I handed in my contract.

'I just got a notion that it was time to get on with the rest of my life. I look back now and to be honest I didn't see myself playing for Ireland, and I didn't see myself as a journeyman, because I didn't think that it was a career. It was something that you'd either go the whole way with and do something great, or not at all. Jimmy was unfortunately diagnosed with a heart problem and forced to retire soon after.'

Shane Byrne played in that Baa-Baas game, and Ruane recalls, 'I was thinking to myself, "What are you still doing playing professional rugby?" Keith Wood was definitely the main man at the time, but fair play to Shane, he hadn't been capped at that stage but kept at it and ended up having a wonderful Irish career.

'Emmet Byrne also played in that game, and I was looking at him, thinking, "You're too small to play international rugby." Again, fair play to him. Both he and Shane had that genuine belief in their ability, whereas I didn't. I didn't think I'd ever play for Ireland. Jimmy did have that belief, because he was good enough, but it wasn't to be for him, unfortunately.'

Ruane then began talking to people in Bank of Ireland, who were the main Connacht sponsors at the time. 'I had done a primary degree and then a post-grad in financial services. Some of their key figures went to all our games, and I just got chatting about banking. An opportunity came up, I went for an interview and got the job.'

He was based in the west, so continued playing with Galwegians, who had a revival under their English coach John Kingston. He led them to promotion in 1999–2000 back to Division One, where they finished second the following season. 'He was magic. He was, I would say, nearly the best coach I've ever had.'

Ruane later relocated to his hometown of Ballina, to settle down with his now wife Elaine, and finished his club career back where it had all started. Ruane had played Gaelic football in his formative years but had also played mini rugby in the Ballina club from the age of eight, where he now helps coach his own three sons, Billy, Tom and Robert. Following his uncles and cousins as a boarder in Garbally College ensured rugby held sway from his secondary school years. 'My family had a pub, so it wasn't really conducive to studying, and I was sent to Garbally, which was a wonderful experience.'

Ruane has four sisters and one younger brother, who also went to Garbally, where, ironically, the long-serving Connacht CEO Gerry Kelly was his maths teacher. Ruane played alongside Kelly's son on Garbally's Senior Cup team, which was coached by Johnny Farrell, 'a huge influence on my subsequent rugby career'.

His father Judd Ruane played music rather than sports, although his mum's family was steeped in rugby. Jean Duffy's brother, Tony, is father of long-time Connacht full-back Gavin Duffy, meaning, of course, that Tony Duffy is also Ruane's uncle. John Duffy, another uncle, also sent his kids to Garbally while Ruane was there, and all the Duffys played for Ballina as well.

Ruane won three Senior Cup medals with Garbally before going to NUIG (National University of Ireland Galway), and having played for the Connacht Schools then played for Connacht Youths. After transferring to Waterford College (where he won an All-Ireland Colleges rugby title), Ruane also played for the Irish Colleges team and the Irish Under-21s.

Having won the Connacht Senior League with Ballina, he was called into the Connacht squad, and so switched to Galwegians. 'In fairness to Ballina, it was on the back of playing for them that I was first called into the Connacht squad.'

In the years after his retirement from Connacht, he regularly attended matches at the Sportsground and also travelled to away games such as the many European meetings with Harlequins. When Kelly retired as Connacht CEO after 13 years in the role at the end of the 2011–12 season, Ruane appeared an ideal candidate. He was encouraged to apply and duly did so. The shortlist was whittled down to himself and Tom Sears, the then CEO of Kenya Cricket, who was eventually chosen for the role.

'When I didn't get the job the first time, I was pretty gutted, I don't mind admitting. Connacht is a small place, and what made it more difficult was people coming up to me saying, "Hard luck with that job" once it had become public knowledge.'

Within 15 months of taking over from Kelly, though, Sears unexpectedly stepped down early in the 2013–14 season. Needless to say, after his last experience, Ruane was hesitant about going through a drawn-out interview process again, but 'ultimately I decided to get over my bruised ego and accept the role when it was eventually offered to me. Obviously I am glad I did now.'

After a 15-year interregnum, Ruane was back in Connacht, moving from their last line of defence on the pitch to their front line off it.

Ruane believes that at times in the intervening years, Connacht didn't help themselves. 'There was a sense of entitlement, a feeling that we should be treated as equals, but maybe we needed to earn that, and earn it by doing things the way they should be done. The attitude was that as long as you give everything you have – and we took that to mean going out on a Saturday and trying your damnedest – then it could mask the things we weren't doing to be a really professional organization. I think Connacht struggled with the idea of moving from an amateur to a professional organization.

'It was a professional organization run in an amateur way, and I'd say that held us back. In fairness to Gerry [Kelly], he was a really good guy and knew what needed to be done, but there were a lot of people that needed to be on the same page, and I have no doubt that proved to be difficult. I'm not sure we were really prepared to challenge ourselves as much as we needed to. Maybe it was too easy to blame others at times.'

Elwood was an honourable exception. 'When we were playing, Eric had standards that no one else could match. "If you're on time, you're late." Even today, if you have to meet Eric, you can be sure he'll be there at least half an hour early. He was just a shining light. I loved every minute of being his teammate.'

Accordingly, one of Ruane's first goals was to bring Elwood back into the set-up. 'All I had to do was nudge him. How could you have Connacht Rugby without Eric Elwood? It's like having crackers and no cheese.'

In time, the role of domestic game manager became vacant, and Elwood was selected after a due interview process.

'He's just part of the DNA. It's the simple things. Pat can come in on a Monday morning, go straight into Eric's office and sit down and chat. Eric is a good listener but will be honest, which is what you need. So when Pat is feeling good or bad about what happened that weekend, he has someone to talk to, someone who has been in his position before and understands the challenges in a way the rest of us can't. They can almost counsel each other. And Eric is so important in reminding us all what Connacht are about.'

Nor will Galwegians receive any special treatment. On the contrary. Elwood treats all of Connacht's clubs as of equal importance.

'Because Eric is so passionate about Connacht Rugby, everyone who comes into contact with him cannot help but be motivated and inspired by that passion. He is prepared to give of his time to anyone who wants to make Connacht Rugby better, no matter what the ask is. If anything, he can be too accessible, so I am working on him learning to say no at times. I'm not sure how successful I will be on that front, though.'

For much of his 15 years working in the banking sector, latterly becoming a director within Ulster Bank's business restructuring division, Ruane never envisaged working full-time for Connacht. Given how he called a halt to his playing career, it's pretty ironic that he's back there, as well as finding it more fun than he could have imagined.

'I love it,' he says, sitting in his neatly kept office behind the Clan Terrace. 'I don't know what I'll do after this.'

After this? 'Ah yeah, eventually everything will come to an end. Not for a while yet though, I hope.'

He also appreciates his good fortune in being where he is. 'We could have sunk without the core of people who work for Connacht on a daily basis, in every department, both staff and volunteers. Along with Gerry Kelly and many others, including Niamh Hoyne, they helped to steer the ship through some pretty choppy waters.'

Even so, when he first came aboard, as he puts it, 'There was plenty of low-hanging fruit. You didn't have to be a rocket scientist to figure out a lot of stuff that needed doing, because the stuff that needed to change was obvious. Finding all the next bits will be more difficult, and probably more difficult in Pat's world too. There are still areas where change is obviously needed. There's still plenty that we need to be better at. Eric has big plans for the domestic game – that's a great opportunity. So we need to figure out how to do it the right way. You could get spread thin doing a load of bits and pieces and not actually have any real sense of what you're trying to achieve overall.'

The local club game is still the poor relation of the four provinces. Connacht has no team in the top flight following Galwegians' relegation from Division 1A on the last day of the 2015–16 season, thus joining Buccaneers in Division 1B.

'We should be doing better, but those clubs know that and are working hard to get back to the level we all want them at.' Improving coaching standards is, Ruane believes, critical for the Connacht clubs.

Corinthians are in Division 2A, and along with Sligo and the two in Division 1B, they are Connacht's only senior clubs. In recent years, Connemara have fallen through the Division 2B relegation trapdoor to join the likes of Ballina, Westport, Monivea and others in the Connacht Junior 1A league.

Ruane is, however, confident about the future. 'We are seeing huge growth at youth and schools levels, and, provided we can keep these kids in the game, there is definitely enough talent out there to support our clubs and Connacht Rugby into the future.'

The last few seasons have also seen Connacht's core support swell to unprecedented levels. After they have finally been granted a whiff of success and a sense of what it's like dining at European rugby's top table, there's a freshness, enthusiasm and eagerness which the other provinces have long since discovered.

'It's hard to mobilize supporters at times, without a doubt, but then again you have to give them something to cheer. We definitely think it's there, but you've still got to be winning to get them here, and I understand that. That's the same in any province. But there are people out there who, if you give them any reason to support, they will support. And the more the wider community feels they're part of it, then the more support you'll have. They don't care whether it's Gaelic football, rugby or soccer. Anything at all. Whatever it is, they'll get behind it.'

To that end, Ruane does not envisage Connacht winning trophies every season but does want them to become regular contenders. 'If you're Glasgow Warriors or if you're Leinster, first and foremost your job is to get into the play-offs, to be in the business end of the season, and then you're in Cup football. That could end after one game or you could end up winning it. Our job is to make sure that we're in the business end of the season. And if you achieve consistency, then you should be in the business end of the season, and then after that, all bets are off. And that's all I think we can hope to do.'

No one is more surprised than Ruane that so many from the generation of the late 1990s are now working for Connacht. 'There is no way that I would have thought that Mervyn was going to be in rugby beyond two years after that. He was the least likely rugby-head.

'I didn't think Nigel would be at all, because Nigel was just a flamboyant kind of free spirit. If he'd said to me, "I'm going around the world backpacking," I'd have thought, "Yeah, that's Nige." Eric? Definitely. I knew Eric would. I thought Conor [McGuinness] just might shoot back to Dublin, but he's also retained that involvement. He's been great. Conor's a really bright fella and is one of the people that I'll go to for a steer on things. If you needed to have a really strategic conversation as to how we should do something, you'd pick up the phone to Conor. He also has real credibility in rugby circles, and that's important.' In fact, the overall role of the Professional Games Board, of which Conor is a member, cannot be overstated.

As for Tim Allnutt, who has been team manager since 2003, Ruane says, 'Timmy is "the glue", as I refer to him. He's the oil in the engine. You see other team managers who do a different type of job, some of them focusing on other areas. But the way Tim performs the role is really important for us; he would do anything for Connacht Rugby. It's amazing, a Kiwi guy who just bought into it and married a local girl [Geraldine]. He's a great fella.' Geraldine's father is also a groundsman at the Sportsground.

Nor could Ruane or anyone have envisaged Duffy coming back one day to work with the academy and then become forwards coach, including Duffy himself. 'I played with Jimmy in that Baa-Baas match, and then he left. He gave up rugby. He went out working in a commercial role of some sort and then came back in. He's a sharp fella. He has a major future in coaching. He has great emotional intelligence. He just gets people and has amazing attention to detail, which is why he works so well with Pat.'

'I have a picture hanging in my living room at home, and it's of me playing a Junior Cup final, down on that pitch,' says Ruane, nodding towards the back pitch at the Sportsground. 'It's in black and white, and was in one of the Galway papers. The pitch was churned up, it was lashing rain, and I was only thirteen at the time. I was playing scrumhalf, and I'm pictured making a dive pass. The other scrum-half, who is about to jump on me, is Mervyn Murphy. I even have photos of me playing against Nigel in school and against Barry Gavin, who now sits on our rugby advisory board. I played against all those guys, before 1997 and 1998. It goes all the way back through school, which is great. I love that.

'It definitely makes it a bit more special when you're working with people with whom you have a long association and who you know are in it for the very same reason I'm in it, and for the very same reason Eric is in it. Because you genuinely love it.'

7

Pat Lam

Virtually everything about Pat Lam the rugby coach reflects Pat Lam the man. He's open, honest, transparent and has found his vocation in life as a teacher; it just so happens that he teaches rugby. And his nomadic life as a player and coach, along with his Samoan/ New Zealand roots, have taught him that both rugby and family demand loyalty, trust and the building of strong relationships.

Both Lam's parents are Samoan. His dad, Sonny, and mother, Anna, first met, and eventually married, in New Zealand after Sonny moved there in the early sixties and Anna followed.

'I've got a lot of respect for him,' says Lam. 'My dad was tough. He was actually brought up by his grandparents, because soon after his birth his own dad left for New Zealand. When he was five years old, his mother's family gave him to his grandparents on his dad's side, the Lams. So he was brought up with all his cousins.

'At 19, he was sent on a ship to New Zealand and met his dad for the very first time. He became a builder/carpenter like his own dad. Dad wanted a better life for us, and he's an unbelievable builder. He still is and does a lot of stuff around the place. When he also got a job in Air New Zealand as a kitchen hand, his pay went through the roof. I remember we went to Disneyland soon after. He rebuilt our three-bed house into a six-bedroom one in his spare time.

'He also decided to go to night school and trained as a pastry chef, and ended up being one of the top pastry chefs in Air New Zealand, becoming a boss over a period of 25 years. Since his retirement, he has a lifetime free flight anywhere around the world, once a year. He and Mum love golf, and once a year they travel around the world to play golf.

'I look at him now and think, "Jeeze, he was such a hard worker." He worked long days to provide for our family, and he was pretty strict and authoritarian. When I left New Zealand for Newcastle at 29 years of age, that was the first time he told me he loved me. It just wasn't how dads spoke to their sons back then. And then I think of his own upbringing as well.'

Lam has an older sister, Antonia, who's a businesswoman, and a younger brother, Damian, called Junior, who's a policeman. 'We had good childhoods. My mum was one of 11, and my granddad, on my dad's side [also Patrick Lam] is one of 23.'

Eh, 23?

'Yeah, 17 and six. My great-granddad had 17 with his first wife and another six with his second. Yeah, the Lams. Lots of Lams. He was Chinese, hence the name Lam with no "b".

'After the war [WW1] the Germans came back to Samoa,' says Lam, in reference to the Germans having colonized Samoa in the nineteenth century before it was taken from them by New Zealand in the First World War. 'That's why you have the Schusters and the Schwalgers, who brought the Chinese in as workers early in the century. That's where you get a name like Bundee Aki, from the Samoan/Chinese influence.

'My mum was one of 11, and her mother lived until she was nearly 103 years old. Yeah, I've got great genes. Her name was Antonia, and when I phoned her she would recognize my voice and know my name immediately. No hearing aid, no glasses. She was great. So we come from a big family, and we spend a lot of time on my mum's side with cousins.

'Mum was your typically supportive rugby mother. One of the reasons I'm not a good cook is because Mum did everything. If I was playing a game at two o'clock, she would have my meal ready at 11, or if I was playing at night, it was ready at four or five. It was like clockwork. I was fed well, and healthily. It could be steak or chop suey or a Samoan dish, lot of chow meins. We were brought up mostly on rice, not so much potatoes as here in Ireland, and plenty of steak, pork, lamb. Plenty of meat. The good stuff. And my gear was always cleaned.

'Mum and Dad were also very sociable, and as a Pacific Islander being educated in a rugby school, it helped me that they mingled quite well with the European community.'

Indeed, as for so many Kiwis, not least those from Samoan extraction, rugby took an early hold and has remained an integral, life-forming experience, albeit no one of his generation could have envisaged it becoming a career, per se.

'I found my identity through my rugby. Remember that I grew up in the seventies and eighties, when being a Pacific Islander wasn't popular. There was a tension there. I've grown up thinking of myself as a New Zealander, but I'm Samoan as well. But growing up I did notice that difference.

'I went into school thinking, "I'm a big guy", like most Pacific Islanders. Rugby is predominantly a white sport, but from a very young age – five or six – I realized, "I'm good at this. I can run through and around people. I can score."

'I was quick then. And when you're good at rugby in a New Zealand school, everyone's your mate. So rugby gave me a real sense of identity. My granddad would give me 50 cents – which was then a lot of money – to score a try. So I used to score lots of tries!'

This is the aforementioned Patrick. 'A good, Irish Catholic name!'

Alas, grandfather Patrick died of a heart attack at the age of 55, when his grandson was only eight. 'He came to all my early games. I think he was trying to make up for missing his own son's childhood, my dad's. My dad always took all three of us to my games.

'His heart attack was also a warning for me and my dad. My dad almost went at 60 because of his high cholesterol, and my cholesterol is high, so he's always on to me to have it checked, and the docs in Galway do the same.'

Lam attended St Peter's College in Auckland, a Catholic

secondary school for boys that has a long-established reputation for high achievement in academia and sports, notably rugby. He was also part of a generation of players that, even by New Zealand standards, was pretty special. He captained both the New Zealand schools and New Zealand Colts (Under-21s), whose teams featured several future All Blacks: Inga Tuigamala, Craig Innes, Walter Little, Jason Hewett, Jamie Joseph, Matthew Ridge, Shane Howarth and John Timu. 'We won everything,' says Lam. 'We cleaned teams up.'

All were earmarked for various provincial set-ups. 'In my last year of school, Graham Henry selected myself, Inga Tuigamala and Craig Innes for the Auckland Under-21s, which was unheard of then, because normally only senior club players were picked at that level.'

Lam made his senior debut at 21 against Queensland in 1990. Auckland's incumbent number 8, Zinzan Brooke, had contracted food poisoning while part of the New Zealand Sevens squad that had won the Hong Kong Sevens, thus ruling him out of the game.

'Queensland was full of Wallabies like Michael Lynagh; in the Auckland team there was only me and one other guy who weren't All Blacks. So it was a massive occasion, and I got Player of the Match that day.'

From the age of ten, Lam had been returning to Samoa for his summer holidays. His parents would put Lam and his brother on a plane to Apia, where they'd spend two months with their cousins. 'And it was great. We loved it.'

Soon after breaking into the Auckland team, they played Samoa in a friendly in 1991. They won well, with Lam scoring two tries, and as a result of this his teammate at Auckland, the then Samoan captain Peter Fatialofa, asked him to play for Samoa in the 1991 World Cup. 'I remember thinking, "Wow, if I don't go to a World Cup now, I might never go to one." In those days, if you had ancestors from another country, you could play for both.'

It would prove to be Lam's first of three World Cups with Samoa, which only strengthened his bond with the country of his parents. Their traits and values are his. 'Family. Entertaining. Laughter. They're always laughing. At a game in Samoa, they're always laughing. If someone gets knocked out, they laugh. If someone's chasing another player, they laugh. Everything is based around culture, dance, music and food. That's why there's not too many individual sports. Samoans need that sense of belonging, that sense of community, of working as a team. That's why Bundee Aki fits in perfectly here.'

After the 1991 World Cup, Lam explained to Bryan Williams and Peter Schuster that, like all New Zealand-born boys, his dream had been to play for the All Blacks. Although Samoa have participated in every World Cup since 1991, the latter had been their first. Williams, a legendary former winger with Auckland and the All Blacks himself, readily understood.

Lam played in the 1992 All Blacks trial for the Possibles alongside Dallas Seymour and Richard Turner. Later that year, when the All Blacks were in Australia on an 11-match, three-test tour (and lost the series 2–1), Lam was called up as a late replacement for Mike Brewer in their penultimate tour game against Sydney.

'I still believe I hold the record as the only player who's played for the All Blacks without ever training for them. I arrived after flying in the night before the match, after their training session, and I was told I was playing the next day. So I was up all night with Eric Rush and Stephen Bachop learning all the plays. I go out there and do the haka. Thirty minutes into the game, we're down 7–3. It's pretty tight, and I get caught by Simon Poidevin. My rib cartilage went. But on my All Blacks debut I wasn't going off! I played on for another five minutes and was caught again. My ribs cracked. So I was taken off. I'll never forget it, because it was the worst pain I've ever known. I was lying under the stadium and could hear all the cheers as they scored again. It finished one of the biggest hidings that the All Blacks ever suffered,' he says of the 40–17 defeat. 'I could console myself with the thought that at least while I was on it was only 7–3.'

His busted ribs ruled him out of consideration not only for the third test but also for the following five-game leg of the tour to South Africa over the ensuing month.

The following year, 1993, Lam was part of the New Zealand

Sevens team in the inaugural World Cup Sevens at Murrayfield. In their pool, they finished above an Irish side including Eric Elwood courtesy of a 24–7 win, before being knocked out in the quarter-final pool stages.

During that tournament, Lam was again named in the All Blacks trial, but both he and Rush injured their knees in the Sevens. His season, as well as the trial, was over. In 1994, the Samoan Rugby Union informed Lam they'd identified him as a leadership figure for their squad at the 1995 World Cup.

He looked at the state of New Zealand rugby. It was, as ever, pretty healthy. He talked with his mum and dad, and decided to commit fully to Samoa.

Vice-captain in 1994, Lam was made Samoan captain for the 1995 World Cup. 'It became a bit of a crusade for me.' In that 1995 World Cup, Lam led Samoa to pool wins over Italy and Argentina before their loss to England and defeat by the hosts South Africa in the quarter-finals.

The game had turned professional that year, and Lam had been drafted by the Crusaders, but a knee injury playing for Samoa against England at Twickenham that December confined him to just three games for the Crusaders in 1996.

Later that year, Lam captained Samoa on an 11-match tour of England, Ireland and Wales, featuring one test against Ireland for the official unveiling of the Lansdowne Road floodlights. Samoa won 40–25, scoring five tries to one.

'The first ever night test match at Lansdowne and we put 40 points on Ireland: a big win. Rob Andrew, who was in the crowd, came to our hotel and spoke to me and Bryan Williams. He asked if he could bring me to Newcastle and flew me there on a day off during the tour. He showed me all the good parts of Newcastle and offered me a contract.'

Good years.

'That was probably where I played my best rugby,' he admits. 'We came over as a family and enjoyed getting away from New Zealand.' Newcastle won the Premiership, their first major trophy, with Lam named Premiership Player of the Year.

'And then I was sold. I was really annoyed at the time, but it was a blessing. Ian McGeechan wanted me at Northampton, and I think my move was at that time a record transfer fee. As I still had a year on my contract, Newcastle received £100,000, and Northampton tripled my contract.

'Geech called me in and told me, "Pat, we're not just signing you for your rugby playing ability. I want you to help change the culture here." I worked closely with him, and I could see what the issues were straight away. It was a split team, so we just started building, having social gatherings and meals together, doing the handshakes, getting everyone involved.'

He remained Samoan captain until the 1999 World Cup, where he led the side to pool wins over Japan and Wales, Lam showing a fair turn of pace for his try in their 38–31 win over the Welsh. After their quarter-final play-off defeat to Scotland in Murrayfield, he retired from test rugby, having played in three World Cups and ten World Cup matches.

Able to concentrate fully on his role at Northampton, Lam was integral to their Heineken Cup success in 2000, with a tour de force as number 8, captain and talisman in the 9–8 win over Munster in the final at Twickenham, despite playing with a shoulder injury that would require immediate surgery. This was Northampton's first major trophy in 120 years, with Lam named European Player of the Year.

He very nearly didn't play against Munster, as Steph was due to give birth to their fourth child on the day of the final. He and Steph had vowed to have all their kids at home – mum, dad, midwife, no painkillers – and he had vowed to be at her side for every birth. Josiah, to the endless gratitude of Northampton and their supporters, arrived three days before the final.

The Lams' five kids are distinctively named: Michigan, Bryson, Nelana, Josiah and Bethany. As a schoolteacher, he was struck by the number of Michaels and Johns and so forth in his classes, often having to identify them by dint of their middle initial: Michael S., Michael D. or Michael P.

'So Michigan came when my wife went to Camp America. As a nurse, she does a lot of community work and wanted to go there. I said, "Jeeze, I like that, I like that name." And Michigan's colours were my school colours, blue and yellow. I wanted something different for my son.

'Bryson is a combination of Steph's dad, Brian, and my dad, Sonny. You combine them and make Bryson. Steph's mum is Nelda, a German name, and my mum is Anna, so that made Nelana.

'Josiah comes straight from the Old Testament story of Josiah. He was the most obedient king, at eight years old, to the Lord. They always say the younger one is the troublesome one, so we thought, "Let's give this boy a head start."

'Bethany is also from the Bible. My wife was reading scripture in which Jesus passed through Bethany, and said, "Bethany, that's what I want." But she also wanted them all to have normal second names, so it's Michigan Mathew, Bryson Joseph, Nelana Grace, Josiah Andrew and Bethany Faith, after her grandmother.'

A good communicator, intelligent and personable, Lam was a born leader throughout his playing career; he'd never ask a teammate to do something he wouldn't do himself. He also seemed a natural fit for coaching.

'Geech thought so. I love the game. I was a schoolteacher, and training to be a schoolteacher was massive for me. You begin to understand not only the art of teaching but also psychology, even if it's child psychology. It's funny, because I initially decided to become a teacher to help with the rugby, with its longer holidays, but I also had a bit of a passion for the job. I didn't realize that when rugby went professional, teaching would help me become a coach. So I still think of myself as a schoolteacher. I'm just doing a subject that I'm really passionate about, not geography, maths, English or whatever. It's a real fit for me.'

In the event, Lam taught for only two years, from 1991 to 1992, during which time Steph gave birth to their first child, Michigan. He was headhunted to do drug education around New Zealand from 1993 to 1995, and he had resolved to retire after the 1995 World Cup.

That tournament had taken him away for four weeks pre-season, and then two weeks after his return home Steph gave birth to their second child, Bryson, whereupon Lam left for South Africa and the World Cup itself, meaning another five weeks away.

'Not seeing each other was causing a strain on us as a young family, so I resolved to give it up. Then rugby went professional, so I was able to keep playing. I was lucky, because I absolutely loved it. Auckland were already the most professional team in terms of the standards they set, even though the players weren't being paid. Then I played the game at the highest level, and work was training in the morning and playing at the weekend. I played this game for the love of it, and the money was a bonus.'

After one more season with Northampton, Lam returned to Newcastle for his swansong in 2001–02. 'I had quite a few significant contracts to choose from but decided to return to Newcastle. I saw it as a great opportunity for myself and Rob [Andrew], whom I had fallen out with, to make amends and rebuild our friendship. He asked me to come back as captain and help mentor my mate Jonny Wilkinson to eventually take over from me. I also wanted to retire with my good friend Inga [Tuigamala], do one more year and finish. I could have signed a three-year deal, but the injuries had caught up with me, and I knew if I was honest with myself my body could handle only one.

'Just after I signed, Graham Henry rang asking me to help him at Wales. I said, "I've just signed for Newcastle." He said, "Well, OK, we'll wait until you finish at Newcastle." Then two weeks later, Geech rang me. "I want you to come and help me with Scotland." I gave him the same answer, and he said, "Well, Scotland and Newcastle aren't far apart. I'll talk to Rob." They came to an agreement that I'd combine a playing contract with Newcastle and a coaching contract with Scotland for one year.'

When he retired from playing in 2002 and left Newcastle, McGeechan and Scotland offered Lam an 18-month contract through to the 2003 World Cup. 'But my wife really felt it was time to go home. She had an inkling that her grandparents, whom she had lived with from age 14 to 19, were not well. I told Geech, "Look, I'd love to do it but Steph needs to go home." He said, "Well, how about you go and live in New Zealand, and we'll fly you back for all the matches." So I was able to take the family home, set them up and work with Scotland until the 2003 World Cup.'

Within three months of their return, Steph's grandmother had been diagnosed with cancer and her grandfather was ill. 'When her grandfather drew his final breath, Steph was there with her grand-mother to hold his hand. Then Steph's grandmother moved in with us, and Steph was also there with her, holding her hand for her final breath. They had been our biggest concern while we were away for nearly six years. We thankfully had come home in time.'

After the 2003 World Cup, Graham Henry came knocking again. Henry had finished with Wales, after a record 54–10 defeat to Ireland in the 2002 Six Nations, and was applying to become the head coach at Auckland. He wanted Lam to be his assistant. Lam agreed, but the All Blacks lost to Australia in the 2003 World Cup semi-finals, John Mitch-ell lost his job as their coach, and Henry was appointed as his successor.

'I thought, "Oh my gosh, I'm stuffed now." But then Auckland rang me. "Pat, we want you to apply for the head coach role." So I applied and got the job.'

In Lam's five years as head coach at Auckland, they won the ITM Cup in 2005 and 2007, when they also won the Ranfurly Shield, and became the only New Zealand provincial team in the professional era to go through the year unbeaten. A record that still stands today. Then, in 2009, he took over from David Nucifora as head coach of the Auckland Blues.

After finishing fourth and reaching the semi-finals in his third season, 2011, an injury-ravaged campaign saw them finish 12th in 2012, whereupon Lam was replaced by John Kirwan. Though it ended a tad bitterly, Lam will always see that experience as an invaluable part of his own learning process as a coach.

'If you look at the Blues now, and since I've left, despite significant investment in resources nothing has changed really,' he notes, and indeed not only does 2011 remain their only Super Rugby semi-final since 2007, but since Lam's departure they've never finished higher than tenth.

'The Auckland team is the "provincial" team, with all its history. The Blues' Super Rugby franchise is slightly different. I played for Auckland. It's my home team, and I came through there. When I took over the Blues, I quickly realized that the organization had no clear vision. I remember the strategic plan that was given to me. I had no involvement, nothing. There was no process of how we were going to get there. There was no shared vision, although we had that as a team. We started off, we built and we got better. In the 2011 season, we reached a home play-off game, then lost a semi-final to the eventual winners, the Reds, in Brisbane.

'Then, all of a sudden, our coaching resources were cut. We brought in Ma'a [Nonu] and Piri Weepu, but I found myself less resourced. That year was horrific, as I was having to do a lot more to grow our game, and this was compounded by injuries.

'My job was then re-advertised. All my mates said, "Go. Do something else. Don't re-apply." But my players were saying, "Pat, you've been telling us to fight all year. We want you to fight. You've got to apply for the job." It was the best interview I've ever given, and afterwards one of the board members said, "Mate, you've made our job harder."'

Lam had one final game in charge, in Canberra, against the Brumbies, coached by Jake White. The Brumbies needed one point to reach the play-offs, but the Blues won 30–16.

Three days later, on the Tuesday, the CEO, Andy Dalton, and the chairman of the board, Gary Whetton, informed Lam his services would no longer be required.

In a dignified but emotional farewell press conference, Lam began by wishing John Kirwan, his former teammate and successor, all the best, and spoke of his pride on his nine years coaching first Auckland and then the Blues. He cited the post-match reaction of his players in his final game as the highlight of his time with the Blues.

Lam had gone to the tunnel entrance on the side of the pitch to greet his players, the first of whom stopped to embrace him. 'That was for you, coach.' This continued, with each player, in single file, until Keven Mealamu, who was last. At the press conference, Lam reflected, 'I look back with a lot of pride and I feel grateful for the time I've had and that moment is what means most to me.'

He added, 'How do I feel? The analogy I have now is that it's always a battle, and if I look at it in terms of being in the trenches in a war, I've been out on the front line taking shots left, right and centre. I feel that this year particularly was the biggest war ever, and I didn't mind being out the front. For all of that time I was out there, I protected this franchise, the people in it, the team and the players. But it appears that I've taken the final hit.'

Looking back now, Lam maintains he had no problem taking the hits in order to protect his team and his home organization, even if he still feels let down. It shows the high esteem in which he is still held that many players have stayed in touch and still call him 'Coach'.

'I came away from there thinking, "Right, what are my big lessons out of this?" The main thing was the organization. Everything from the management team down has got to be aligned and heading towards a shared vision. Because I knew we had the culture right. I knew we had the leadership right. I knew we had the game, but we did not have the resources to be efficient at it.

'Then we had our awards dinner. I said goodbye to all the players, played golf with my management team and then left.'

Samoa asked Lam to help them out on their 2012 tour of Wales and France, during which they also played Canada. 'I was happy to jump in as the technical adviser/attack coach.'

Wins over Canada and Wales helped Samoa secure a highest-ever world ranking of seventh and a second-tier seeding for the 2015 World Cup draw.

That made him feel better about rugby life. He returned to Auckland, where his contract with the NZRU would run until the end of December. Come January, he'd need a new job.

8

'See Something, Do Something'

Sunday, 6 January 2013

Pat Lam was walking the darkened night-time streets in Auckland, chatting with his wife Stephanie about their options. His four-year stint coaching the Auckland Blues had finished in July 2012, and so had his salary at the end of the calendar year. With his voluntary period as technical adviser to Samoa also over, his coaching career was effectively in limbo.

'We both have a strong faith, and she suggested, "Let's just pray",' he recalls. 'So, she's praying: "Lord, we trust in You to open doors." Two minutes later, I kid you not, the phone rings. I wondered, "Who's ringing me at this time?" It was my agent.

'He said, "Connacht's got an offer on the table for you." I said, "Connacht? OK, that could be interesting." There were others, potentially, but concrete offers don't normally occur before March/April, near the end of the season. So all of a sudden here's me thinking there are potentially three or four out there, but this is one in front of me now.'

He and Stephanie continued to walk and talk, whereupon she said, 'That's the one. I believe that's the one.'

'Oh, really? You think so?' said Lam. He was a little surprised but also intrigued by this turn of events.

During the course of Samoa's preceding November tour of Wales and France, and following it, Lam's agent had lined up four interviews with prospective employers. One was Connacht, who flew him to Dublin. There he met Steve Cunningham and Conor McGuinness of the PGB and the CEO Tom Sears in a Dublin hotel.

'I want to ask you a question. What is the vision of Connacht Rugby? I need to know what the vision is.'

Sears said, 'To be the best Irish province in five years' time.'

'Oh, I like that. You guys are the bottom team, aren't you? You're the fourth?'

'Yeah.'

'Oh, I like that. That's like Samoa. I love that.'

The interview went well, as interviews tend to do with Lam. The man can talk.

Rugby had taken Lam to Dublin, Limerick and Cork, but never to Galway. Interview over, in a cab back to Dublin airport he asked the driver, 'Hey, what's Galway like?'

'Oh, that's the best part of Ireland. It's a fantastic place.'

At the airport, he randomly asked, 'Excuse me, do you know Galway?' 'What's Galway like?'

One person said, 'The whole of the west is fantastic. The people are friendly and easy-going. The countryside is beautiful. We go there on holidays.'

He began researching Connacht and, naturally enough, started on good old Wikipedia. He read about their long struggle against the odds, the threat of being closed down in 2003, and their march on Lansdowne Road. He downloaded *The West's Awake* documentary and was riveted.

He had also met representatives from three other UK clubs. 'I won't say who they were. When I got home, Connacht wasn't my first choice. But in January, when Connacht made their offer, the other clubs with whom I was in contact couldn't make a decision before March. So, bird in the hand and all that.

'If Connacht had waited until March, then I might have had to choose. But Connacht were the first with a firm offer, and the more I looked, the more I thought, "I think I could do something here." I know what I can do and what I'm about: culture, leadership, the game, and I looked at them. "Wow, look at what they do. This group fights for everything. I could bring a game there, and then I can grow on the culture that's already there. It's united, it's us against all the rest."'

He rang his agent. 'I'm keen to do this.' Soon after, Lam signed the requisite contracts and his appointment was confirmed on 12 January.

Hence, by dint of Elwood's decision and his conveying it to his employers early in the 2012–13 season, he facilitated Connacht finding and securing Lam. Otherwise, Lam's appointment might not have happened.

Right man, right place, right time. And it's been more rewarding than he or Stephanie could ever have hoped.

The whole family, apart from their eldest, Michigan, moved to Galway. Then 20 years old, he is now managing a surf shop in New Zealand, having graduated from Auckland University with a degree in Commerce. He was also in the Auckland training squad, before injuring his shoulder.

Ironically, he's an out-half. 'Although I was a back-rower, everybody said that I was to blame because I always played in the backs anyway,' says Lam. 'But at Newcastle I played with Jonny Wilkinson, and then Paul Grayson, and they taught Mich how to goal-kick. So he's an 80 per cent goal-kicker, which is great.'

Bryson was 18 when they moved to Galway, and is now studying at NUIG. 'He has some great mates from Galway and absolutely loves being a student there.'

Like Bryson, Nelana, 15 when they moved, has now completed her Leaving Cert at Yeats College. 'That is a real credit to my kids, because it's a totally different system from New Zealand.' Nelana wanted to be a primary schoolteacher but, not having Irish, applied to the teachers' college in Auckland that Lam himself attended.

Her transition to Galway was the toughest, as she missed her friends back home, but, having been due to return to Auckland in February 2016, she had a change of heart.

'In January, she goes, "I think I might defer for a year, Dad." I said, "Why?" She said, "I really like Galway now." A good friend of mine, Peter Burke, who was in IMC cinemas, had got her a part-time job during her year in transition which is now full-time, and she's made some good friends here.'

Josiah, now 16, is at St Joseph's College, aka the Bish, and also plays with Galwegians. An out-half cum full-back, he's in the Connacht Under-16s and Under-17s set-up. The youngest, Bethany, is nine, and is a pupil at Maree National School.

Initially, Lam had arrived in Galway somewhat wounded after his removal from the Blues. He sensed a hunger and a desperation to succeed rather like his own.

One of the first to ring Lam to congratulate him was Eric Elwood. Lam told him, 'Look, Eric, I promise you, I know it's your hometown. I know it means a lot to you, because I've watched all the videos. I'm just leaving my hometown, and I know how important it is to me. I guarantee you I'll give it everything to help your home province.'

Remaining in touch by email, Elwood invited Lam over to Galway prior to his projected arrival and starting date of 1 June. Lam arrived at the beginning of April, thus allowing him to take in the last four weeks and four games of Connacht's season.

'That was priceless,' he says. 'Absolutely priceless.'

It was also generous of Elwood, as not every coach would have been so open. 'It didn't just allow me to see the professional team but also the organization.'

There was one small problem. When he asked his benchmark question – 'What's the vision?' – few were singing from the Sears hymn sheet.

'I thought, "OK, we've got a problem here. I was really happy with what they told me at the interview but it clearly was not an established collective vision." So I watched Eric and the other coaches with the senior team, and Nigel Carolan and Jimmy Duffy with the academy, and met the people upstairs. I tried to get the whole picture and begin to understand how everything worked.'

Elwood's last meeting with Connacht's Professional Games Board was also Lam's first. The PGB were holding a meeting in Athlone on the same day as the European Challenge Cup final, Friday, 17 May, when Leinster hosted Stade Français at the RDS Arena in Dublin. Connacht had a vested interest. Leinster won, thus securing a place for Connacht in the Heineken Cup the following season.

As well as Cunningham and McGuinness, the rest of the PGB – Liam Rattigan, Jimmy Staunton, Pat O'Connor and Simon Heaslip – were all present for Elwood's review of the season.

'He was asked, "How can we improve the culture and what are your thoughts on the culture?" And Eric answered, "Well, I'll tell you this, the team has a good culture. As an organization, well, you asked me to be honest . . ." And he let rip. I'm sitting there listening as Eric is being blatantly honest, which was great. This was exactly what needed to be said.

'I could see they were a little taken aback, and finally Eric said, "I don't know if this is the right thing to say, but you asked me a question and I've given you an honest answer."

'So Eric leaves, and I'm getting my presentation ready. They're discussing what Eric has said when I interrupted, "Can I just show you my first slide?" And I put it up: "Vision drives the leadership and leadership drives the culture, the culture drives the performance and that's what creates the legacy".

'I added, "You guys told me that the vision was to be the best Irish province in five years' time. I've got here, and no one's aware of that vision. So you're talking about culture, but the problem is you haven't established a vision, because that determines what we as leaders do, and that in turn drives the culture." The change in the collective culture and vision of Connacht began at that meeting.'

By then Lam had taken in Connacht's last four games on successive Friday nights through April and into May. In the first, Connacht won 32–24 against Edinburgh in Murrayfield, then lost 34–18 at home to Ulster, drew 23–23 away to Treviso and lost 20–3 at home to Glasgow. 'That whole transition period gave me an insight into the players, and I was able to put my plan together.'

As well as being wounded, Lam had arrived in Galway as

somewhat damaged goods, at least publicly, following his removal as the Auckland Blues coach. His appointment as Connacht coach was not widely acclaimed by the Irish media, many of whom had championed Eddie O'Sullivan for the job.

None of this truly bothered Lam, albeit he recognized that Connacht could be a crossroads in his coaching career. 'When my time in Auckland was finished, I honestly still had a positive attitude towards coaching. I saw myself as very fortunate to finally be joining many other good coaches in being sacked. I remember bringing the kids into a room. "Great news, guys, we'll be going somewhere new, but I don't know where yet." Once me and Steph decided on Connacht seven months later, we brought them all together again: "Great news. We're going to go to Ireland. We're going to stop in America, see Disneyland." It was important to give that message to them, because if I was down and gloomy, that would affect all of them.

'But I also knew my next job was the most important. Once you're sacked, your next job is crucial. It's make or break. I needed somewhere that was aligned to my vision, my plan, the rugby, culture and leadership. I needed a place that had the vision to go from fourth to be the best. That's where I was in Auckland. It doesn't matter what you're doing, the expectation is to finish first, to be the champions. And everyone outside is "anti". At Auckland, everyone is anti-Auckland. By contrast, Connacht were in fourth place. They were ripe.'

At the end of the 2012–13 season, with Elwood gone and the squad on holidays, Lam stayed put in Galway. There was always someone around with whom he could have one-on-one meetings; essentially, however, it was an opportunity to use the information he had gleaned from his watching brief during the final month of the season to make detailed plans for his first campaign. He also wanted to make some changes.

Traditionally, strength and conditioning is the primary focus of pre-season. Lam had his S&C staff outline everything they wanted from pre-season and the first few months of the campaign, so he could include 'skills blocks' into every single day of training. If the forwards were doing weights, the backs did skills, and vice versa, perhaps only 10- or 20-minute blocks at a time, but skills became part of the daily routine. Lam planned the daily schedules for months in advance. 'I was conscious of what they were used to. I didn't want to make wholesale change. I wanted to add to the usual routine and make sure there was buy-in.'

At the end of June, the players returned for pre-season. On the first day, he welcomed them all and made his PowerPoint presentation. 'This is who I am.' It took about 40 minutes.

He'd introduced this idea at the Auckland Blues, albeit only at management level. It was also a case of necessity being the mother of invention. 'I realized when I arrived that for my whole plan to work I had to get to know these guys. What's the fastest way I can do that? To tell them what's important to me and then have them do the same. Basically it's accelerating the process.

'I knew they would always be respectful, because I had come in to the head coach's position, but I wanted to give them an early sense of who I am, what is important to me, what I am actually about and put it out there.'

He regards this honesty in relationships as critical, and he likens an organization such as Connacht to a large family. 'And relationships start with you giving. If you don't give first, how do you expect them to give? So I really opened up. I gave them my coaching philosophy. I have a one-page coaching philosophy, which Geech encouraged me to do if I wanted to coach. I always ask my staff, and all my players, to keep me honest in this. "This is why I coach. And if you feel I'm not [following my philosophy], challenge me."'

He told them the details of his family background, his Samoan and New Zealand heritage, and about his own family. 'At the end of it, I said, "Fellas, I want you all to do just a ten-minute presentation on what's important to you. Just put together pictures and stuff, and present it." That was to happen throughout pre-season.'

Lam nominated his three captains and the three longest-serving players, John Muldoon, Michael Swift and Gavin Duffy, to make the first presentations. Thereafter, it was random, so every player had to compose a presentation and hand it to video analyst Conor McPhillips, to allow him to load them up.

Then, at the outset, middle or end of a meeting, Lam would say: 'Let's have someone's presentation. Who'd like to go next?' The entire squad made their presentations in the eight weeks of pre-season.

'What amazed me was that some of them had been working together for three years and didn't know some of the stuff revealed in those presentations,' says Lam. 'Everything was about connecting everybody together, making them more open with each other.'

The players all learned something about each other in a way that rugby players don't do over lunch or even over pints after a game. There's a safety net in just talking about work: in their case, rugby. They now opened themselves up in a way they had previously never done. 'Guys became emotional around grandparents or family or friends that they'd lost. You could see the watery eyes. They were sharing from the heart.

'My number-one question is "What's important to you?" That's the first thing I want to know. Some guys didn't even know that other players had partners or even kids. Or they didn't know the names or ages of the kids.

'My number-one theme for my first season was "relationship-building". The second season was about "challenge", because I quickly realized that many people, particularly Irish people, don't like to challenge things. I was in a restaurant with the management. The food was cold and wasn't good. The waitress came to the table and asked, "How's the food?" They said, "Great." That's so not me. I'll do it nicely and say, "It's a little bit cold, can I get it warmed up?" And they warm it up.

'For any successful team, like the All Blacks, challenge is important. Not challenging to be a pain, challenging to develop. Part of my whole philosophy concerning leadership is "See something, do something." See something positive – reward it, acknowledge it. See something negative – challenge it. And that was the only way we'd improve our culture. That was the second year.

'The third year became about "ownership". I found that, at the end of the second season, a lot of guys were going, "I should have done this" and "I should have done that." Or, "Yeah, I did this well and I should have done this." I said, "Stop telling me 'should have'. Let's own your development. Let's make it happen." That's been the three seasons.'

Lam arrived with what were, especially by Connacht's standards, some grandiose ambitions and wasn't shy about communicating them to the players. Not only would they become Ireland's leading province, but, for example, to this end they'd become the best counter-attacking team in the League.

'I've a very simple philosophy and vision of the way to play. I want our team – no matter the weather conditions, who the referee is or the fixture, be it a European Cup or a friendly game – to have the ability to go through a team, go around a team, or go over a team. That's the vision.

'So effectively I ask myself, if we need to go through a team, do we have a structural system? Because at the higher level, I totally disagree with the saying "Play what's in front of you." It's actually "Play what's on." Because in any given situation there are four or five different decisions you can make. Every player sees different options, so choosing the best one becomes the team focus.

'Our main philosophy is to attack from anywhere on the pitch but to have a structure. In defence, it is all about time and space. Take time and space away from the opponents, and you spoil their rhythm. That's it. As simple as that.

'And then in attack it's on the ball and off the ball. Who's on the ball? Who's off the ball? They go hand in hand. If a team sends one, two, three or even four guys to secure the ball, that's great. The ball has been won, but if the players off the ball haven't got into a shape, you'll be stopped easily. Effectively everything we do is based on that principle: that we can attack from anywhere.'

Many coaches and teammates contributed to Lam's philosophy, but it also stemmed from his captaining so many of the teams he played for. 'Ultimately as a player, and especially as a captain, you have to make calls, and when that happens, you want the bullets in your pocket. If I was going to fire a shot, but I've only got one bullet, I'm struggling. As a captain, I wanted that awareness on the field to say, "We need to go here, can we go here? No, we can't. We don't know how to get there." I wanted a situation where all my decision-makers on the team can see space. And if they see space, and I can see space, then we're able to attack as a team.

'It used to be said about me as a player: "He's in the backs all the time." I love to express myself. I did not see any point in being a rugby player and not getting my hands on the ball. If you're not involved, what is the point? And in the old days, before subs were introduced, you had to go 80 minutes. You had to share the workload, and if you have a structure which ensures the workload is shared, you can go for longer and you enjoy it. When you came off the pitch, you wanted to think, "We all shared that."

'But ultimately the biggest thing I wanted as a player was absolute clarity that we knew how we'd beat that team. When I was playing for Samoa, we knew how we would beat Wales,' he says, referring to Samoa's seismic 16–13 win over Wales at Cardiff in the 1991 World Cup. 'That was a big party, mate,' he admits, fondly recalling the night.

That clarity came from the then Samoan coaches, Bryan Williams and Peter Schuster, and a playing group that had leaders. 'Graham Henry and Ian McGeechan were the best tactical coaches I had. The Samoan coaches were very big on player empowerment. Bryan Williams challenged us to think about the game, so we owned a lot of it.

'The game should be, and certainly was for me, an expression of what I wanted and enjoyed as a player. That is what I now apply to my coaching. And I have to believe in it. If I don't believe in it, the players will see through me, because as coaches we have the biggest influence. And I absolutely believe that this game can beat any team. All you need is the players to be able to do it.

'Yes, our squad is not full of experienced internationals, but that doesn't matter. Maybe they'd be better players, which, of course, might make some things easier, but you still have to work the culture. The individuals still have to come together and be a team.'

Like building a house, Lam's first season was about establishing foundations, and, as he's detailed, specifically about building relationships. Hence, the way he talks with the players now is not the way he talked with them then.

'But I was able to establish very clearly the way I wanted us to play, and to do that I needed the toolbox to be fuller. The skill toolbox was a little low. That's why I was trying to get Dave Ellis over but Dave was still on another contract, so he couldn't get here until September.'

To hasten this improvement in individualized skills, he made all the players buy their own rugby ball. 'That went quite well, because I was new and it was different, but it all had a purpose.'

Yet some players looked askance at the notion of carrying around a personalized rugby ball like a child's toy, or at any rate smirked at the notion.

'I didn't care. This is what I wanted. And it lasted the whole year, because I put everyone into mini-teams. Everyone had to have a ball with their name and a quote – any quote they wanted, anything that meant something to them or interested them. Just put it on.

'I think what made it acceptable was because they knew that historically they haven't been as skilful as the other teams. So I explained, "If you're going to be skilful, you have to be comfortable with the ball." And I added, "Hands up those of you who had a rugby ball when you were young and looked after it?" Nearly every hand went up. That's what we did as kids. "That's my ball." So I said, "It's pretty ironic that you got used to it back then, but now, when you really need it, you don't have one!"

'I told them, "I expect that ball to be taken everywhere, in the car, or next to you wherever you go." When I walked past them, they had to have a rugby ball with them. I'd go, "Yeah", and they had to pass me the ball, and in a different way from before.'

Randomly, he might ask a player to demonstrate a new skill. Then, noticing there were fewer individualized balls, he awarded points in mini-games to those who had remembered to bring them to training. 'Guess what happened? At the next session, everyone had their own rugby ball.'

It wasn't a dictatorial message. It was the carrot rather than the stick. He also detected that those who bought into this concept the most were also performing more efficiently in the skills sessions.

Another custom initiated by Lam was 'the Connacht handshake'. This may seem a tad cheesy, and probably did to some within the squad, but in Lam's view it was 'crucial' in a number of ways.

The idea emanated from his time as a 21-year-old with the New Zealand Sevens. Wayne Smith was one of the coaches and Gilbert Enoka, a former volleyball player turned sports psychologist, or as he describes himself 'a mental skills coach', was part of the backroom team. Enoka, who has worked across a variety of sports, in latter years has worked almost exclusively with the All Blacks.

'He talked about connections and the weakest link, that we needed to introduce a handshake. That made a really big impression on me. Whenever I was appointed captain, I made a handshake compulsory. With Samoa we had our own handshake, and I just know it works.'

By the time he arrived at Connacht, Lam had been conducting morning handshakes for over 20 years. He wanted to introduce this custom at Connacht, but with a Connacht twist.

In truth, historically there is little sense of identity with Connacht as a province, certainly not to the same extent as with Ulster or indeed Munster. Ulster, obviously, has always retained its identity as a province in its own right, as has Munster, what with its history of strong competitiveness against touring international sides – notably their historic win over the All Blacks in 1978. Hence, with the advent of professionalism and the Heineken Cup, they could tap into that sense of being Munster, making Thomond Park a fortress from the off. By contrast, Leinster had perhaps more to do to develop an identity as they moved into the professional era, and their rivalry with Munster was also something of a catalyst for this.

Connacht had nothing like the same historical competitiveness as Munster, but, as Lam discovered, despite having only five counties, it retained the same GAA-rooted county and parish-based rivalries. He also realized the extent to which the Connacht squad was infused with players from outside, be they from the other provinces or from abroad. Yet barely inside the front door of the main entrance to Connacht's offices, on the right-hand side adjacent to the lift upstairs, is a simple map of Connacht, with the names of the five counties written in white against a green backdrop.

'That was there when I walked in; Eric must have put it there,' says Lam. 'I studied that map and began to tour the province, driving to Sligo, then Leitrim, Roscommon and Mayo, and around the county of Galway. I could then say that I'd been there. I'd been to all five counties.

'I told the guys to go away and nominate three players to devise a handshake. They had one week to do so. Then, for the first week, every morning everybody had to shake hands and verbally name Sligo, Leitrim, Mayo, Roscommon and Galway. They had to say it. Repetition. Eventually, we didn't have to say it. It was just bang, bang, bang, bang, bang, and everyone knew, subconsciously, what it represented. The five counties.

'The handshake was also more about relationships. I talk about three types of people in this world. Number one – those who wake up, the sun is shining and they say, "Beautiful day!" Or they wake up and the rain is horizontal against the window. It's cold, and they go, "Yeah! Great day. No one is going to stop me having a great day." Unfortunately, not many are like that!

'Then there's the guy who wakes up and even if it is a lovely day says, "Not another hot day. I don't want to see anyone today. I'm going to get burnt today." Real negative. Fortunately, there are not too many like that either.

'The third, and what most people are like, they wake up, they see how the day is going and their day normally depends on which one of those two types they first bump into.

'I said to the boys, "Challenge yourself to be more like the first. Have that positive mindset. You'll also make a big difference to other people's day." And that's where the handshake comes in. I shared that message first before I introduced the handshake: we all need that positive energy. Some days we don't have it, but when you shake hands the positive energy will rub off on you.'

Every season the handshake is different, and hence Lam will nominate another three players to invent a new variation, be it combining forehands, backhands, closed fists or open-handed, but always with five connections to represent the five counties. 'More importantly, it binds them, and new players buy into it.'

Connacht were embarking on a journey of self-discovery, as players, as a squad, and as a province. Perhaps only an outsider, or at any rate a visionary, could have pulled it off.

9

The Foundation Year, 2013–14

Pat Lam turned 45 on 29 September 2013, in the first month of his first season as Connacht head coach. His wife, Stephanie, presented him with a six-foot plank of seasoned wood. It hangs on the wall in Lam's office bearing the following inscription: 'To accomplish great things we must not only act but also dream, not only plan but also believe'.

'Steph bought me that for my 45th birthday. She said, "That sums you up." She knows that I'm a big dreamer. A vision man. She also knows I won't do anything I don't believe in. And if I don't believe it, nor will anyone else.'

When Tom Sears first informed Tim Allnutt that Lam would be the new head coach, he was intrigued and enthused. 'He's a global celebrity in rugby terms. I'd grown up watching him and loved the way he played. I didn't know much about him as a coach, but everyone I spoke with – coaches, players and agents – said, "He's a great bloke" and "a real good guy". After he got the job, I spoke to him a few times on the phone, and then I went to meet him off the plane in Shannon.'

It was 4 April 2013.

Allnutt had acquired Lam's Mazda seven-seater, which he'd driven to Shannon airport. Allnutt pulled up in the car park, finding a space well away from any other car. 'There were twenty spaces near me, but this lady pulled up right beside me. When she opened her door, the wind caught it, crashing it into Pat's door. I'm sitting there going, "You've got to be joking!" So our first conversation was, "Hi, Pat. Great to see you. Welcome to Connacht, and oh, there's your car over here. By the way, mate, there's a little dint on the door there", and I had to explain what happened.'

Allnutt was immediately taken by the warmth of Lam and Steph, who gave him a big hug and a bar of Toblerone as a thank-you for collecting them. 'I was at ease with him straight away. He's personable and has an aura about him, and with Eric still in situ, he just came in and observed.'

Allnutt was taken with the way Lam conducted one-on-ones with both players and the backroom staff, and with the way he drove that Mazda seven-seater, with his family, to various parts of Connacht: Carrick-on-Shannon one weekend, Sligo the next, and all over the province.

'Gee, man, you've seen more of Connacht than I have.'

'I just want to see what makes them tick.'

Much of that first conversation on the way back from the airport was about the weather in the west. This was a subject Allnutt had come to know better than the weather in the Land of the Long White Cloud. Allnutt had come over on holiday simply to visit his older brother Simon in 1998 and never left. They hail from Waimate in South Canterbury, about two and a half hours south of Christchurch. His parents Marie and John had three boys, all of whom played rugby, cricket and basketball.

When Tim Allnutt was 17, Dr Oliver Bourke, brother of former Irish president Mary Robinson, had put him in contact with Ollie Campbell and he played with Old Belvedere for a year while working at Belvedere College.

He went back to New Zealand but returned to Ireland to hook up with his brother Simon, who was then playing in Castlebar. Allnutt trekked around Scotland for a while, and by the time he came back to Ireland in 1998, Simon had joined Corinthians and was playing with Connacht.

When his brother was injured, Allnutt was brought into the

Connacht squad to train with them. After an injury to Mervyn Murphy, Steph Nel promoted Allnutt to the team, and he played all six games in the group stages of the 2000–01 season. The following season, he was again an ever-present, not just in Europe but also in Connacht's inaugural Celtic League campaign.

Allnutt was made captain in 2002 when Connacht made a wonderful start in the League, winning their first five matches – including a victory over Leinster in Donnybrook – whereupon the wheels came off his and their season. In the fifth of those games, a 24–23 win over Bridgend at Brewery Field, Allnutt suffered a bad knee injury which ruled him out of the remainder of the season.

He returned to captain the side again in 2003–04 under Michael Bradley, playing half of their 22 Celtic League and six of their Challenge Cup games before being dropped for the two-legged semi-final against Harlequins. 'I wasn't playing well, and Brads and I had an honest chat. There was an opportunity of a contract but it wasn't certain, and to be honest I didn't want to be a bit player. Then I was offered the job as team manager. I hadn't had designs on being a team manager. It was just something that fell that way when John Fallon decided to move on.'

Allnutt, as captain, had been part of the march to Lansdowne Road in 2003. 'We hummed and hawed, but a few senior players like myself and Dan and Eric decided we wanted to lend our support. It was about the province but it was also about people's futures. They were some weird old days back then, some pretty grim times to be honest.'

In the midst of that threat to their very existence, Connacht lost a Challenge Cup quarter-final first leg to Pontypridd by 35–30 at a sold-out Dubarry Park in Athlone. 'I remember walking around the pitch afterwards, chatting with Dan [McFarland], who had been through this with Richmond,' says Allnutt, in reference to the London club that had been placed into administration and were merged, along with London Scottish, into London Irish in 1999.

'He became a spokesperson for the players – helped by his father, who had a legal background – but at that point we just honestly didn't know what the future held. Everyone's heads were down. That game wasn't going to keep us alive, but we just felt we'd let a lot of people down by not winning.

'Since those days, the relationship with the IRFU has blossomed. But we had to earn their trust, and I get that, because we were usually going up there with our cap in our hand.'

Even so, it was a tricky time to become manager. 'I worked in tandem with Gerry Kelly as CEO and learned on the job. To still be involved having finished playing was brilliant but quite difficult, trying to be the disciplinarian with guys who had been teammates and mates for the previous four seasons. We were a professional outfit, but we were also pretty amateurish. It was about trying to grow, and we had to tread really carefully with the IRFU. We had to be seen to be standing on our own two feet, but it took a while to get there.'

For 11 seasons he's been a consistent thread, working with Bradley, Eric Elwood and now Pat Lam. He's seen his own role grow in tandem with the growth on and off the pitch. 'There were some difficult times, but the one thing I've always loved is our fight. We had to fight for everything, so we celebrated every victory, partly because you didn't know when the next one was coming and also because of the effort required for a victory. We never won by 20 or 30 points. I'm sure it was torture as a spectator, because you could never relax for the last ten minutes of the game.

'The season before I joined was a shocker. They were being beaten by 40 or 50 points. I remember walking into the old Connacht Branch in Lisburn Industrial Estate. They had a big frame with all the newspaper clippings, but it was usually "Connacht destroyed by Munster" or whatever. That was weird. You'd wonder why they'd put that on the wall at the time, but it was part of the history. When everything moved here, it gave us a real lift,' he says from his tidy manager's room in the Sportsground.

Allnutt is part of a strong Kiwi connection to Connacht. Maybe it's the remoteness, the landscape and the climate. 'We look at players worldwide, but the Kiwis seem to settle in here quicker and easier than players from elsewhere do. And Connacht people have an affinity with New Zealand. The All Blacks played here twice in front of the biggest crowds that they'd ever seen here [at the Sportsground].

'When I was a young fella, the All Blacks played here in 1989. A behind-the-scenes video was produced after that tour called *The Good, the Bad and the Rugby*. After they beat Connacht, Frano Botica was interviewed and said, "Oh, I was lining up a conversion and took a couple of steps back and I stood in some dog shit!"' I thought, "Where is this place? That's bloody ridiculous!" I didn't think I'd be sitting here one day.'

He never forgot Botica's comment. 'One of the first things I did as manager was get rid of the dog shit. But it's a great place. Myself and Dan [McFarland] always agreed that people from the west of Ireland are special because they have worked so hard for everything and they take nothing for granted. Any sporting team from here that's ever won anything has had to work bloody hard for it.

'In his first season, Pat got a real taste of what rugby is like here. It's like a player coming in from abroad. There's a settling-in period, which sometimes could take six or seven months for a player to find his feet. And I suppose it's the same with the coach. Pat had a lot of different ideas. He'd inherited a squad which didn't have his stamp. He had also come from the ITM Cup with Auckland and then Super Rugby with the Blues, both of which were short bursts. Here, it's pretty much an eleven-month season. It's very attritional, and with a small squad he quickly realized we had to strengthen certain areas. When you're in the bubble here, you don't always see everything, but Pat came in and opened our eyes.'

Lam's first signing was Craig Clarke, who had just captained the Chiefs to their retention of the Super Rugby title. 'Connacht had already identified him, and we just had to get him over the line,' says Lam. 'They'd mentioned him to me while I was in New Zealand, and so I rang Craig. We talked about what we were going to do, and he signed not long after. But all the prep work had been done by Eric and Dan.

'Craig was a real culture man and a real down-to-earth family man,' adds Lam. 'He actually had a big impact because he had a different leadership style than Connacht were used to, and I know John Muldoon and other guys, like Mick Kearney, learned from him.'

Jake Heenan was another arrival in the summer of 2013. 'When I got here, we had an issue at 7, as they had only Willie Falloon. Jake came through when I was doing the Blues Under-18s. He was in the Auckland academy, and I knew there was a long list of 7s there, so I spoke to him. He was keen to come, and we signed Jake on a three-year deal.

'I first spotted him as a schoolboy way up north in Whangarei,' recalls Lam. 'Then when I was at the Blues Under-18s, one area of weakness was 7. Jake stood out straight away because there were a lot of boys from the Pacific Islands but he was playing as a 6. The way he tackled and went over the ball reminded me a lot of Richie McCaw. I thought, "Wow, this guy is good, let's move him." Halfway through the trial, I moved him to 7 and of course he made the team, and they won the league. He also made the New Zealand Schools team and Auckland signed him to their academy, but he was competing against Luke Braid and Daniel Braid, and the Pryor brothers, Dan and Kara, and Nepia Fox-Matamua as well. There were a lot of 7s. Jake was also good friends with my son, Michigan, and spent a bit of time around my home. I knew he was a good kid. So when Connacht said they were looking for a 7, I said, "I know the man! That's the one you want."'

With Falloon injured, Heenan had to hit the ground running, quickly becoming a regular until he too was sidelined halfway through the season.

Lam liked Heenan's professionalism. 'He brought his notebook to team meetings and worked well with the other players. Remember, he was also captain of the New Zealand Under-21s that went to South Africa, so he had a big impact immediately. The players all saw his attention to detail, which impressed the younger players. For such a young guy, he seemed to have a pretty wise old head.'

Another key signing was Dave Ellis, initially as a backs-cum-skills coach, changing to simply the skills coach in year two. Ellis's arrival was delayed until midway through September 2013 due to a coaching commitment at an Australian school, but his influence would be profound.

Lam had first met Ellis in July of 2012, following his departure from the Auckland Blues, when he was asked to do some coaching at the IRANZ, the International Rugby Academy which was the brain-child of former All Black Murray Mexted and is based in Palmerston North.

Ellis was there, overseeing the various camps throughout the year, and Lam was one of the guest coaches he invited.

'They asked me if I could run the coaches programme. When I was doing coaching philosophy and, say, team attack, myself and Dave worked together with the players, so I came to know him well.'

Then, chewing the fat over lunch together at the training centre in Palmerston North one day, Ellis asked Lam, 'Pat, how do I get a gig in one of the professional teams?'

'I didn't realize you were looking, Dave. You're part of the furniture here.'

'Yeah, yeah, I'd be keen to try it.'

'OK, I'll keep that in mind.'

If Ellis hadn't spoken then, Lam would never have known. After taking over at Connacht, Lam and Ruane were going through their finances and working out what they could afford to add to the coaching ticket. Paramount amongst these was a skills coach.

'I knew straight away he was the perfect fit. When I looked at the group's profile, I knew what I needed. Developing skills was massive, and I needed someone to be on the ground to drive that programme. That was Dave.

'His strength is his knowledge of a skill, whether it's catching, passing, tackling or breakdown and, along with his rapport with players, his ability to break it all down, to simplify it. He does a lot of good work with decision-making as well.

'If he's working with Jimmy on line-outs, and there's a way Jimmy wants the ball delivered, Dave can pick up on that. If the backs want to do some team attack or team defence, he can grab the detail that we'd like to focus on as coaches but which we lack the time to do.

Dave can do the one-on-ones and the small group sessions. He runs that whole skills programme every day. He's one of the busiest coaches.'

Ellis even devises specific individualized programmes for players who are recovering from injury. 'He works closely with Paul Bunce, our head of fitness, and Garrett Coughlan, our head physio. He'd simply ask them, "What can the player do?" If the player has a shoulder injury, Dave will have him working with the other hand, or doing some footwork. Even with injuries, players' skills are constantly being worked on thanks to Dave.'

The Ellis effect was immediate.

'I remember his opening meeting upstairs,' says Lam. 'He got all the boys into the team room, and he had medicine balls. He talked through this concept of skills and put four guys on each of the medicine balls. Balancing on their knees, they had to catch and pass. They were falling off initially, but balancing on the medicine ball forced them to catch and pass at arm's length, while keeping their core as still as possible. He has coloured cards which he uses to signal different skills drills.

'It was all new to the boys, but basically he was breaking the skill down into component parts, and in a whole new way. So for players to be able to pass off the base of a ruck, he had them leaning their heads against the wall and they then passed from underneath their torso, with their arms extended, and so the pass is going in a straight line, not loopy and not drifting back.'

So when you see Connacht players, no matter the position, step in at scrum-half, or when they pass the ball along the line without checking or breaking strike, with no inside-shoulder pass, this all comes from the Ellis skills sessions.

'And he keeps it interesting too. He does each session with different coloured cones, or coloured balls or cards, and all sorts of gadgets to stimulate the learning process.'

You don't have to have been an outstanding player to be an outstanding coach.

'No, you don't. You just have to have the knowledge. I always say the four things you need as a coach are: one, you have to know your stuff. Two, you have to be able to get it across while understanding that players learn differently. What works for one might not work for another. For example, Bundee learns differently from John Muldoon. The third one is your planning, your preparation and your detail. My PPD – planning, preparation and detail. The fourth one is that he has to be a team man. Those are the four things I look for in all the staff, whether it's the coach, the physio, the doctor or the trainer. I'd say we probably hire at number one, and generally we fire at number four, maybe number three!' concludes Lam, laughing.

'Initially, Dave arrived as the backs coach, but he's not a backs coach,' says John Muldoon. 'He's a skills coach. And he is very good at it. He's not as hard on the lads as Pat would be, but he'd still individually pick lads out.

'Initially Dave was quite quiet and everything was really pedantic, like, "Pass with your hand, guide it." We were doing it after weights and your arms would be sore. It would be 25 one-handed passes off your left and then 25 off your right.

'After about three or four days, I won't name names but Pat showed clips of two forwards, one from the academy and one senior. He goes, "Right, watch this. Lovely pass, lovely pass." He was flicking through clips. "Nice pass, nice pass, nice pass." Then he shows the second player, with no comment. "What does everyone think of that?" Everyone is thinking, "Ooooh, that's not good", but not saying anything. "Right, what do you think of this?" he asked, showing more clips. It was one of the academy lads, and it was just lazy. It was so bad. But again, no one spoke. "No answer then? What did you think of that, lads? Lads, come on." This is Pat's first year and no one wanted to criticize the young fella. Now everyone has their head down, saying nothing.

'Pat said, "Right, I'll ask you a different question. Who would you pick? Hands up if you'd pick the first lad." And even the young lad himself put his hand up! Straight away. And that was one of our very first dealings we had with Pat. "Hmm, so it's going to be like this." And that's how it would be. He was always asking us what we thought.

"What do you think of that?" "How can we improve on that?" He wanted feedback, feedback, feedback. At the end of the video sessions and training sessions, he'll pick out players to ask them what they think.

'It's funny, he's a real teacher, but he gets the lads to criticize each other so that it hits home with them more. Now the lads don't even need Pat to show them the video because the chances are if someone has done something wrong on the pitch, they'll be told by someone else anyway. You'll see lads turning around, going, "Who the f*** is in this ruck?" And then someone will run by going, "Sorry, that was me." "Ah for f*** sake." It doesn't even have to be shown in the meeting then.'

However, when Lam informed the squad at their first team meeting of the pre-season that he wanted Connacht to be the best Irish province within five years, in accordance with his remit, Muldoon admits he was sceptical. He'd heard it before, and Lam's ideas also raised Muldoon's eyebrows.

'One of the first things he did was make a presentation of who he was. "This is who I am, this is my family, etc." That was a Monday, and then he said, "Next Friday, we'll start off. Mul, you're going to do one; Swifty you're going to do one too."'

Muldoon admits, 'I was like, "What? All the lads know who I am!" I made my presentation, and in it I had a section about my granny, and her being 100 years old. Afterwards, some of the lads said, "Jesus, I didn't know that your granny was 100." Or, "I didn't know this or that." Everyone learned a little bit more about everyone else.

'Then he started to bring training sessions to the different counties. It adds to the travel, and it's time-consuming compared to rocking up at the Sportsground. But you arrive there and you see the enthusiasm. Then a few weeks later you're warming up for a match in the Sportsground and there are kids shouting, "Remember me?" In fairness to Pat, it's worked.

'Everyone seems to know him, and the thing I think that people love about him is he'll always give someone two minutes of his time. Always.'

Lam's effect on players has been equally profound, Muldoon admits. 'He's turned around players that I was thinking, "Mmm, I don't know", and these players are now pushing hard for selection. And he is hard on players. He'll get to a point that if you're not good enough, then that's it. And once you're out of his loop, it's very hard to get back in. But he will give you every opportunity to work hard and get back.'

Entering his eighth season as a member of the senior squad, Ronan Loughney admits he liked Lam from the very off. 'From a team bonding point of view, I thought his PowerPoint presentation, and then promoting everyone else to do one, was really good. It encouraged me to start talking to people more, because you're always having the craic and there's always banter, but to talk about your family background means you're revealing stuff about yourself and learning more about your teammates on a personal level. Some players had lost parents early in life, which was a brave thing to reveal in their PowerPoints.

'Players revealed how much of an influence their grandparents had been, or talked about their siblings or whatever. It may seem like a slightly enforced friendship, but it wasn't, because these are people you get on with really well anyway. It certainly was a cue for me to talk to people more and to get to know them better.

'There were plenty of other things as well. He had the '70s party at the end of our pre-season in the marquee, in which you had to do a dance routine. And I know some of the lads were cringing at the idea of doing the dance-off! Again, though, it took you out of your comfort zone, even in front of your mates.'

Lam's insistence that everyone carry their own rugby ball also generated a reaction. 'Some of us had to take a bit of a knock to our pride,' admits Muldoon. 'We were thinking, "Damn it, I can do that. I think I've got good handling skills." Obviously we didn't know that he would change our game plan, that our shape and style of play would change drastically. From the first day, he told us we'd have fitness sessions, and then straight away we were doing skills. We were like, "Ah, sure we've done this before, and after a few weeks there'll be more rugby sessions and the skills will be out the window." But after two weeks, we're still doing skills, all the way to the end of our pre-season. I went into Pat and said, "Pat, we need to knock the skills on the head now." And he said, "No, we're not knocking the skills on the head." I said, "But we're on our feet for five/six hours a day. It's too long." He was making us bring in lunchboxes, and we were having meetings after meetings. The lads were just, "We're absolutely drained here." But he insisted otherwise. One of the first things he said was, "This is a job. You're in here from 9 to 5." It was cruelty.'

No pain, no gain. In every sense.

After beating Zebre at home in their first match under Lam, Connacht lost their next eight League matches in a row, their only reprieve being another win away to Zebre in the Heineken Cup. Muldoon recalls, 'At that time, we were still getting used to him. The other problem was that we had been there before. I had certainly been there before, so we were kind of going, "Oh, Jaysus, not another losing streak." But we improved as the season progressed. We had more of a shape.'

After the opening win over Zebre, they lost 21–10 away to Cardiff, 18–7 at home to Ulster, 43–26 at home to the Ospreys and 23–3 away to Treviso. 'That was a disaster,' admits Lam.

They became more competitive, losing 23–17 at home to Saracens in their first Heineken Cup game. 'We should have won that,' reflects the coach. And 16–13 away to Leinster. 'We definitely should have won that too. We were robbed in that one,' he says. There were also more bonus points in losing 19–12 at home to Glasgow and 24–21 at home to Scarlets.

Connacht's execution had been breaking down sporadically, but after each defeat Lam kept believing and saying that he and they were making progress.

Conor McGuinness became a constant conduit between Connacht and the PGB. 'Conor was good, because he hired me and he was always asking, "Are you sure?" And I would show him on the video that we were getting there. That's what you want from Board members: you want them to ask, to challenge and question, not just accept.

I appreciate that Conor always talked to me in person. If he was talking about me, it was the same as he was saying to me anyway. That's why I respected him.'

Of course, it was always going to take time. Lam made that abundantly clear to everyone at the beginning, especially the PGB, which had been set up in advance of the 2011–12 season. The PGB were particularly important to help fill the void when Tom Sears unexpectedly stepped down in September of Lam's first season.

'All of these games were informative for me. I was learning so much about the refereeing, what these guys can do and the mentality and the shape of the team. This was a massive learning curve for me, but the Edinburgh game was the big one.'

Indeed, the sequence culminated in an embarrassing night in Edinburgh. In the last eight minutes, Connacht collapsed, conceding three tries and 21 points to lose 43–10. 'We shipped 21 points in the last seven or eight minutes,' Lam recalls, before adding, albeit with the benefit of hindsight, 'but that was the best game ever for me.'

He didn't think so that night, though. 'I remember that was the first time I lost my rag in the changing-room. And I also remember at the time questioning if I had come to the right place.

'I lost the plot. I got really angry. I said, "I'm not sure that I've come to the right place, and whether all of the things that I read about you were true." It was heat-of-the-moment stuff because I was so gutted with what happened. I don't normally let rip like that until I see the video.

'We flew back that night, I went home and after that game I completely changed the defensive system. I went through the video and thought, "Holy heck, what is going on here?"'

He freeze-framed Connacht's defensive alignment, noticing that Dan Parks and Fionn Carr were both defending a five-metre blindside channel when only one was needed. Connacht had simply been overloaded on their blindside and undermanned on their open-side.

'We had eight on one side when we needed only five or six, and they'd exposed us down the sidelines. We were like headless chickens. The last five minutes of that game was like the light-bulb moment!

'I could see the majority of guys were working hard but just working in the wrong places. So I needed to educate them.

'I didn't get to sleep. I stayed up all night, and I remember writing a system that would make it easy.'

He emailed every squad member, advising them to each bring an A4 notebook and pens to Monday's team meeting. He was going to be a schoolteacher again.

' "All right, everyone ready? We're going to go through this step by step."

'I started to put a basic shape and numbers system on our defence. "In this area here, we're going to have one person only, plus one." There's always a plus-one at the back. "We're going to have ten on the front line." Basically I just went through every position on the pitch. "This position here, six on that side. This position, seven on that side." And so on. And they all wrote down their sums. "Everyone got that? Write it down!" I wouldn't move on until everyone had it. I walked around the room like a schoolteacher, looking at everyone's notes, and asked, "Have you got it? Yeah? Good. Good."

'I had to provide a system which ensured accountability. With a clear system, there's no excuse. You're either doing it or you're not doing it. And it was designed to keep it as simple as possible. The desire to go hard was still there, but they were just in terrible positions, so I broke all that down and we trained it and trained it all week long.'

Next up were the French aristocrats Toulouse: four-time Heineken Cup winners at home to the Pro12's bottom-placed side. And in front of a 16,000-plus crowd at the Stade Ernest-Wallon on 8 December, with Clarke captaining them for the first time, Connacht won 16–14.

'We just executed our new defensive system perfectly. And we changed the game plan. Toulouse had a massive forward pack. We were a smaller but hard-working team, so we decided to get separation between their backs and their forwards. Their back three were Yoann Huget, Clément Poitrenaud and Hosea Gear, and we planned to kick the ball long and then chase hard, because we knew they'd run it back. If we kicked it short, their forwards wouldn't have to go far.

'But the main thing was changing the shape of our D [defence].

And because they all had to write it down and study it, and we trained it all week, the boys went straight into those positions quickly. We had shape, we put pressure on them, and it worked a treat. It really did.'

Connacht would not have beaten Toulouse had it not been for the scale of the defeat the previous week in Edinburgh.

'That Toulouse game was big for me, the team and the board. That went all around the world. You could see at the final whistle we were jumping up and down because I was really proud of the boys. We won on a structure and a system. We put a lot of work into that one.'

Six days later, Connacht hosted Toulouse in the return game.

'The second game was a big source of frustration, because on the plane home from Toulouse we'd identified clearly that when Toulouse looked at that first game, they'd see how much space we left on the outsides. We trained all week to cover those spaces, but we went on to the field and unfortunately we still shot up and they put the kicks in and scored two tries.'

Maxime Médard scored them both and Toulouse were 22–9 up at half-time, going on to win 37–9 as Connacht wilted.

'Half the guys had been in hospital during the week because a virus had swept through the squad. Marmo [Kieran Marmion] was 48 hours in hospital, only coming out on the morning of the match. We had an injury crisis at 9, as Paul O'Donohoe and Frank Murphy were both sidelined, so we had to play Marmo.'

Marmion was integral to Connacht that season, as he has been for all of the last four seasons since being thrust into the team in the midst of a previous injury crisis at the start of 2012–13, when he became an ever-present in his rookie campaign.

Connacht beat the Newport Gwent Dragons at home a week later, although they lost Jake Heenan to a shoulder injury for the remainder of the season. They were competitive in the Christmas derbies, losing 22–16 away to Munster and 16–8 at home to Leinster, before beating Zebre at home in Europe. But there would be more harsh lessons, notably their ensuing pool finale away to Saracens on the latter's Allianz Park artificial surface.

Connacht lost 64–6.

'That was horrendous,' admits Lam. 'That was an unpleasant day, but I learned another big lesson from this game. There was a three-week gap before our next game, and so the boys were officially on a break after that game. In the feedback following the game, I discovered the players were still planning their holidays the day beforehand. We weren't mentally right.

'We played a team that we'd almost beaten at home in October because we adjusted our tactics to counter their blitz defence. But once you fall behind against them, they're ruthless, especially on that artificial pitch. It was terrible, and the game just went from bad to worse. To this day, every time we are due a break, we play the game, then we come back to review the game on the Monday, and then we take a break. Since that day, we've never lost the last game before a break, because the holidays will only happen after our Monday review. It's a totally mental thing.'

Against Saracens, Clarke suffered a concussion, forcing him to take an indefinite break from the game. He retired at the end of the season, one year into his three-year contract. Muldoon says, 'Dan McFarland, our forwards coach, was very upset to lose him. He was a seriously good signing and a very good speaker, probably the best speaker I've ever known as a captain. He always seemed to know the right thing to say at the right time. I remember one or two lads saying to me, "Ah Jesus, this lad's only through the door and he's been made captain." But I said, "Hold on a second, there's more to it than that. He's got a proven pedigree." I was probably a little bit put out that someone came in and was given the captaincy so soon, but after a couple of weeks working with Craig I could see his quality. And I knew he was a top bloke as well, which helped.'

Returning from that post-Saracens break, Connacht lost 8–6 away to Glasgow, the concession of a try to Mark Bennett restricting Connacht's interval lead to just 6–5 despite having first use of a ferocious wind.

'That was a shocker,' says Lam. 'That was another game we should have won. We were going really well in that game, but again one defensive system error let Henry Pyrgos break out and cost us that match. So at this stage it's all about re-enforcing "Do your job". We were losing games because of breakdowns in concentration and someone not performing their role.'

But Connacht then won four in a row during and immediately after the Six Nations, against Edinburgh at home, Zebre away, Treviso at home and the Dragons away.

'The weather was improving,' explains Lam. 'All those "learnings" from the first half of the season were coming into effect. The guys had been together for over six months. They were adapting, and it was getting me all excited for what's coming ahead.'

But for that defensive glitch against Glasgow, Connacht would have been chasing a sixth successive win when losing 32–30 away to the Scarlets. Cue the start of Lam's difficulties with officialdom.

'It was after that game that I got my first warning,' he says, in reference to having his knuckles rapped by the Pro12 for his post-match comments about Scottish referee Neil Paterson.

'I think the best way to sum that up is that we should have won that game, but we had a couple of bad calls which cost us at the end. Speaking to the media afterwards, I mentioned the tough calls and I got a slap on the wrist. I got a big slap on the wrist!'

Next up came another long night, in Ravenhill, when Connacht lost 58–12 to Ulster. Plenty of defensive system errors.

'Yeah, that was a terrible one,' admits Lam again. 'And speaking of referees,' he adds, in reference to Ian Davies, 'a world record happened in that game. The penalty count was 9–0!

'I went up to him afterwards, and I said, "Do you know you've set a world record there? Honestly, in my whole rugby career as a player or a coach I don't think I've ever known a game where we never got one penalty at all. Don't get me wrong, I'm not saying that the nine against us were wrong, but are you trying to tell me that Ulster is the most obedient team that ever played?"'

Lam went through the game on video and, suffice to say, did not feel that the penalty count was entirely fair. One of the net effects was that Ulster had 17 line-outs to Connacht's three.

'It meant we could not launch anything in the line-out. Nothing!

That compounded that result. We spent so much time on defence in that game, and eventually it just broke.'

Connacht completed the season with three more defeats, losing 32–23 at home to a strong Munster selection, 22–15 at home to Cardiff and 45–20 away to the Ospreys. This left them in tenth, two places worse off than the previous seasons, but the statistic Lam derived most encouragement from was their try tally, which increased from 32 to 42, albeit they conceded 11 more, 54.

That tally of 42 was also at least ten more than they'd scored in a decade of League campaigns, dating back to their 50 in Michael Bradley's first campaign of 2003–04. Eleven bonus points (four for scoring four tries or more and seven for losing by seven points or fewer) was not only seven more than the previous season but also showed how close they'd been in a number of games.

This was also pretty much the squad Lam had inherited, so henceforth he could put more of his stamp on the squad's make-up. And this in a season without a CEO. Hence, Lam, Tim Allnutt and Conor McGuinness oversaw player contracts with the IRFU.

During that first season, Lam and Stephanie hosted an evening with the squad, and he also conducted 50 one-on-ones at his home. Those that were married with children also visited with their families, so that Stephanie and the kids could meet them as well.

'It was what I call the foundation year, laying out what we wanted to do game-wise, culture-wise and leadership-wise,' says Lam. 'Anyone who wanted to be on the leadership team had to make a formal application and go through an interview process with myself and Tim Allnutt. I also filmed each interview. Plenty applied but only some were interviewed, based on a survey I'd undertaken with the players; 12 or 13 applied and we settled for eight. We changed the whole leadership structure. And that group changed dramatically over the next few years.'

The Lam revolution was underway.

10

John Muldoon

John Muldoon reckons he was about 13 or 14 when he and his brother Ivan, older by 13 months, fired a rugby ball at each other from opposite ends of the hallway in their home in Portumna. The hallway was just over a metre wide and both walls were adorned with framed family photographs. Those two walls, the photographs and the light bulb, demanded accuracy.

Yet by the end of the year, the ball was bald from brushing against or rebounding off those walls, and general usage. A few photographs bit the dust too, as did one or two light bulbs.

When Connacht, in recent years, developed more of a running and passing game under Pat Lam, Muldoon was asked, 'Jeeze, where did your ball skills come from in the last few years?' He'd often afford himself a wry smile and think back to those teething stages with his first rugby ball.

You can't teach an old dog new tricks? Muldoon thinks he was a puppy when he first learned how to catch and pass.

'I've always felt that I have good skills; I just didn't use them. In the weather at the Sportsground, we just did "one out" runners. That was never my game, but Pat came in, shook things up, and the game plan now probably suits me better.'

By rights, though, Muldoon had no business playing rugby, much less ultimately becoming the stuff of Connacht folklore. He was born on 30 November in 1982 in Portumna; its Irish name Port Omna translates as 'the landing place of the oak'.

It's a market town in the south-east of Galway, close to the Tipperary border and west of the point where the River Shannon enters Lough Derg; hence its long history of bridges and ferry crossings between the two counties. On the south-western edge of the town lie Portumna Castle and Portumna Forest Park.

Muldoon, like his dad and his father before him, hailed from Gortanumera, about four miles outside Portumna, and his mum from Cappataggle in County Galway. 'Her home house is literally a stone's throw from that last toll bridge before Galway.'

Pure Connacht stock, but the area is very much a hurling stronghold.

During Muldoon's playing career with Connacht, Portumna GAA club have won four All-Ireland Club Senior Hurling Championships in 2006, 2008, 2009 and 2014, producing all the Cannings and Hayes hurling All-Stars.

There's also innate strength in the Muldoon gene pool. His father has two brothers and two sisters, and one of Muldoon's uncles, Pat, was a renowned exponent of tug of war while another, James, rowed for the Garda club, competing in the Montreal Olympic Games in 1976.

'Apparently one of the crew missed a stroke coming to the line in the semi-finals, and the team that caught them on the line went on to win the bronze medal. Yep, one of them missed a stroke! My oul lad rowed for the Guards as well – not as well as my uncle – but he reckoned yer man just switched off. He thought they were cruising over the line and he missed the stroke.

'My family wouldn't really talk about stuff like that. I only found out the other day, after an article appeared in the paper, that they missed a stroke. I knew my uncle competed in the Olympics, but any time you asked him he was a bit blasé about it. My dad told me the other day that his brother did hold a lot of records and was a renowned rower in Dublin. I think he rowed into his early forties, but my family are not too good at detail.'

Both his father and uncle were Gardaí in Dublin. 'My dad was based mostly in St James' Street. We have a farm as well, and as my granddad grew older someone had to move home to help with the farm. So my dad moved back, but for another ten or 12 years he was still a cop.'

His dad returned to Portumna a year or so before Muldoon's birth. Hence, he grew up there, along with his older sister Olivia, older brother Ivan and younger brother Conor, working long hours on that farm as well as attending Portumna Community School and playing a truckload of sports.

His parents had met and married in Dublin, and both sides of Muldoon's family are steeped in hurling. 'A couple of our cousins have been captains of Galway minors that won All-Irelands, and my dad's nephew, my first cousin Brian Feeney, was captain of the Galway hurlers.'

There was also Muldoon's aunt on his mother's side. 'They're the Kennedys. There were eight boys in the family, and I think all of them bar one played for Galway at underage, and one of them, Greg Kennedy, played for the Galway seniors.' It goes on. Muldoon's mother's sister is the wife of Pat McDonagh. 'He is Mr Supermac.'

Muldoon had what he describes as 'a typical country childhood. I grew up on a farm, so we worked during the day and at weekends. You had to get your jobs done before school if you had training later, and we also went out on the farm after school if we didn't have training.

'We played every sport and watched every sport on TV. Our local school is a two-teacher national school, it's still going, and right across the road lies a hurling pitch which is part of the school. On some days there could be 12 or 13 lads, and 12 or 13 girls, aged from ten to 15 or 16, playing sports. Anything that we could get our hands on – footballs, rugby balls, American football, soccer, hurling. Anything. I'd say I had a typical eighties/nineties upbringing. We weren't spoiled. We weren't running around with money in our pockets, but we never wanted for anything either.'

The only organized sport was hurling, through Gortanumera

national school. He can only guess what age he was when he first had a hurley and a sliotar in his hands. 'My brother has a little girl who runs around with those little plastic ones. Likewise, I'd say from the age of two or three we were all running around with a hurl in our hands.'

At around 11 or 12, Muldoon also began playing soccer with a local team, 'just to do something different', whereupon the 1997 Lions tour to South Africa was the hook with which rugby ensnared him.

'We didn't have Sky Sports, but one of our mates who did used to record the games for us. We'd sit around watching them that night or the following day. We didn't fully understand the rules. I was 14 and Ivan had a bigger grasp of the rules as he had started playing rugby in the [Portumna] school the year before.'

Rugby had turned professional two years previously, and Sky's packaging of that Lions tour struck Muldoon. 'The whole buzz and atmosphere around that tour just pulled me in. I knew about soccer but not about rugby. I don't know why I bought into it, but my brother was playing the year before, and he used to bring me out to the garden to make himself better. I was like his bloody tackle bag. I'd stand there and he'd tackle me.'

It didn't deter Muldoon. His first memories of rugby had been of the Five Nations and watching Simon Geoghegan. 'My oul lad said, "Oh, his family is from down the road." I said, "Where down the road?" He said, nodding, "Ah, just four or five miles down the road there."

'Eric [Elwood] was also playing, and my dad said, "Oh, he's from Galway." It helped give you a little sense of affiliation. I'd like to think it was when Ireland beat England [in 1993 or '94], but my memory might have been influenced by seeing those clips in later years. But definitely the 1997 Lions dragged me in.'

With Muldoon inspired by his brother, the previous September he'd decided he'd try his hand at the oval-shaped ball. On the first day of term at Portumna Community School, the 120 or so boys and girls are split into two halves of the school's main hall, and those who wanted to play the various sports, be it hurling, Gaelic football, soccer, rugby or whatever, went to different parts of the room.

Sheer numbers decreed whether they'd have a team in any given sport, but Muldoon canvassed his mates to try rugby as well as hurling. The third-year boys were already providing the bulk of Portumna's Junior Cup team, so Muldoon reckoned he'd be playing alongside his brother in that team anyway, but he also wanted to get an Under-14 team up and running, to also ensure there'd be a Junior Cup team in the subsequent year.

There were, indeed, enough for an Under-14s team, with Daithi Frawley his first coach, but that was just as well for Muldoon.

'Turns out I was completely wrong. I never played a game with the Junior Cup squad the whole year,' Muldoon recalls with a rueful smile. 'I was the only player in the squad not to play a minute! And this out of a squad of around 25 players.'

The following year, now inspired by the Lions, Muldoon was captain. 'Growth spurts I reckon,' is his rationale for that. 'I remember going into my class in second year as one of the smallest lads, and I came out one of the tallest. My dad is 6 ft 4 in. I never managed to catch him, but my uncle who rowed is 6 ft 3 in. or 6 ft 4 in. as well. My other uncle, Pat, who did tug of war, was more of a squat fella. It's funny because me and my brother Ivan are tallish and lean, and my younger brother Conor is small and fatter! Very similar to the three brothers in my dad's family.'

But another factor had fast-tracked his improvement. Muldoon and his older brother had also decided that playing for Portumna wouldn't be enough.

They joined Nenagh, half an hour's drive away, because some of their cousins were part of the Nenagh team being coached by their cousins' dad. Again, to a degree, Muldoon admits he was hanging on to his older brother's shirt tails.

His older brother has probably been the biggest influence on Muldoon's career. Ivan was exceptionally tall at 14 and 15, when playing back-to-back Schools Junior Cup campaigns and, as his younger brother describes it, 'running over the top of people. He grew another little bit going into fifth year but never grew after that and, a bit like Shane Jennings, moved to number 7.'

The brothers had considered the Under-16s in Ballinasloe, but when Ivan went to a meeting at that club he discovered that there were only five teams in the league. That amounted to eight games, four at home and four away. Their Nenagh-playing cousins told them that they played about 14 or 15 games a season. 'It was a no-brainer, and I think we ended up playing twenty games that season in the North Munster League, a higher standard league.'

Gerry Kelly encouraged them to relocate to the Connacht Junior League with Ballinasloe, with whom they reached an All-Ireland semi-final. But even so, there weren't enough matches for their liking, so they went back to Nenagh, winning an All-Ireland title by beating Ards in the final.

Meanwhile, back in Portumna, whereas Ivan had captained them to a Connacht Junior Cup, Muldoon's team lost in the semi-finals. His two years on the Senior Cup team were no more rewarding in terms of silverware.

In his first, Portumna lost their semi-final to Sligo in a second replay, after two drawn games, and in his final year they lost in the semi-finals again to Ferbane. 'Conor O'Loughlin was on their team,' says Muldoon of a friend who would graduate to Connacht in the same year. 'I'll never forgive him for that.'

That aforementioned Lions tour had also prompted Muldoon to attend his first Connacht match, the re-arranged Tuesday-afternoon game against Northampton at the Sportsground in September 1997. 'I mitched from school but got caught because the bus dropped us outside the school grounds. We had changed out of our uniforms, but one of our teachers who is a neighbour saw us. I had to go home and beg my mother to write a note explaining that she knew we were absent from school. We told her what we'd done, and she forgave us and wrote the note. So we got away with it. We'd picked a good one. I didn't go to another Connacht game for a while after that. We tried to mitch another day, but Mum smelled a rat and said, "You're not going to that game."'

Approaching his final year at Portumna, 1999–2000, Muldoon trained with the Connacht Youths and desperately wanted to make the Irish Youths. The previous season he had been considering 'knocking hurling on the head', as he puts it, after he had just been part of a successful Minor winning hurling team with the club, but in March 1999 one of his best friends and neighbours Keith Hayes, whose brother Damien played for Galway, had died in a car crash.

'He was like the up-and-coming Joe Cooney,' says Muldoon, in reference to the great Galway star of the eighties and nineties, a five-time All-Star who won two All-Ireland and three National League titles. 'Keith had just played in the Under-18 final a few weeks before and had put in a Man-of-the-Match performance when scoring 2–9 from play, so obviously that shook the whole of our small community. His brother Damien was also on the team, and we'd all been in school together and grown up together.

'Damien came in one day and made an emotional plea for us "to win it for my brother". So I wasn't going to let my buddies down, and I had to commit to that fully, while also training and playing with the Connacht Youths.'

The Portumna Minors retained their Galway hurling championship crown, and on the back of that he was called into the Galway Minors, as well as making the Irish Youths in rugby. As both squads went into training in February 2000, Muldoon turned down the Galway Minors and played for the Irish Youths against their Scottish and Welsh counterparts.

Whereupon one of the Galway Minors selectors called him to see if he'd reconsider. Muldoon pointed out that he hadn't played hurling in several months but was prevailed upon to train with them. 'I rocked in, but still in rugby mode, and when I arrived to training I realized I'd forgotten my hurl! That's the honest to God truth. There were four Portumna lads in the squad, and I had to borrow one of theirs. It was too small, but I couldn't admit I'd forgotten my hurl.

'My oul lad, who I'd say hadn't been at one rugby match in his life up to then, asked me, "How did that go?" I said, "Ah, I forgot my hurl." If looks could kill! Yet two days later, the Galway Minors called

Above: The Connacht squad of the late 1990s. (*Back row. L–R*) Nicky Barry, Martin Cahill, Johnny Maher, Barry Gavin, Mark McConnell, Graham Heaslip, Junior Charlie, Willie Ruane, Eric Elwood. (*Front row. L–R*) Simon Allnutt, Billy Mulcahy, Rory Rogers, Nigel Carolan, Pat Duignan, Conor McGuinness.

Below: Warren Gatland, Connacht coach 1996–98.

Above: Conor McGuinness – Connacht's #9 – in a famous win against Ian McGeechan's Northampton.

Left: Taking a break in the south of France during the 1997 European Challenge Cup campaign: (*L–R*) Brian O'Byrne, Gerry Thornley (author), Billy Mulcahy and Willie Ruane.

Below: Nigel Carolan breaks through the centre against the French giants Racing Club.

Above: Friends of Connacht marching along Baggot Street towards Lansdowne Road, January 2003.

Below: Delivering a letter of protest to IRFU headquarters.

Above: Connacht coach Michael Bradley talks to his team before a Celtic League match in 2004.

Below: Analysing options – Michael Bradley with Eric Elwood.

Above: Connacht stalwart Michael Swift.

Right: Gavin Duffy.

Below: All-time top try scorer for Connacht, Fionn Carr.

Eric Elwood. (**Above and right**) Playing against Northampton in 1997 and (**below**) applauded by teammates as he leaves the pitch at the end of his last home game for Connacht in April 2005.

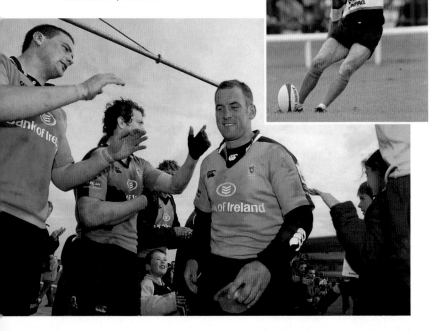

Top left: Connacht CEO Gerry Kelly announces Eric Elwood as Connacht coach, March 2010.

Top right: Former teammates, now opposing coaches. Michael Bradley of Edinburgh and Eric Elwood of Connacht after a Pro12 match in 2012.

Below: Eric Elwood with his family as he steps down as Connacht coach in May 2013.

Above: Previous Connacht coaches: (L–R) Michael Bradley, Warren Gatland and Eric Elwood with (*second from left*) former Connacht CEO Gerry Kelly.

Below: July 2012. The Aviva Stadium. Then IRFU president John Hussey presents the seal of office to the incoming and 125th union president Billy Glynn of Connacht.

again. "You're in the squad. You're starting training four nights a week." Damien Hayes said to me, "Oh, there's someone looking after you." I couldn't believe it, and it meant I had to lose a load of weight.'

It also meant Muldoon won an All-Ireland Minor medal when Galway beat a Cork side containing the would-be Munster and Irish scrum-half Tomás O'Leary in the final at Croke Park. 'I played a club game about two weeks later and never picked up a hurl again. That was it. At that stage, I knew what I wanted.

'I rang the hurling coach at the time to tell him I was packing it in. He said, "Yeah look, we've seen this coming for a while." I'd say 80 to 90 per cent of the people from home would have understood that I was playing underage rugby with Ireland. Rugby probably suited me better, and I liked the physicality of it. I've always been a realist: I knew I was better at rugby as well, and I just enjoyed the game more. I don't know why.

'I think there's a little bit more reliance on teammates in rugby. In hurling, one or two really good players can mask the whole team, and I think you end up having better relationships with lads in rugby.'

In that season, he'd been combining schools and underage club rugby with club and county hurling, not to mention his Leaving Cert. 'It was a busy old year that. I did all right in the Leaving, actually, which surprised me, because I didn't do a lot for it. My farm work as well was limited enough. If you ask my oul lad, he'll tell you I did nothing.'

But just out of school and about to start his first year of Production Engineering in GMIT (the Galway/Mayo Institute of Technology) something had to give. That was September 2000.

There'd been another turning point in his last Connacht Senior Schools Cup campaign with Portumna, when Frawley invited the then Connacht hooker Bernard Jackman to take a session. Afterwards, Jackman hosted a Q and A with the squad.

Muldoon asked him, 'I know you're professional, but is this like being a professional in soccer? Do you work at anything?'

'No,' said Jackman.

'How many times a week do you train?'

'Once or twice a day.'

Connacht's season was winding up in February, and Jackman then returned for Portumna's quarter-final, after which he presented the Man-of-the-Match award. He chose Muldoon.

'I actually don't know if I've ever told him this – I think I did say it to him one night on the piss – but "Birch" gave me his Connacht zippy-up jacket. Their season was coming to an end, so he probably didn't even need it, but I remember at the time thinking, "Oh, wouldn't that be class, being a professional rugby player?" And then I made the Irish Youths as well.'

In 2000, he moved in with his brother Ivan and a few other mates to a house in Galway. Still eligible for the Nenagh Under-18s, he combined this with the Irish Under-19s, with whom he travelled to Chile for the FIRA Under-19 World Championships. 'We lost to Uruguay. Yeah, that was a year to forget. I think my game stagnated that year, living in Galway, going to college, and playing for Nenagh and the Irish Under-19s. I was getting by without being as fit as I could have been.'

Living with his brother and John Burke, a cousin and a neighbour who was playing with Nenagh, they stayed somewhat fit by training with the GMIT squad in Galwegians. In advance of a planned night out in Galway, four of them were late for training after dinner. 'There were lights on. Up in Galwegians, if there's lights on that was a good start,' says Muldoon. 'But we looked around, and there was no sign of anybody.'

A man in a hooded Galwegians jacket informed them that as only about five of their GMIT fellow players had turned up, they had relocated to Flannery's bar. The man invited them to train with the Galwegians Under-20 squad. The Nenagh Under-20s had hammered their Galwegians counterparts that season, which was mainly made up of the Nenagh Under-18s squad, and Muldoon was not keen. But Burke prevailed upon them to do the session.

'It was grand,' says Muldoon. They put on their runners, put their boots over their shoulders and headed for home to shower and attack the night.

'As we were leaving, yer man ran down the road after us,' recalls

Muldoon, who left the Galwegians man talking with Burke. It transpired that John Kingston, the coach whom Galwegians had brought in from Harlequins for two seasons, had been watching the session, at the end of which he told the man in the hooded Galwegians jacket: 'I'll have him [Burke], him [Muldoon] and those two [Muldoon's brother Ivan and Ray Hogan].'

'Yeah, OK, but I have no idea who those guys are.'

'I don't f****** care, get them down on Thursday night for training.'

Burke arrived back to tell his housemates the news. Kingston wanted the four of them at training two nights hence. The fifth member of the household, who hadn't been to training, was Brian McClernan. He ended up playing with 'Wegians for a dozen years and is now their head coach.

The AIL was big then, as big if not bigger than the provincial game.

'You have to remember Galwegians were in a semi-final against Dungannon three weeks later, and they were asking us to go training with them. I said to John, "You're talking shit!" Because he was prone to it. And he said, "No, I swear. He'll be ringing us tomorrow."'

The five housemates, including McClernan, trained with the Galwegians senior team that Thursday night, and after the session they were then asked to train again the following week.

'So we rocked down the following week, sat down in the dressing-room, and who am I sitting across from? Eric [Elwood]. They hadn't told us all the Connacht lads were training too. As well as Eric, Dan and Swifty were there.'

Muldoon, then 19, stared at the ground.

They began training regularly with Galwegians, and Kingston prevailed upon them to join the following season, 2001–02. In the meantime, they played with Galwegians in a friendly against UL Bohemians. Whereupon Connacht made contact to say that their head coach Steph Nel wanted to expand their Connacht Colts squad with four or five new contracted development players.

Buttressed by their five newcomers, the Galwegians Under-20s had nearly beaten a Buccaneers Under-20s sprinkled with Connacht players in the provincial final. Nel had been amongst the Sportsground crowd that day.

'I think we got 1,500 euros or something for the year,' recalls Muldoon. Hogan was injured, but the Muldoons began life with Connacht at the start of the 2001–02 season.

The Connacht Under-20s soon broke new ground that season by winning the interprovincial title but, ironically, the older Muldoon discovered the game was not for him. 'My brother hated it, absolutely hated going to training every day, and hated the environment. He just walked away, and he ended up becoming a cop but played for ten-plus years with Galwegians.'

Muldoon made the Irish Under-21s for the next two seasons, playing in two Under-21 World Cups, in South Africa in 2002, and England in 2003, with Ciaran Fitzgerald and Michael Bradley the respective coaches. He describes the 2002–03 season as 'weird'. That was the year the IRFU academy, of which Muldoon was the first Connacht graduate, was regionalized into four provincial branches. But after the first of those World Cups, he had only a week's holidays before returning for pre-season with Connacht.

'By Christmas, I was flat. I was struggling to put on weight. I was really badly out of form.'

He recalls a pre-Six Nations Under-20 friendly between Connacht and Leinster in Athlone. 'I should have been one of the main players in the Under-20s but just bombed out. By the end of the Six Nations, Brads had dropped me. I didn't know where my head was. I wasn't playing well and I'd get frustrated. I remember thinking, "Jaysus, this couldn't be going any worse."'

After the Six Nations, Muldoon was telephoned by Nel. 'I was getting a proper development contract, one of the fifteen-grand ones. I was like, "This is nice. Proper work." I didn't tell a sinner.'

At the end of that 2002–03 season, Johnny O'Connor, Gavin Duffy and Colm Rigney had decided to leave Connacht and join Wasps, Harlequins and Leeds, and a few weeks later, Nel phoned Muldoon again.

'Your contract has been changed.'

Muldoon felt his heart flutter.

'You'll be on a full-time contract.'

'What do you mean full-time?'

Muldoon couldn't believe his ears.

'It wasn't even the money. Immediately, I decided to drop college. I decided, "I want to go at this hard."'

After a training week with Connacht, he met two of the players in Galway, one of whom said, 'Did you hear that Steph's after handing in his notice? Rumour has it that Brads is taking over.'

Muldoon was taken aback. 'No, that can't be true.

'Remember, Brads has just dropped me from the Under-21s in the Six Nations. Then one or two of the Connacht players rang me, asking, "What's he like?" I tried to play down my own worries. "Yeah, he's grand," I said, but wondering if Brads was ready for this.'

At an ensuing Under-21 squad session in readiness for the World Cup in Oxford, one of the first players Muldoon bumped into was the Shannon and Munster back-rower Stephen Keogh, who revealed to Muldoon that Bradley had offered him a contract at Connacht.

'So Stephen Keogh, who played in the same position as me, a 6 or an 8, has been offered a contract by Brads! I just said, "Look, I'll think about this when I come back." So we went to the World Cup, with Brads still the coach of the Under-21s.'

Muldoon's form picked up. 'Maybe the contract was a bit of a weight off my shoulders going to the World Cup. I played in all of Ireland's five games, and as the tournament continued, my form got better and better, and I ended up enjoying it.'

Muldoon had graduated from underage rugby. Henceforth, he would be a fully contracted, fully fledged Connacht player.

11

Devoted to Connacht

The 2003–04 season was an interesting time. Although the League had shrunk from 16 clubs to 12, as the Welsh RFU trimmed their numbers from nine to five, it expanded from an eight-game, two-section competition into a 22-game home and away format. This not only meant 22 games instead of eight, but a mid May finish instead of early November. The provinces, including Connacht, were now full on.

John Muldoon made his competitive debut as a replacement in a home win over the Border Reivers in October, and his full debut as one of eight changes for the Ospreys game later that month. A notionally stronger selection had lost at home to the Scarlets a week before this seemingly weaker team beat the Ospreys 33–22. Nonetheless, Muldoon was amongst those dropped for the ensuing win at home to Ulster.

Muldoon was granted his second start away to Edinburgh in mid February, but, although Connacht won again, he was dropped for the next defeat to Cardiff.

'Brads is a top bloke. You couldn't meet a nicer fella, but he had this rotation policy back then. He'd play a team for two or three weeks, and then he'd bring in virtually a whole new XV. It was like lambs to the slaughter.

'The lambs beat the Ospreys four tries to two at St Helen's in Swansea, but we were all dropped the following week. The same thing happened a few weeks later. We went to Edinburgh, won again, four tries to three, but were dropped again. We were like, "Brads, do you not see, we're the good team?" But Brads was cute.'

In early March, Muldoon – a replacement away to the Border Reivers – set up a try, made a couple of turnovers and big hits, and came off the pitch feeling good about himself. Only to be dropped from the match-day squad again. The following week, playing for Galwegians, he suffered an ankle ligament injury that sidelined him for six months.

'I suffered a thing called bone bruising, which wasn't a great injury to get at the time. If you have bone bruising now, there are ways to deal with it, but back then they didn't really have any precedent for it. One specialist would say, "There's nothing wrong with you." Another would say, "Oh, total rest for four months."'

The lay-off was a blessing. 'I was in the gym twice a day, as I couldn't run. I went from 99 or 100 kilos to 107 or 108 kilos, so I piled on a stone in weight. It did me the world of good. It turned me from a frail young fella into a bigger man. I became a more physical player.'

Returning for a pre-season friendly the following August against Newcastle, Muldoon rolled his ankle. 'From that day onwards, I've always strapped my ankle. Every game, just for pure psychological comfort.' Even so, after turning 22 in the November, he played 24 games for Connacht that season. 'It was a little by default. I played at 6, 7 and 8 because Swifty and John O'Sullivan were carrying injuries. John had had his breakthrough year the season before, but he was probably lighter than me, trying to play as an abrasive back-row, and the following season his body just broke down before he moved on to Munster. But whenever the main lads came back, I'd get dropped again. So I felt I was still trying to change Brads' perception of me.'

In the Challenge Cup semi-final first leg at home against Sale, Muldoon suffered a thumb injury which ruled him out of the second leg 59–9 thrashing – not a bad one to miss.

After that second leg, Bradley called Muldoon into his office and informed him that Connacht had a new contract for him. It was a week ahead of schedule. Muldoon didn't even have an agent at the time but agreed to sort it out with Gerry Kelly.

Bradley then asked him, 'How are things with you anyway?'

'Yeah, good,' said Muldoon, a little surprised to be asked.

'We missed you the last few weeks. How much longer before your thumb is right?'

'About two weeks.'

'Good, we need you back.'

From that day on, their relationship changed.

'The following year [2005–06], he offered me the captaincy and I turned it down. I was too young.'

Nevertheless, Muldoon was becoming a mainstay. He played another 26 games in 2005–06, starting all but two, and was again an ever-present in their run to the Challenge Cup quarter-finals. In 2006–07, he started another 23 games. There were some notable scalps in these years, but Connacht remained consistently near the foot of the table.

'We were like a good FA Cup team. On a given day in a pressure situation we could beat teams, but week on week, consistency was a big issue for us. Basically we probably had 16/17/18 players. In certain positions we might have two lads, and in other positions we had only one, and if that one lad was injured we were f*****. And invariably they did get injured. We just didn't have the squad. But at the same time, lads played above themselves quite a bit.

'The culture of the place and the team camaraderie were always very good. We just weren't good enough. Ultimately, we just didn't have a good enough team. It's harsh to say, but it's the truth. We didn't have the money to invest. We didn't have the facilities. We didn't have the crowd.

'We travelled to France quite a bit and had a lot of good victories over there. Montpellier stands out, and Narbonne. In Brads' last year, we beat a good Bourgoin side to reach the semi-finals and put Toulon under the pump for a long time. Things were starting to change and improve slowly.

'Playing South Africa here before the 2007 World Cup was pretty cool. We filled out the Sportsground, and games like that made you think if we could tap into the goodwill here, people would come to matches. The Interpros were picking up each year around Christmas, with more and more supporters.'

There were low days too. 'A lot of low days,' he admits.

Muldoon recollects a home end-of-season League game against the Dragons on May Day, 2004. It was a week after an estimated 6,000 had turned up for Connacht's Challenge Cup semi-final second-leg win over Harlequins (although they came up four points short on aggregate over the two legs).

'It was well before the Clan Terrace had been built. I was injured, so I watched it from the open side of the ground. It was towards the end of the season on a lovely sunny day. There were about 300 or 400 there, and I was thinking, "This is a disgrace after the great atmosphere the previous week. It's a lovely day, 2.30 on a Saturday afternoon." I was wearing sunglasses. It was even before they had put up the railings, and before the new building on the far side. It was like, "Ugh, this is woeful." There were even a couple of lads with their dogs. I know all about the cliché: "There were fans there with their dogs!" But there actually were. I was like, "Oh no, this is brutal. Where are we going?"'

Another that stands out for Muldoon was a 23–0 defeat away to the Dragons in May 2007, and Muldoon admits he lost his rag in the dressing-room afterwards.

'I felt that we should have won the game and that one or two of the team were happy to play and pick up a pay cheque. I had a bit of a pop in the dressing-room. I am sure I was called every sort of name afterwards. Some said, "Ah, f*** off, will you?" One or two lads understood but reckoned that probably wasn't the time or place. I remember putting my head in my hands afterwards and going, "Right, that's me done. I'm not f****** staying here. I just can't do it".'

Midway through the 2008–09 season, when a contract was put in front of him, Muldoon was genuinely of a mind to leave. 'I felt they completely low-balled me.'

He let the contract offer sit without any further response for a month, and when Gerry Kelly and Bradley pointed out to him that it was still unsigned, Muldoon explained that this was because he wouldn't be signing it.

'They asked me, "Are you not happy with it?" And I was like, "I told you when you offered it to me I wasn't happy with it." About two days later, I walked into Brads' office and said, "Just to let you know, Brads, I'm close to signing for another team." He looked at me. "Oh, I didn't even know that you were thinking about going." I said, "What did you think when you offered me a contract five weeks ago and it's still sitting on the table?"

'They were offering me a 5 per cent increase on a wage that I knew was already low. I wanted to leave Ireland altogether, but then Ulster came in with a very good offer. I had an opportunity to go to England too, but that contract was pretty average. It would have been less money, but it was all incentivized, with the possibility of doubling my money the following season.

'Their rationale was that the Pro12 is a lesser league, and while some players coming from the Pro12 to the Premiership had done well, others have crashed and burned. But I was prepared to back myself. So both offers were tempting.'

It was Christmas week, 2008. Bradley texted him: 'Enjoy your Christmas, you've ruined mine.'

Muldoon ignored a call from Kelly, who then texted: 'Please answer.'

He rang Kelly and told him, 'You're too late, Gerry. I've decided.'

Bradley rang him. 'Have you been on to Gerry?'

'Well, yes. Kind of.'

'Well, don't make a decision until after the Munster game.'

That Munster game was on Sunday, 28 December. A crowd of 5,000 packed the Sportsground, and Ian Keatley kicked four penalties in a 12–6 win.

'We'd beaten Munster for the first time in I don't know how long,' recalls Muldoon. (Since 1986 to be precise, and for the first time in Galway since 1979.)

'So I decided to stay! Thankfully!'

Would he ever really have left? Could he?

'The main factor was that we were definitely getting better, but the problem was that the other teams were as well.' Indeed, no sooner did Muldoon think they were closing the gap than at the end of the 2010–11 season Ian Keatley decamped to Munster and Sean Cronin and Fionn Carr to Leinster.

'Just as you think our squad is becoming more settled, you lose those lads and you think, "How the f*** are we going to close the gap?" Then Macker [Mike McCarthy] left in 2013. Just as we were growing, one of our legs was chopped off.'

Even so, in Elwood's first season of 2010–11, Connacht rose to ninth of 12 in the League. 'I enjoyed working with Eric. I enjoyed his energy. He made a big difference. Myself and Eric have similar personalities, so we got on well. We saw things similarly, whereas if you had a different personality, he struggled with you and you struggled with Eric.

'It was unfortunate the way it finished. Eric wanted Connacht to change so much. But the players and the organization weren't moving as quickly as he wanted, and that ultimately became too much for him. We improved massively under Eric, and our results show that. It was just that everyone else was improving even more quickly than we were, and they were signing phenomenal players.'

Muldoon had won two caps on the summer tour to Canada and the USA in 2009, and in the summer of 2010, he had been part of the Irish squad that toured New Zealand and Australia. But barely half an hour into the test in New Plymouth against the All Blacks, Muldoon suffered a broken arm. He had been relatively lucky with injuries, but his recovery from this one over the summer months was compounded by a groin injury for much of the following season. After ten weeks of rehabbing, he broke down in training and finally underwent a groin operation. Due to an injury crisis, he was then rushed back for their opening Challenge Cup game away to the Italian side I Cavalieri Estra in October. Connacht, embarrassingly, lost after leading 18–3.

Muldoon played in the win at home to Bayonne the following week, noticing a modest improvement in his groin over the next few weeks, all the while being assured that the return of other players would allow him time on the sidelines and the physio's table.

'The Irish management must have been looking at me going, "What's this gobshite doing?" I should have put my hand up and said, "I'm not playing." Because effectively I killed my international career in those few months. I stupidly put myself forward and said, "Yeah, I'll play." We were short on numbers.'

To compound this, in the second of the back-to-back defeats against Harlequins that December and with a lay-off due immediately afterwards, Muldoon broke his arm again. That sidelined him for another three months and effectively scuppered his season.

Regrets, he has a few, but playing when patently not right in those months in 2010 is uppermost amongst them. 'I should have been big enough and bold enough to say, "No, I'm not fit, so I'm not playing."'

About the only silver lining was that he could rehab his groin. Able to run again, he made himself fitter. He returned for Connacht's game in Aironi in late March on the bench. Aironi were bottom of the table with 17 defeats in 17 games, but although Connacht trailed for the entire match Muldoon was left on the bench. And left there. Until the last five minutes, when he was brought on with Connacht trailing 25–13. He didn't touch the ball and made one tackle.

Again, left on the bench until the final 15 minutes of the win at home to Edinburgh a week later, Muldoon called into Elwood's office the following Monday. He was bitter, bitter that he'd played earlier that season when not fully fit. It was one of the more difficult discussions between Muldoon and Elwood. McFarland joined the debate and told Muldoon his form had not been good enough.

Muldoon reckoned it wasn't as simple as that, but in any event it was the first time in six seasons he hadn't been a de facto first choice, and what's more he was captain.

In the two weeks before Connacht's next match at home to Cardiff, Muldoon put in extra hours on his fitness. Then, at half-time against Cardiff, with Ray Ofisa injured, McFarland informed Muldoon he was being brought on. He pulled on his jersey and his scrum cap, shoved his gumshield into his mouth and walked out of the dressing-room.

McFarland said, 'Where are you going?'

'I need a few minutes to myself,' said Muldoon.

'You've to listen to tactics.'

Muldoon ignored him and ran out on the pitch ahead of everyone else, and did a few sprints at the Bohermore end of the ground. When his teammates returned and regrouped at the College Road end, he had to run the length of the pitch to join them. He did 'all right' for 40 minutes, but Connacht lost. A week later, with Ofisa still injured, Muldoon started at Ravenhill against Ulster, who pulled away late on. Away to Munster in the last game of the season: a similar story. It was only his eighth game of the season for Connacht, and only his sixth start.

'I did all right. Didn't do anything bad. Didn't do anything good.'

He returned at the start of pre-season as fit as he'd ever been, but the following week Elwood announced that Gavin Duffy would be the new captain. Muldoon was disappointed but not too surprised.

'I walked over straight away to Gav: "Gav, congratulations. If you need anything from me, come to me whenever you want. I'm here for you."'

Muldoon gradually found his form in pre-season and, fit and in form, was an ever-present in all of Connacht's 28 games in 2011–12, starting all but two of them. He regularly picked up Man-of-the-Match awards and was Connacht's Player of the Season. Connacht, and Muldoon, competed in their first Heineken Cup campaign, with sell-out marquee fixtures against Toulouse, Gloucester and Harlequins. There was the torment of that 14-match losing run, but they did at least bring it to an end with their first ever Cup win over Quins.

In the Pro12, a three-game winning run (including a home win over Ulster) helped Connacht finish in a new high of eighth position. They were competitive in every game and might have had a few more wins – witness their tally of seven losing bonus points.

Playing when unfit in December 2010 had probably contributed to him losing the captaincy, but on mature reflection, perhaps it had been for the best.

'I was foolish to have played when I wasn't fit. But you learn, and in a way I walked away from the pressure of responsibility. I took a complete step back. I helped Gav every time he asked, which wasn't too much because he had his own opinions, but I had a good year. If you'd asked me at the time, I wasn't happy, although I would never have admitted it to anyone. But it probably was no bad thing.'

Furthermore, but for this interregnum as Connacht captain, the 2015–16 season would have been his eighth in a row – which sounds unlikely or at any rate too big an ask. It also meant that when he was subsequently re-instated as captain in 2014, he was both more ready and fresh.

Muldoon's form in 2011–12 also earned him one last game in an Irish shirt the following season. This was the non-capped match against Fiji at Thomond Park in November 2012, when chosen as an ill-fitting number 7. It also brought him more ill-fortune in an Irish jersey.

'Every time I played for Ireland I got f****** injured,' he laments. 'I was carried off with a knee injury. That bolloxed my knee for three months.'

It ruled him out of Connacht's remaining second Heineken Cup campaign – the games against Biarritz (home and away), Harlequins and Zebre – as well as the big festive Interpro derbies.

Muldoon returned the following February, making his first start in Connacht's first win over the Ospreys since 2008. This kick-started a run of three successive wins, and although they'd manage only one win in their final five games, away to Edinburgh, Connacht achieved a new high of eighth in Elwood's final season as head coach.

'I remember walking down Shop Street a couple of weeks after the season ended and some Connacht fan said to me, "Just f****** give up that Irish jersey. It doesn't do you any good. Get rid of that other green jersey!"'

So the records show three caps, all away from home, against Canada, the USA and New Zealand.

'I'm proud to have the caps, but I suppose I didn't really ever feel like I was part of an Ireland team. I felt more like a tackle bag for whatever number of years I was up there [in Dublin], on and off for three or four years. Yeah, I just felt like a tackle bag to be honest.'

Looking back, having been Connacht's captain and Player of the Season before winning his first two caps in 2009, he admits he didn't adapt well to his delayed start to the following season. The broken arm in New Zealand had even more repercussions.

'Basically I missed a full season when I should have been in the prime of my career, and undoubtedly that soured my experience of playing for Ireland. I was in the wilderness for a year afterwards and was never capped again.

'Even when I played really well for Connacht every week the following season [2011–12] and was called back into Irish training camps, Sean O'Brien and other lads had passed me out. I was back to holding a tackle bag and feeling like I wasn't really a part of it. You're called in one week, gone the next, called in again. There's lads looking at you as if you've four heads because you've played for Connacht on the Saturday, you've been called up Sunday evening and you get handed sheets with 95 line-outs and 15 variations, and you've line-out practice the following day. Then you're gone again on Thursday night to play with Connacht on Friday. You're not up there training the following week and then you're back the next week. I'm not paranoid, but I know there were lads looking at me thinking, "This useless Connacht . . . he hasn't a clue of the line-outs."'

He remembers one day when a fellow member of the Irish squad asked him why he didn't know all the calls. 'How the hell am I supposed to learn all these off a page?

'Another prominent international', as Muldoon describes him, grabbed the page and asked, '"Who the hell gave you this?"'

'He proceeded to draw an X through about 25 of the 95 line-outs, admitting, "I don't even know them myself." He literally got rid of about 25 in one fell swoop. I was grateful to him for that, but even so, I just never really felt part of it to be honest.'

It can also go with the territory of being an Irish back-rower. James Coughlan, that fine Munster number 8, never won a cap. 'You think of the players I was competing with,' says Muldoon, 'Stephen Ferris, Sean O'Brien and Jamie Heaslip, and you'd have to be very good to take them out. Unfortunately, that's just the way it is. I'm a realist. I know if those three boys are fit that they're going to start ahead of me or any other back-rower. So you're not going to get too many international caps with those three ahead of you.

'Do I feel that playing for Connacht hindered our chances? Not in the last three to four years. Definitely not. From 2001 to 2010 it most certainly did, and for good reason. We weren't good enough. There may have been a couple more Connacht lads who were good enough to be involved in Irish squads but weren't, and one or two lads from other provinces who were no better but were picked. But when you're in the shop window you get more opportunities.'

That non-capped match against Fiji in November 2012 would be Muldoon's last time in an Irish jersey, but with Pat Lam's arrival in 2013, Muldoon could devote himself to all things Connacht.

12

The 2014–15 Season

Out of little acorns and all that. The seeds for Connacht's second season under Pat Lam had been sown early in 2014, when he and Tim Allnutt undertook a scouting mission to their native land. They flew from Heathrow the day after the 64–6 defeat to Saracens.

From Lam's perspective, it was as much a mission to sell Connacht as anything else. 'I was pretty much winging it at that stage. I didn't have a strategic plan. I was sharing my vision. "We want to be the best province in five years. This is what I'm doing. We've brought Dave Ellis over. Craig Clarke has been there. I'm trying to build from bottom to top. That's the vision."'

As Allnutt puts it, 'I'd been dealing with agents for years and we were often stonewalled back in the day because we hadn't the money to spend on players. But going over with Pat opened a massive number of doors. We met the biggest agents and sold his vision.'

Specifically, they met with Bruce Sharrock, the non-executive chairman of Esportif International in New Zealand, and former All Black Craig Innes. Aside from Innes having been a former teammate of Lam's, the new Connacht coach knew them both from his time with Auckland and the Blues. He knew the key was to convince them that Connacht were every bit as professional an entity as the other three Irish provinces. 'I knew they were the same as I had been. They knew about Leinster, Munster and Ulster, but they had no idea who Connacht were. But Tim and I put together a pretty good PowerPoint and the win over Toulouse had helped too. I truly believed in this vision.'

The first player they met in Auckland was Tom McCartney, at the Skycity Hotel. 'Pat sold his vision to Tom,' says Allnutt. 'Tom had been one of his leaders in the Blues, and they trusted each other. Tom was fighting with Keven Mealamu and James Parsons for a starting spot with the Blues, and was captain of the ITM Cup team. He wanted to come abroad and test himself, so it wasn't a hard sell.

'Tom is a real no-nonsense bloke. There was no small talk. He knew what he wanted from the rest of his career. When we left, we thought, "Hmm, that's what we want." That feeling was proved correct. He's made a massive difference to us. He's added to our game and to our leadership group.'

Connacht were struggling at the time with injuries at hooker, and had plenty of young forwards. 'I knew straight away Tom McCartney would be a perfect fit,' says Lam. 'I'd brought Tom through Auckland and into Super Rugby with the Blues. I've had a long association with him. I knew the character, the ability and the professionalism, which was the big one – leadership stuff. So we organized a meeting. We were in New Zealand for just three days. Tim stayed a little longer, but we had left prepared.'

And in the fallout to that Saracens thrashing, the PGB were more inclined to sanction signings!

Mils Muliaina, capped 100 times by the All Blacks, was their most high-profile capture from this trip or at any time in Connacht's history. 'I knew his agent [Innes] well,' says Lam. 'He told me Mils was available, and I was like, "Really?" So I rang Mils. Mils was an easy one. Mils added massive value, because Connacht had their first All Black. It gave us recognition around the world, and that was an important part of the journey. We were striving for wider recognition. The win over Toulouse and signing Mils helped, although I knew from the start that he was not the Mils Muliaina of his heyday. He was playing in Japan, but also for the Chiefs in Super Rugby. I know their coach, Dave Rennie. I knew what Dave was doing too, bringing in Mils' experience. Likewise, Mils brought that to us too.'

With the retirement of Frank Murphy, Paul O'Donohoe, Dan Parks and Gavin Duffy, as well as Clarke and Brett Wilkinson, an already youthful Connacht back-line was looking even more callow entering the 2014–15 season. Hence, in Lam's three key areas of game, culture and leadership, the biggest void was in the latter, which had ramifications for the culture.

After his first season at the helm, Lam recognized the need for the squad to challenge each other more. 'Following on from Craig Clarke, who was in a strong leadership role, Mils Muliaina had had ten years in the All Black leadership group. So even in our meetings in this room here, where challenging wasn't normal, Mils would always challenge. He'd say, "Fellas, you just talked about this outside. Bring it up. Bring it up." He changed the whole environment, making sure that any issues within the team were discussed. He really brought that All Black leadership culture into Connacht.

'After my first year, when I played a young back-line, I needed to bring in a more senior influence, and I knew that Mils would bring more professionalism. No one should underestimate his impact.'

Muliaina played only 11 games for Connacht before leaving under an unfortunate cloud at the end of the 2014–15 season, but he was a key signing. 'Mils gave us a huge amount off the field,' maintains Allnutt. 'Acquiring Mils made it "OK" to sign for Connacht.'

Indeed, Muliaina's capture went some way towards persuading Bundee Aki to be a part of the Connacht vision. Lam also needed more ballast in midfield, all the more so as young centre Eoin Griffin had also moved on to London Irish for a couple of seasons. Soon after Lam and Allnutt returned from New Zealand, Aki's CV landed on their desk.

Allnutt recalls, 'I know we got criticized a lot by Munster and Leinster, who were trying to sign him and claimed we outbid them. But we outbid them because we knew if a player has an offer from Munster on the one hand and Connacht on the other, certainly at the time he was more likely to choose Munster, so you have to give him a reason to come here. The figures being thrown around were exaggerated, but we packaged our offer in a way that was attractive to him, and having Pat at the helm helped. The same with Mils and Tom.

'In about a one-month period, we had signed Mils, Tom and Bundee. They were three different releases in New Zealand so everyone was wondering, "Who is this Connacht Rugby?" I've family back home, and they kept saying, "Jesus, you guys are getting great press over here." When Steve Hansen complained about players taking "the easy option" of leaving New Zealand after Bundee agreed to join Connacht, that just gave the story legs. We were in the press for a long time, which was awesome for us.'

The one caveat was that the trio's Super Rugby and ITM Cup obligations delayed their arrival until October. Yet even without their new marquee arrivals, Connacht made a much better start to their second season under Lam, winning their first three games at home to the Dragons (16–11), away to Edinburgh (14–13) and at home to Leinster (10–9). 'That was the game Marmo did the big step,' recalls Lam of his scrum-half's stunning try against Leinster at a typically sodden Sportsground. Connacht recovered from a 9–3 half-time deficit to win courtesy of Marmion sniping between Cian Healy and Ian Madigan, and then side-stepping Rob Kearney for one of the tries of the season. It was his 58th consecutive appearance following his debut on the opening day of the 2012–13 campaign. It also ended a run of 11 successive defeats in Interpro derbies.

Their fourth game pitted them against another unbeaten side, Glasgow, the coming force in the Pro12 and finalists the previous season. Connacht trailed 29–21 entering the last ten minutes, but an 80-metre intercept by Mark Bennett sealed a 39–21 win for Glasgow.

A week later, Connacht led Cardiff 24–10 entering the last ten minutes but contrived to leak two late tries and so drew, before getting down and dirty to beat Treviso 9–6 away. They had accumulated 18 points, compared to five at the same time a year previously. 'We'd now had more than a year together and a good pre-season,' says Lam.

They began their European Challenge Cup campaign with a handsome bonus-point win at home to La Rochelle, but were then faced with a Sunday–Friday, five-day turnaround from Exeter away in Europe to Ospreys away in the League.

With the attendant travel and squad juggling, Connacht lost both games 33–13 and 26–11, with Aki making his debut at the Liberty Stadium just a week after his arrival. Connacht had lost at the Liberty on their previous nine visits, and the Ospreys were then unbeaten League leaders. 'We were going really well,' says Lam. 'These were the form teams at the time, Glasgow and Ospreys. Good teams.'

Connacht responded by hammering Zebre 43–3 at home, a game notable for Muliaina's debut and also McCartney's more low-key first outing off the bench. The attendance, for a game against Zebre, was almost 5,500.

That figure was bettered the following Saturday, when all three new Kiwis were in their starting line-up for a 14–8 win over the Scarlets. Matt Healy was the match-winner when chasing down his own perfectly measured kick from halfway along the touchline in front of the Clan Terrace. Connacht retained their top-six place.

Returning to Europe, they beat Bayonne 42–19 at home, but even more satisfying was their 29–27 win against the same opponents seven nights later at the Stade Jean-Dauger after Lam changed his entire starting XV. Their 20-year-old academy scrum-half from Monivea, Caolin Blade, was the match-winner in a young and inexperienced line-up when his two late tries helped Connacht recover from a 27–16 deficit in the last quarter of the game. 'That was a totally new 15 that went over there,' says Lam. 'We brought all the young kids, and we pulled that one off. So that was massive.'

Approaching Christmas, Connacht travelled to Dublin to play Leinster in the RDS Arena. With Connacht trailing 14–11, Leinster went to the corner with the last play of the game. Although Matt Healy successfully kept the ball in play, it landed in the in-goal area for Zane Kirchner to score, so Connacht left Dublin empty-handed.

There were no thrashings, however, no late collapses as had happened in the previous season. On a rainy pitch in Ravenhill on St Stephen's Day, Connacht were unlucky to lose 13–10 to Ulster, the bonus point at least keeping them in the top six for the New Year's Day rendezvous with Munster.

In front of a crowd of 7,745, Connacht won 24–16, Marmion sparking a fightback from 13–0 down with another superb individualistic try before half-time. Craig Ronaldson and Aly Muldowney added tries after the break. In maintaining their unbeaten record at the Sportsground so far that season, Connacht had beaten Munster for only the second time in 41 meetings and the first in six years. 'Big win,' says Lam. 'January, terrible weather and they were stacked: Paul O'Connell, Peter O'Mahony, C. J. Stander, Tommy O'Donnell, B. J. Botha, Simon Zebo.'

Ultan Dillane was in his third year with the Connacht academy, having been plucked from under Munster's noses in Tralee. He'd made his debut against Leinster as a replacement two weeks before, started against Ulster and then was brought on halfway through the second half against Munster. 'He was buzzing because he was up against Paul O'Connell,' recalls Lam.

'I'd met Ultan in the academy during my transition period. He had a lot of injuries at the time, but talking with him I thought, "He's a nice kid." And then Jimmy Duffy was the one who said, "This kid's tough. You can go down an alley with Ultan Dillane. And he's explosive." He had skinny legs, but he was no holds barred. He just kept having niggly injuries, so he had been rehabbing a lot of the time; then we gave him a chance against Leinster. He had been training with us, along with a few of the academy guys.'

After the Munster game, Lam and the others had seen enough. Dillane was offered his first full contract by Connacht. A star was rising.

Aside from the three Kiwis settling in, Connacht were now a year and a half into the Lam era. Their new backs coach Andre Bell had made a discernible impact. His arrival on a two-year deal at the start of the season also freed up Ellis to do what he does best, and, unlike the previous campaign, Ellis had also completed a pre-season with the team.

'I didn't want Dave tied up with the backs,' explains Lam. 'I wanted him to work across the board with skills. So we were short and I needed a backs coach. We advertised for the job, and there were a few applicants.

'Andre and I had never worked together before, but Joe [Schmidt] and I both knew him from back home. He brought real value, but his main contribution was instilling confidence in the backs, because he empowered them and gave them belief. He knew his stuff, was a good talker and had good drills.'

Other factors were at play in Connacht's new-found consistency and established place in the top six. 'Muldoon was now up to another level as captain,' says Lam. 'In my first year, I had three captains, because I didn't know anybody, and I knew that Craig Clarke wouldn't know anybody when he arrived. He was the obvious one, but he didn't want that role.'

After the retirements of Clarke and Duffy, Muldoon was then the obvious choice. Younger than Michael Swift, Muldoon had done the job before.

Initially, Muldoon had seen the rationale, and even the ingenuity, behind Lam's idea of naming three joint captains. Duffy had been captain in the 2012–13 season but had picked up a few injuries and was 31. Similarly, Muldoon had been even more restricted in his appearances and was also 31, while Swift was 35. Clarke, who had just captained the Chiefs to their retention of their Super Rugby crown, was an obvious choice. But at that point he was an outsider and more-over would not arrive until after the season had started. 'I'd say Pat didn't want to rock the boat by walking in and straight away making Craig Clarke captain. I could see the logic.'

As events transpired, following their early-season run of nine defeats in 11 games, Lam named Clarke captain for their Heineken Cup pool win away to Toulouse and thereafter, until his career was cut short after that defeat to Saracens. But Muldoon admits that working alongside Clarke helped make him a better captain second time around.

'Craig was outstanding. As he was only just in the door, I won-dered, "Should he be captain?" But after a few weeks I decided, "Yeah he's the right man." I learned a lot from him. He's a very quiet indi-vidual, but he had the knack of saying the right thing at the right time. In that sense, I'm still nowhere near as good, but I picked up a few things from him. How he delivered his words. The timing. The accuracy. And, if you've nothing to say, don't say anything. Yeah, he was very good.'

Muldoon admits he was also more mature than in 2008.

'I was too hot-headed then. I wasn't able to control my emotions and find the right things to say. Even now, sometimes, I have to try to calm myself down. Amid the emotion of saying something at half-time, I have to go, "Whoa, take a break." I try to speak calmly. "Slow down, slow down." Even getting a small simple point across, it's how you deliver it.

'I used to be too headstrong and not see the overall picture. I wanted us to succeed and improve too quickly. And by no means am I now the finished article. At times, I struggled to understand how other players wouldn't want to do something my way. Now, I think I'm a lot more relaxed. If someone isn't pulling their weight, I'll tell them but without becoming too upset with them. If they don't want it badly enough, someone else will take their place. A few years ago, I was probably less patient. You can encourage players too. I learned that from Clarkey. You don't always have to say what you feel. Even if there's a bigger problem, highlighting a smaller point can sometimes achieve better results.'

In other words, Muldoon has learned that less can be more. He also concedes he adapted better to Lam's methods in year two. '[In his first season] Pat changed the game plan and while some picked it up very quickly, others took a bit longer. In the first few games, we struggled a little bit, and I too struggled a little initially.

'We'd gone from the choke tackle to chopping low. Swifty, myself and a few others had become really effective at the choke tackle. Now we were chopping lads around the kneecaps, and I struggled big time to change, and so did Swifty.'

Coming into Lam's second season, Muldoon also felt that Connacht were better than their results and final standing the previous season suggested.

'We had a good pre-season, and the likes of Marmo and Robbie would be an awful lot better with a year behind them. I genuinely went into the season thinking, "Yep, we could have a good year here."

We were also playing a more ambitious brand of rugby and were becoming more used to it.'

Connacht were now not only winning more games than they were losing for a change but there were also no thrashings, as in those Saracens and Edinburgh games. 'In the first season with Pat, we spent a lot of time trying to hone our attack, and at times we had forgotten about D [defence]. That Edinburgh game was the one that really hit home. After that, we worked on D more, and you could see the improvement.'

Connacht's win over Munster was their seventh thus far, along with a draw and just four defeats, in the League. They'd also won three games out of four in their Challenge Cup pool.

It also meant they'd won seven and drawn one from their first eight games of the season at the Sportsground.

Muldoon could sense a change in how opponents were now perceiving them. 'They're kind of looking at you thinking, "Jaysus, this is no easy ride now. Connacht are getting harder to play against." You got a feeling that teams just didn't enjoy playing against us any more.'

As well as Muldoon's captaincy and form, midway through this season Lam could see the effect that Connacht's Kiwi imports were now having. 'Bundee and Tom had taken everything to a different level at training and in matches, particularly with Bundee's X factor. Marmion and Matt Healy were on fire now as well.'

Alas, there was nothing like the same buzz in the ground eight nights later when Edinburgh came calling. On a howling night in the west, they won 16–13. Connacht took first use of the wind but conceded an early try, which meant a 13–7 lead was an insufficient buffer after the interval, despite a brave second-half display. A succession of penalties by Sam Hidalgo-Clyne ended Connacht's unbeaten home record.

With a penalty count of 14–10 against Connacht, that was also the night that Lam's problems with Welsh referee Leighton Hodges rose to another level. 'Leighton penalized us off the park with what I believe to be some wrong calls,' says Lam.

'Their try came from three penalties one after the other. Bang,

bang, bang, they scored, and that effectively was the game there. We defended massively. We were holding them up, but 13–7 became 13–10 became 13–13 became 13–16, and the penalties that he awarded against us were just so debatable. I put it through the Pro12 channels and they said, "Yes. Yes, sorry, Pat, you're right there." But I came away from that game going, "All right, we're going to play differently into the wind next time", because that was probably the worst weather we had. And we should have kept the ball and not kicked it. We got penalized so many times off the park just by defending, defending, defending.'

And it's not as if the wind might never be a factor at the Sportsground again.

Another home defeat a week later against Exeter left Connacht chasing a runners-up slot in their Challenge Cup pool. 'We blew that game,' says Lam. 'We really should have won that one.' But victory away to La Rochelle a week later by 30–20 earned a quarter-final away to Gloucester. This game also featured a first try for the province by Niyi Adeolokun.

Not only has Nigel Carolan helped transform the Connacht academy into a rich conveyor belt of home-grown players, but he has an acute eye for talent in the underage, youths and club scene, and is well connected. He recommended the Nigerian-born winger to Lam after being sent a video of Adeolokun by Trinity's long-serving American coach Tony Smeeth.

In April 2014, Adeolokun was given a trial game for the Connacht Eagles, their second-string team, against Enisei at the Sportsground. Eagle-eyed Connacht indeed.

Lam had liked the footage of Adeolokun and was in his coaches' box when the Eagles played Enisei that midweek afternoon. 'I watched his defence. He was raw, but I could see from the video he was quick. He didn't get many chances with the ball, but I loved his work-rate.'

At Lam's behest, Carolan brought Adeolokun to his office. 'I knew from Tony Smeeth that Niyi had completed his degree [in Business and Event Management in DIT], and so straight away I knew he was smart and had a good work ethic, because to earn a degree you obviously have to work hard.

'He told me about his background and I asked him, "Well, what's your big goal?" And he said, "I want to be a professional rugby player and I want to play at the top level." I could see he really wanted it too. I said, "Do you want to play for Connacht? Will you move down?" He said he would, and right then and there I said, "Mate, I'll sort it out and get a contract for you." And on the back of that, he arrived for my second season.'

Adeolokun had set up Connacht's first try of the season in their opening home win over the Dragons, and impressed Lam and co. sufficiently to be awarded an improved two-year deal in November of his first season. But the try against La Rochelle gave a hint of the jewel Connacht had unearthed.

Entering the last five minutes, Connacht trailed 20–16 when Adeolokun, on as a replacement, beat three players to score a spectacular try from his own half. With the game's last play, Healy then scored another of his kick-and-chase long-range tries for the bonus point, which earned Connacht a top-eight seeding and a place in the quarter-finals of the Challenge Cup for the seventh time.

But then came a 32–14 defeat away to the Scarlets. Connacht were still sixth, but the Welsh region had moved alongside them on 33 points thanks to this four-try win. 'Yeah, we played badly in that game,' admits Lam. 'That wasn't a good game. Wales wasn't a happy place for us, although we did win the following week away to the Dragons.'

A seven-try romp at home to Treviso cemented Connacht's place in sixth position, opening up a six-point gap over the Scarlets. But, with a five-day turnaround and another trip to Wales, Connacht lost 18–17 to Cardiff. 'That's the one!' says Lam. 'That's the nasty one. That's the one where everything happened on and off the field. Because I thought, "If we win this we get a jump." That's the one that went to the 88th minute.'

It was also, as he puts it, another 'learning', especially for his young out-half Jack Carty and centre Craig Ronaldson. Leading 17–11 entering the last play, Connacht had a line-out on their own 22.

'All we had to do was keep the ball, play our system. Jack whooshed the ball straight down to them. About 50 metres out. Now we're defending. And we defended and we defended. The referee, Lloyd Linton, penalized us, so they tap and go. We defend, and defend again, until Mick Kearney was penalized for offside. It was a touch-judge call and a yellow card, so he's gone and we start again with 14 men. Defend, defend, defend.'

With the clock passing 83 minutes, Lam went down to the sidelines. 'The ball comes to Alex Cuthbert, he gets tackled, knocks the ball on. Jake wins it on the ground, and we kick it out. I'm running on to the pitch, and I hear Leighton Hodges [a touch judge this night] say, "Hold on. Hold on, he hasn't blown the game up." Linton asks if there is anything he needs to see, and Hodges says, "Yeah, hands in the ruck." So Linton goes back and gives Cardiff a penalty, where they knocked on, for hands in the ruck.

'There was no ruck. There was a knock-on [by Cuthbert]. I've seen it all from the sideline. It was only 20 metres away and I just couldn't believe it. I'm going berserk, to the point that I'm getting warned on the sideline. I'm saying, "That's just wrong." '

Cardiff kept going through the phases and eventually their Argentinian winger Joaquín Tuculet scored his second try for Rhys Patchell to land the conversion with the game's last kick – 18–17 to Cardiff. Instead of retaining their seven-point lead over seventh-placed Scarlets, the latter's win over Leinster the next day trims it to three, with Edinburgh just a point further away.

When Conor McPhillips shows Lam a replay of the third penalty against Connacht in overtime, it merely confirms what his own eyes had seen. When Lam complains to the media again about Hodges' call from the sidelines, he is charged with 'misconduct' by the Pro12. 'I went to a judiciary hearing, and I had to accept that it was misconduct because of the rules. So I had to pay a fine of €8,000, with €5,000 suspended. That was a costly defeat!'

The Cardiff game also prompted a downturn in Connacht's season. After a three-week break for the closing rounds of the Six Nations, Connacht were beaten 42–20 away to Munster, before a Challenge Cup quarter-final defeat away to Gloucester. Connacht trailed 14–0 at half-time but came roaring back in the second half and pounded the home line for no reward at the end.

'It was after this game that Mils was arrested, and so from then on there's all that going on in the background,' says Lam, in reference to Muliaina's arrest outside Kingsholm, which was even televised by Sky Sports. The claim of sexual assault against Muliaina had been made a month earlier after Connacht's League defeat in Cardiff. Muliaina left for Zebre at the end of that season, although he was cleared of sexual assault the following October when Cardiff Crown Court dropped proceedings after hearing there was insufficient evidence.

'It wasn't good publicity, but the way it was done was completely wrong,' says Lam. 'All the boys knew too that Mils was accused of something that he hadn't done. But he wasn't allowed to say anything and that just made it worse.'

Thereafter, Connacht's season unravelled. They were beaten 27–20 at home by Ulster and 31–13 by would-be champions Glasgow, now on a rich vein of form as they worked towards their first title. After 20 rounds, Connacht thus slipped out of the top six for the first time in the season.

A bonus-point win away to Zebre and a bonus-point defeat at home to the Ospreys left them in seventh place, seven points behind the Scarlets: their best-ever finish but also short of their stated goal of top six and automatic qualification for the European Champions Cup.

That final League match of the season also marked Michael Swift's 269th and last game for the province after 15 years' service. It was also only his second game of the season after hyper-extending and fracturing his knee in February.

Swift was determined to make it back for one final appearance for a variety of reasons. On 2 February, the day after Connacht beat Treviso 53–5 at the Sportsground, Swift's father Jim, a Wexford man who boxed at underage level for Ireland before moving to London to work for the London Underground, passed away suddenly. His father had never missed a game since relocating to Galway four years previously, and he'd been in the Clan Terrace to witness the victory over the

Italian club. Now Swift wanted to honour his dad while also saying a proper goodbye to the supporters whom he had come to love over the last 15 seasons.

'That was my main motivation,' said Swift on the week of the Ospreys game, 'and he's buried just across the way from the Sportsground. So it's pretty special. Just to play one last game was for him, really.'

Muldoon recalls, 'I first came across Swifty in 2001 when I joined Galwegians. He's a few years older than me, and I would have kept myself to myself quite a bit. I always go out with the lads, but had my own friends as well. But me and Swifty probably developed one of the best relationships in Connacht.

'I always sat in the same corner beside Swifty, and I loved sitting beside him for thirteen-odd years or whatever it was. We'd text each other over the summer, and when we'd come back, Swifty was always an early bird, into the dressing-room with his coffee. We'd sit down and have a chat for 15 minutes before anyone else came in. We talked about the seats beside us being poisonous, because whoever sat either side of us was usually gone within three years!

'Sometimes a new player would put his bag on Swifty's seat, but I'd chuck it into the middle of the changing-room, and he'd do the same for me.

'We always had huge mutual respect. We both played at 6, and when you're young and a little immature you'd view someone in the same position as your opposition. But maybe because we started sitting beside each other I never felt that immature rivalry with Swifty.

'The thing I admired most about him was the way he revived his career in 2010. He was off the radar with Connacht and was playing badly for 'Wegians. He was just about to be released by Connacht when he reinvented himself as a second row for about four years. And he was phenomenal.

'During any of my own hard times I thought about how Swifty had reinvented himself. I used Swifty as an inspiration.

'I also loved the way he embraced Connacht, that his mum and dad moved to Galway. He wasn't from here, but you'd never think it.

There have been times as captain that I thought how fortunate I've been, considering guys like Swifty, Gav and Eric have put as much into Connacht Rugby as I have, if not more.'

Connacht's seventh-placed finish meant a play-off away to Gloucester, with the winners hosting Bordeaux-Bègles for a place in the European Champions Cup.

More heartbreak, and more controversial refereeing, this time by Romain Poite. Connacht led 25–18 with a minute of normal time remaining, before Poite's highly debatable penalty against Connacht at the breakdown led to Gloucester drawing level through a try by Billy Meakes, so taking the game into extra-time.

After James Hook kicked Gloucester ahead, another superb Healy try, converted by Jack Carty, put Connacht back in front before Poite sinbinned Dave Heffernan. Late tries off a maul, and by Jonny May, from long range, ended Connacht's hopes and season.

It looked like a crushing anticlimax from the outside, but not on the inside. Lam and Connacht took more positives from their campaign. They had scored 49 tries in the League, another hike from the 42 of the 2013–14 season, never mind the 32 the season before that.

'I did a presentation at the start of the next season and said if we'd conceded six fewer tries [than the 48 conceded,] we'd have been top six. Then I went through all the tries we had conceded. Some were soft tries. So there was a real focus on our defence.

'But the mindset had completely changed by now. The skill level had improved out of sight, and when we put together highlights of the tries we scored, guys could see that stuff from training was coming off.

'There was also a better understanding of the patterns and the plays. Most of the guys had now been two years with me and were moving into a third season. So we were really firmly establishing the game. The culture had grown massively, and the leadership of the team had changed. And the age of the squad was coming down.

'The progression was happening really fast. Dave and Andre had settled in nicely, and the staff and the players were getting to know me.'

Dan McFarland moved on at the end of that 2014–15 season, and promoting Jimmy Duffy from the academy was the obvious choice. 'He knew the players and that was the key. The relationships were just getting stronger and stronger.

'How I was talking to the players in year two compared to year one was totally different. When I first started, I didn't know any of them. By the second year, I knew which ones to put my arm around and which ones I sometimes needed to come hard at.'

Lam had also learned from his own mistakes.

'Without a doubt. I made a lot of mistakes on the way, but I call them all my "learnings",' he says with a chuckle.

Connacht had fallen short of their stated goal, but they were still on the rise.

13

The Wanderer – Dave Ellis

Kiwis have a tendency to wander. It comes with the territory, and rugby has been their best means of seeing the world. But even by New Zealand standards, Dave Ellis has led a particularly nomadic existence.

Internet searches reveal little more than that he was born in a small town in New Zealand, which he left at 22. After a career playing and coaching around the rugby world, he ended up in Connacht, coaching a professional team for the first time in a life defined by rugby.

'It took me a long time to get here, and I wandered, yeah,' he says with a smile. 'Maybe my wandering days might be over, though. But I can't complain about my life.'

Probe further and he explains that his is a relatively typical story of a player whose career was restricted by injury, thus turning him towards coaching. But there's way more to it than that. 'I still played on, on one leg, till I was in my thirties, and then you realize, "Jeeze, I've never done anything. What do I do now?" Coaching just became the thing I did from there. But I wouldn't change anything. You learn a lot in different places. Some guys nowadays are spoon-fed to the very top and don't experience some of the unusual situations which I did.'

Playing and coaching have taken him to Australia, Canada, the USA, Asia, South Africa, Hong Kong, Argentina and, lastly, Connacht; this will be his final overseas port of call. Different cultures, conditions and particularly standards have contributed to his some-what unique brand of skills coaching.

'One thing that usually never changes is the desire of the player. Once you have some players who want to do something, that's the key – which is what's so good about here. The boys are just enthusias-tic. They want to get better. They've been kicked around for quite a few years.'

The small town Ellis left is Putaruru, in Waikato, about an hour and a half south of Hamilton. 'It's inland, bushman country. It's pig-hunting, loggers, timber mills and farming.'

His father, Eric, was a railway worker, and his mum, nominally Margaret but known by everyone as Jean, was a homemaker. Ellis was the youngest of six, by some distance. 'I was a mistake,' he reveals cheer-ily. 'Rumour is that when my mother got the phone call she said, "Doctor, you must be wrong?" That was me. We don't know how Dad did it.'

He had three older brothers and two sisters – Lorna, Peter, Barry, Gordon and Erica. There are 20 years between him and Lorna, and ten between him and Erica.

He describes his childhood as 'wonderful', adding, 'My parents were old-school. We had no money. Dad was the income, and Mum did work outside the home as well when she could. We lived in town till I was about 12. Then we moved into the country, and it was great.'

Initially, they lived in the railway yards. 'The train ran past my bedroom when I was a kid, probably about as close as Willie's car out there,' nodding to Willie Ruane's Mazda about 20 yards away. 'The whole house would shake. We had outdoor toilets and outside wash houses. Mate, it was a wonderful life. I see a little bit of old Ireland that resembles New Zealand and what my early life was like, I guess. My brothers used to beat the crap out of each other; they'd fight and bicker, full fisticuff fights, and my mother would chase them with a broom and kick them out of the house. On Saturdays, my sisters would turn up with all their teammates after a netball match, and my brothers with the bloody rugby team, and Mum would feed them or they'd have fish and chips on the floor. I was just hanging around them.'

He reckons he started to play rugby when he was three. 'Three years old and three stone three, I think. The whole town played. There was no club at that stage. Everybody just mucked in, including Grant Fox, who went on to play for the All Blacks, and Wayne Smith, who played in my first XV at school.'

Ellis was younger than Smith by two or three years but recalls possibly playing a couple of senior games with him. Ellis was a little scrum-half or, as Kiwis say, half-back. 'Smithy always tells stories that I was his half-back, but I think I only played two games with him.'

That was at Putaruru High School. By contrast, Fox, whose parents were 'a little bit more well-to-do, went to high school in Auckland.'

As for so many Kiwi boys, rugby was a rite of passage, whether he liked it or not.

'Growing up, that's all you did. Winter would come, and my dad would usually drag me up; I wasn't overly keen and was a bit shy. There were millions of kids everywhere. Somebody would throw you a jersey, usually about ten sizes too big. You were in bare feet, frost on the ground and it was, "Off you go, boys." And it was great.'

He reckons he was 12 before he had his first boots, prompted by being picked for South Waikato – big, black, square-toed, old-school, agricultural boots. They had white laces, which he removed and washed regularly.

His last year on the Putaruru High Schools firsts was his best.

'It's a bit of a comic-type story, really. All our big rock stars had left at the end of the previous year, the Wayne Smiths and so on. We were the motley crew who were told by the headmaster, "Well, boys, last year was a real strong team, and we understand that some of our best players have left, and we don't really expect that much from you this year. But we're behind you." Which, of course, just pissed us all off, including the new coach, Graham Walker. He was a wonderful coach. I couldn't speak more highly of him. That year changed my life. He was our PE teacher at school. He was strict. We trained every day of the week, which was unusual in those days. He made us as fit as hell. He gave us a bit of buy-in as well. He didn't just lecture us, and we won everything. We broke records all over the place. It was a great year.

'The headmaster was a surly old bugger. I only stayed at school to play rugby, and he knew it. So as soon as the rugby season was over, I was called into his office and told to sling my hook! But I wasn't the only one; there were a couple of us in the same boat.'

Ellis played with Waikato age-grade sides until their Under-21s, then senior rugby for the Putaruru club in the Waikato first division for three or four years after leaving school. 'I thought I was OK. I was bloody weak with one hand, that's why I'm such a stickler with it these days. I was weak off the left to right. I had a rocket off the right, and could only kick off my right foot. That's why I try to push the guys to do left and right, if they can; try to work both sides of the body. Because once I started teaching it, I realized how easy it is to learn, if you learn it in an easy way.'

On leaving school, he had no grand plan, and his life rather took its own course. 'I bummed around a bit. I worked in a big mill in town. I was a logger out in the bush for a bit, where my boss told me, "You've got to go to Australia." It was a small town, nobody went anywhere, really.'

In 1980, he suffered an ankle injury playing for Putaruru, 'and I just kind of lost my mojo. When I came back, I struggled and I didn't get on with the new coach. I played in a Waikato senior trial, won Player of the Day and thought, "I've made it." But I wasn't even named in the squad, not even in the Bs. I couldn't get my head around it.'

Ellis had won a bottle of whiskey as his prize for Player of the Day. 'The boys in the team joked, "You should have given that bottle to the coach." George Simpkin was the coach, but I took it home to show my mum. I never made the Waikato team, which went on to be a really strong one.

'I ran into him [Simpkin] about 15 years later, and his first words were, "You should never have left New Zealand." And I went, "Now you tell me." You've got to remember that in those days coaches never gave feedback. Or very rarely. They were quite gruff. You were either in or you were out, and as a player you never questioned the coach.

'Even though New Zealand is praised for the way we do things, in those days we had so many players that they were being turned over all the time. It was the Aussies who first began to examine the scientific side of rugby. I was in my late 20s, early 30s then. They changed the dynamic of the game, in my opinion, in our part of the world anyhow, and then New Zealand adapted. Nowadays, the Aussies have too much science. They're stuffing themselves up.'

In any event, that Waikato trial had left his fledgling career in limbo. The bible of New Zealand rugby, *Rugby News*, always carried advertisements for players abroad, usually in Australia, and Ellis applied for three of them by letter. He told his mum, 'The first one that comes back, I'll take.' He was true to his word.

'The two other teams were quite good teams; this one, Smithfield, were in the Sydney second division at the time. They were a great bunch of guys, though.'

About eight games into his first season with Smithfield, Ellis did more than break his tibia. 'I also mashed up all my cruciate and anterior ligaments. Just a mess. A surgeon said I couldn't walk again. I asked him, "How can I live and how can I play rugby? You've got to help me play again."

'He made a special cast for me with a hinge, which was revolutionary in those days, and in fairness he did as good a job as I could afford. I had only been with the club for eight weeks, but they paid for everything. They had a whipround every week to provide me with money for beer and food. They did that for the whole season. That's why I stayed for two more years. You can't leave people who do that for you. It was a humbling experience.'

Even without whiprounds, rugby was a limited source of income – perhaps providing free accommodation and, if he was lucky, a car. While playing for Smithfield, he also worked as a labourer in an arms and weapons workshop.

'That was one of my best jobs. Walking down King's Cross every morning at about six o'clock as a 22 year old was bloody interesting!

'That was an eye-opener, especially coming from a small town in New Zealand. I moved in with a bunch of other Kiwi rugby players until even I found them too messy. I had to leave. I'd gone from being a young player in New Zealand to being perceived as an experienced one in this Aussie team. Local papers were interested in this Kiwi. That was different. I was a bigger fish in a smaller pond.'

Ellis played two consecutive seasons in Smithfield. In one game, he came up against the future Australian World Cup captain Nick Farr-Jones, then uncapped and playing for the Sydney University club. 'I was fortunate enough to be on good form both times I played against him.

'Their team was better than ours, but I was lucky to have good games. Dave Brockhoff, then the Wallabies coach, came to me and introduced me to his beautiful daughter and lovely wife. He asked me if I'd consider playing for Australia. I was blown away by all of this. Dave and my club coach said they wanted me to go somewhere where the competition was better. Ironically, they suggested France and, I think, Munster. But I was a bit scared and turned them both down. Then they offered me Queensland, and I was even listed in the Queensland squad in one of the local newspapers, though I'd never set foot there.'

This led to him driving to Queensland with a buddy to meet members of this would-be new club. 'It just didn't do it for me. I didn't have a feeling for it. I went back to Sydney and told my girlfriend, "I don't know, and I don't know if I want to play for Australia either." So we never went.'

Instead, perhaps inspired by the ten-hour drive to Queensland, another idea struck him. 'Then I went walkabout. I wasn't seeing anything of Australia. My girlfriend also wanted to see more of the country.' They went as far as South Molle Island in the Whitsundays, in the heart of the Great Barrier Reef.

'I worked on a bloody island in the tropics as the laundry boy driving the laundry truck. We had a blast, although I missed rugby almost immediately. I realized that when I was playing rugby, I was somebody. Now I was just that guy driving the laundry truck. It's funny, when I look back on it. I didn't think so at the time, but my ego got the better of me there.'

Out of the blue, a mate rang him imploring him to come to Darwin and play rugby. 'You'd kill it up here,' said the friend. So he relocated to Darwin, the smallest and northernmost city in Australia at the tip of the country, and joined the South Darwin club. 'Tropical rugby. Bloody hot. And about ten levels down from where I'd played in New Zealand, but good guys and the heat was quite an equalizer.'

One of the highlights was an annual game which his club hosted between the Mosquitos, a combination of both uncapped Kiwis and ex-All Blacks, and the Casuarinas, named after a native Australian tree, consisting of Aussie players, including former Wallabies. 'That was full-on. Rugby and beer, really. There was a massive drinking culture.'

During this time, he made his first foray as player-coach, when switching to Casuarina for a year. Also, as captain of the Northern Territory team, he led them against touring international sides such as Manu Samoa and Italy. 'But I didn't play in their big game, the year they beat Scotland. I was in America by then.'

In 1985, he and some equally disgruntled teammates formed their own club in tandem with the university there. 'We called ourselves the Pirates, so we could affiliate with other Pirates teams around the world. I'd always had this vision of a World Pirates tournament in Darwin, with a big tent and a fun day. We started with an interim coach, but I ended up as their player-coach for a couple of years.'

In their first year, the Pirates reached the semi-finals and then won three Darwin Premiership titles in a row from 1987. This was, he reckons, possibly his biggest legacy to the sport he loves. 'The beauty of it was that we hadn't just created the club and the team; we created the culture. We brought in our own rules. The university gave us great support. It had been an institute of technology and then became a university. They helped both financially, as well as providing training facilities. They also let us, as senior players, establish a culture and the things that were important to us.

'We wanted to play a high-skill game with integrity. My goal was to give nothing to the opposition, no reason for them to hate you. So on the field you're bloody good guys, and off the field you party like you wouldn't believe. Other clubs would come to the Pirates simply to party.'

The inaugural Pirates first team was initially earmarked for a C grade, equivalent to a Golden Oldies. Other players, however, from the Northern Territory squad and from other clubs soon came on board, so that the Pirates could field both A and C grade sides.

By the time Ellis moved on, the Pirates had teams at grades A, B and C, as well as a women's team, which he coached, and Under-18s, -16s, -14s teams all the way down to what he calls 'the little tuckers', or Under-8s. And all within six years.

'That was the achievement of my rugby life, until I came to Connacht. A lot of other people laid claim to being there at the outset, but I know who the exact group was, and I think that was really neat. To me, that's a legacy that will always have an effect on rugby. They're still going. I think they just won the last Premiership, but nobody would know me there now.'

Yes, he enjoyed Darwin and is uncertain how long he stayed there. 'Oh, too long. I couldn't tell you exactly. Maybe eight years.'

Not that he was permanently there, of course. He played in Darwin's summer, their wet season, and in their off-season travelled to play elsewhere – be it Sydney, the USA or Canada. 'I was probably never more than six months in any one place at any one time for about eight years.'

In Canada, he played for a club called Cowichan on Vancouver Island. 'A beautiful place. Terrific experience. Probably one of the highlights of my rugby life socially – just wonderful people – and we played at a good level. We had some Canadian reps [representative players] in that team. Big men. I played for them for two seasons, then went back to Canada again to coach a team called Nanaimo, also on Vancouver Island. I got paid for that!'

There was also a stint playing Sevens rugby in Singapore. 'Boy, you could write a chapter on that alone. This was back in the Bugis Street days, before it became clean,' he says in reference to Bugis Street's wilder times, before it became the more wholesome, family-friendly shopping location it is now.

All the while, odd jobs supplemented his modest rugby income. 'At the university, I drove the courier van. I built swimming pools in Darwin, laid hardwood floors in Canada, cut trees down in America, logged through the bloody Rockies.'

By the early nineties, his early thirties, coaching was taking hold, and he'd also become a father. 'I've got a colourful history there too!' he admits. 'On that first trip to Canada, my daughter was born. Her mother, Lisa, and I were really good friends but probably weren't made to be together. I tootled off and had a good time in Canada, such a good time that unfortunately when my daughter was actually physically born in New Zealand, I was on a ski field in Banff, in the Canadian Rockies. Not a good start. I went back a couple of years later to try to rekindle things, but it didn't work out and I returned to Canada.

'She's a wonderful, beautiful girl,' he says of his daughter, Ashlee. 'I love her to bits. I have had very little contact with her in her entire life, which will always be a regret of mine. But she's a good kid, and she's doing well. She's living on the Gold Coast and must be 26 now.'

On one of his subsequent trips back from Canada to New Zealand, he met his first wife Cathy, whom he married in 1999. 'She dropped sticks basically and came to live with me in Canada. From there, I had a very interesting time getting into the United States for a coaching job. We had a bit of trouble going through Customs there, because by this time I was an "over-stayer in Canada", but we managed it.'

The coaching gig was in Breckenridge, a town at the foot of the Rocky Mountains in Colorado. 'A beautiful part of the world if you ever get a chance to go there,' he says, adding, 'Again, not a high level [of rugby]. I'm not kidding myself here. I'm not coaching the All Blacks, but great people. Eclectic as hell. All sorts of nationalities, some crazy-arsed Americans that I just loved. It was paradise. The Rocky Mountains were like from here [the Sportsground] to Eyre Square. You could walk there. My job as a logger was like a daily take from an old Disney movie, with all the animals and wildlife. I loved it. I spent two seasons there. I would have stayed longer, but my mother passed away while I was there.'

His father had died of a heart attack when Ellis was 17. 'I was out and about with him when it happened. That was my introduction to death. The first XV formed the guard of honour at Dad's funeral, which was kind of cool. I didn't take it very well, but Mum was strong. In those days, parents were stronger. After my dad died, Mum was straight on with life.'

After returning to New Zealand for his mum's funeral, Ellis then brought Cathy with him back to Darwin. 'She hated it, and I didn't blame her. She was a little more refined, and there was quite a drinking culture. You didn't go there for a long-term relationship, so I left after a year.'

He began presenting coaching courses in Australia through a friend of his who was with Northern Territory Rugby Union. This entailed acquiring a level-three coaching badge.

'I was keeping all my files on computer in those days and lugged it everywhere, even to Canada. I was creating image files and things like that, drawing diagrams of my drills and writing notes. I was using a database programme called FileMaker Pro, and I went to a lecture by a guy called Barry Honan, an ex-Wallaby. He produced the Honan Drills, which are still used in coaching today.'

The lecture was part of a three-day coaching course in Brisbane. 'I went up to Baz [Honan] after the lecture, which was hard for me because I was so bloody shy, and said, "Excuse me, Barry, I thought maybe you'd be interested in something I have." I showed him some of my stuff on printout and he said, "Right, what are you doing for lunch?"

'The next minute I'm in Barry's house, and he's pulled out all his stuff. He could do things on computer programmes that I couldn't, and I could do things that he couldn't.'

Ellis never returned to the course, instead staying on in Honan's house. 'Maybe we should make coaching products?' Honan suggested. 'The world needs these things.'

Ellis was keen, and after three days he flew back to Darwin, played a semi-final and final for the Pirates, and returned to Brisbane. 'I worked at Bazza's place every day from the crack of dawn till midnight, and we formed a company called DigiRugby, with a database containing about 350 rugby drills.'

They toured Australia to market their products. 'The package had folders and kit boards and all sorts of shit, and we sold it through Harvey Norman and places like that in Aussie.'

They also travelled to South Africa and New Zealand, enlisting coaches and compiling more and more video footage. Wayne Bennett was brought on board from the Brisbane Broncos for their rugby league package DigiLeague. Leading Australian women's netball players were enlisted to make DigiNetball, and ditto DigiCricket with legendary Australian cricket players.

'Even though I wasn't big on cricket, I was on the perimeter of the Gabba with my camera, filming so we could use footage. It was Queensland v England, and I'm right there. And we also became friends with Wayne Bennett. It was a wonderful little gap in my life.'

This staging post lasted three years, with no playing or coaching. Through marketing this product, Ellis had met John Harmer, an Australian who coached the Australian women's cricket team and would subsequently coach their English counterparts. He had a profound influence on Ellis.

'He was just a great guy, and he opened me up to biomechanics. So all of a sudden I was becoming a little bit "skilly". He taught me about skill sets, and that's what triggered my interest in the skills side of things. I saw the futility of drills on their own, because drills are all well and good, but if you don't know what you're doing it's just a dance, as my sister would say.'

Through working with the Australian women's netball team, Ellis developed his own colour-coded system. 'This was coloured cones, balls, cards and bibs, all to do with decision-making, as well as skills. I developed that in the background as I was working with Baz.'

By chance, the former All Black-turned-TV pundit Murray Mexted came to Brisbane to advertise the International Rugby Academy in New Zealand (IRANZ). This was Mexted's brainchild, created with help from the NZRU and based in Palmerston North. Wayne Smith had told Mexted about Ellis and his DigiRugby programmes.

'I wanted to go there and learn how to coach,' says Ellis, 'but Murray was offering me a job as his skills coach.'

'No, I want to come to your course,' said Ellis. 'I want to pay you money.'

'No, no,' said Mexted. 'I want you to come as a skills coach.'

As the NZRU were advertising for skills coaches and drills packages, Ellis applied. He was invited to Palmerston North for the interview and flew back to Brisbane to inform his wife that they and their baby son, Cory, were relocating to Cathy's home city, Auckland.

The NZRU contracted Ellis and provided him with the funding and equipment to devise a computer skills programme for them. Ellis began travelling around New Zealand, presenting his programme and skills drills with his coloured balls and cones. 'It was like a roadshow, presenting courses with sports psychologists and rugby coaches.'

Ellis devised CDs, be it about kicking, passing, tackling, rucking, mauling, line-outs or scrums. 'I filmed them, made them all, and they were given free to all the coaches. They came to [NZRU] courses and took what they wanted. It meant everybody was on the same page.'

With his NZRU coaching products and also IRANZ up and running, Ellis combined his roadshow with overseeing skills drills at the three-week-long camps in Palmerston North. There, he also made individualized skills assessments of each player who attended the camps, backed up with personalized CDs. The three-week camps increased from about three a year initially to the point where they took up half his calendar year.

Plenty of future All Blacks passed through the IRANZ. 'Want me to rattle off a few?' he asks proudly. 'Well, let's just go All Blacks. There was Aaron Cruden, Cory Jane, both the Savea brothers, Julien and Ardie, Israel Dagg, Codie Taylor, Liam Squire . . . I'm missing some real famous ones, I know I am.'

Others who travelled to the academy from abroad included South African François Steyn, English hooker Tom Youngs and Australian prop James Slipper.

He describes Dagg, then 17, as 'skinny and cheeky', adding, 'The best player of them all at about 17 or 18 when we first saw him was Aaron Cruden. Just a complete natural footballer. He knew the game inside and out. You only had to tell him something once. He'd say, "Yeah, got that" and would implement it. From a young age, he saw everything.'

IRANZ also set up camps in South Africa and Argentina. The IRANZ also had a team, coached from 2003 to 2007 by Dave Rennie, who would guide the Chiefs to their back-to-back Super Rugby titles in 2012 and '13. 'I was Dave's assistant, so I used to work a lot with "Rens". Others who were invited to coach at the camps included Graham Henry, the aforementioned Smith, Steve Hansen, Eddie Jones, Wayne 'Buck' Shelford, Brian Ashton from England and Dick Muir from South Africa. And it was, of course, through the camps in IRANZ that Ellis first met Pat Lam and had their fateful chat over lunch.

Nor did the travelling stop there. Through his work at IRANZ, Ellis was also invited to Hong Kong for the first time by their rugby union, and ditto by the Argentina Rugby Union (UAR). There he brought in Dennis Brown, another IRANZ employee, as his forwards/assistant coach. They coached at the Monte Grande club in Buenos Aires and Tucumán.

'Big family clubs, with rugby and hockey, and I love the food. I'd been to Argentina promoting DigiRugby to a symposium of about 2,000 people. I stood up to talk about DigiRugby in English to a whole bunch of Spanish-speaking people. It was one of the scariest events in my life.

'This time we visited Iguazú Falls and all that sort of stuff, all paid for by the Argentinians. They fed us, put us up in a hotel, paid for all our travel for a month and didn't want us to leave. They still contact me now to ask, "When are you finished? When are you coming back?"'

Their wives or partners were also invited, which in Ellis's case was now Esther. Ellis had two sons with Cathy, Cory (16) and Brody (14), before they broke up and divorced in 2007. Both Cathy and Ellis have remarried. Brody lives in Portland, Oregon, with his mum and her American husband, while Cory is living in Galway with Ellis and Esther.

Cory loves Galway, and wants to stay, but has little interest in rugby, while Brody is a budding artist. 'I've never pushed any of my kids. I coached them when they were young, and it was fun. They liked having me around, but I never pushed any of them.'

Ellis and Esther married after his first season with Connacht, and their first in Galway, in the summer of 2014. He had met her before his last coaching expedition to a school in Australia. 'I took Esther to this place called Rainbow Beach, which we both thought is really beautiful. So we went back there and married on a beach in Aussie.'

Some career. Some life. Rugby truly has helped Ellis see the world.

'It has, and to me coaching is my repayment to the sport for giving me everything. I think that now, at my age, I've painted myself into a corner. I say, "This is tiring", but Esther says, "If we go home to New Zealand, you've got to find a job, buddy." Of course, I'm reluctant as all hell to do that, because I've never had one. I've had lots of jobs and I've always been a good employee, but there's always been an oval ball in the background.'

His methods appear to work, but he maintains he's no great innovator. 'What I've learned over the years is there are no new ideas, only different ways of looking at them. Everything that's old is new again.

'It's the same with Buncey [Paul Bunce] in his industry [fitness], and this supposed new way of lifting, or new diet. "Ah, Jeeze, that one's around again?" But I've always enjoyed working in the background.'

A decade working with the IRANZ was the longest job, per se, he's ever had. 'By a long chalk,' he admits. 'Esther and I had actually bought a house in Palmy and moved the boys there, but I needed a change.

'Soon after my chat with Pat, he was in talks with Connacht, but I couldn't wait. I decided to coach a first XV at a private school in Toowoomba, in Queensland, where they pay more than I make here. Great climate, I think it rained for one game, and great facilities, and all the equipment – tackle suits and tackle bags – that I can't get here, they had in spades there.

'I enjoyed it there, and that would be a good retirement for me. The headmaster wanted me there for seven years, but then Pat called. I wanted to be a pro coach. I've always wanted to be a pro coach, and I thought, "If I don't do it now I'll never do it."

'Part of my job for the rugby academy was to coach coaches, but I always felt a bit of a pretender, and one coach actually pulled me up on it one day, saying, "It's all theory." Thank God I can face him now, but he had a point. His remark made me think about it. "Yeah, I've got to get my hands dirty." I was offered club positions in New Zealand, but that didn't float my boat.'

Back in 2007, his compatriot and then USA Eagles coach Peter Thorburn had invited him to America for a coaching camp along with the former All Blacks skills coach and current Australian skills coach Mick Byrne and All Blacks scrum coach Mike Cron.

'We coached 50 or 60 of the best players in America, and about 70 coaches came to watch us, in San Diego. It pissed with rain, the coldest day ever in San Diego! We were there for a couple of days, and I bloody loved it. I bloody loved working with Mick and Mike. Thorbs subsequently asked me out of the blue to do some more coaching with the Eagles at their last camp before the 2007 World Cup. Coaching at club level didn't appeal after that experience.

'I had a ball coaching the school team in Queensland, because they were my team. I could do whatever I wanted with them, and it was like having a pro team because they were there 24/7. But I just needed to try a pro team like Connacht.'

By the time Lam contacted Ellis in the summer of 2013, he was already in Australia, and wouldn't walk out on his school until the end of the season. This delayed his arrival in Connacht until late October, with his first game the 19–12 defeat at home to Glasgow in November, their sixth League defeat in a run of eight.

His first impressions?

'We've got a lot of work to do. At first, I wasn't sure of my role. I came in as backs coach as well. But we looked at all these young

Connacht guys and thought, "We could be good." And one thing that Connacht has that is a key part of a good side is ticker. They've got ticker. I've so much respect for Mul [John Muldoon]. He epitomizes rugby to me. If I were still playing, that's what I hope people would think of me, the way I think of Mul. He plays hard, a good man. So I thought, "I've something to work with here."

'They have a lot of good bloody hard-working players like Swifty, salt-of-the-earth guys. They've bloody worked their arses off for the club for so many years. I guess that's what stoked my desire, even if that first year was a struggle.'

An initial one-year contract has been extended to a four-year stay, for which he is also indebted to Esther. 'Esther has been wonderful and has always supported my decisions. I doubt I could do what I am doing without her support and the balance she brings to my life. As I have learned over the years, all rugby, rugby and more rugby would bog down my mind and I would lose the ability to be objective or try new things.'

And in all his travels, he's never known anywhere like the west of Ireland. 'My favourite part of Ireland is Connemara. I love going to Ballyconnelly, Roundstone, Renvyle, wherever. It's just a beautiful part of the world.

'When we go for a drive now, Esther knows what's coming, because I always say, "Oh, can we just turn right and drive that way?"'

To Connemara. After all his wandering, Ellis had found his rugby home from home.

14

A Season of Opportunity –
2015–16. The Opening Run.

When Pat Lam needed to fill the void left by Dan McFarland, after their former prop ended a 16-year association with the province and a decade as forwards coach, Jimmy Duffy was the natural fit. His was a road less travelled than, say, that of Dave Ellis, but it was no less circuitous or unlikely for all that.

Hailing from Renmore, about a 15-minute walk from the Sportsground, Duffy was born and bred in Galway and both his parents come from the city. Galway through and through. His father Joe, who used to be a truck driver, is now retired. His mum, Mary, worked as a secretary in the Eye Department of the University Hospital Galway. His younger sister, Emer, is an Advanced Nurse Practitioner in the Accident and Emergency ward, while his younger brother, Raymond, is a Guard in Balbriggan.

His dad also played rugby for OLBC (Our Lady's Boys Club) on the back pitch in the Sportsground. 'As a kid, I would have been in the changing-rooms across the way in the old place on many Tuesday and Thursday evenings, but I played mainly soccer and football.'

Indeed, he describes himself as a soccer 'fanatic'. A centre-half mostly, and sometime right-winger in under-age football with Renmore, he went across the water or to Dublin for trials with several

English clubs, including Everton, Nottingham Forest and Man City. 'But it was quite difficult to get out of Galway, as there were lots of very talented soccer players around the city. Some guys made it, like Con Hogan, who went to Coventry City. But it was very, very difficult to break into England. Dublin soccer was really strong at the time too, with clubs like Cherry Orchard and Home Farm.'

He also played Gaelic football with the St James GAA club and didn't start rugby until 15 or 16 in St Joseph's College, aka 'the Bish'. 'A PE teacher in school asked me one day to give it a try, because they were short on numbers. I absolutely loved the vibe straight away. I loved the craic. It was markedly different from soccer and Gaelic football. It follows you off the field, something that I very much leaned to then and thereafter. I think I was pretty hooked from that day.'

Playing at lock and in the back-row, mostly at number 8, Duffy won a Connacht Schools Cup with the Bish in 1994 but injured his knee the next season, missing all of it. 'It was tough at the time but great memories.'

He broke into the Connacht set-up soon after school and looked set for a promising career. He played for the Ireland Under-21s and A sides. Duffy was also part of Connacht's travelling squad to Northampton in the 1997–98 season and was in the away dressing-room after that famous win in Franklin's Gardens.

'I was only 19 and it gave you a little glimpse of what could be, and for me that was a big driver. I wanted more of it, and Gatty solidified us quite a bit. We had quality players then, but not enough, and I genuinely felt there was a real lack of ambition in the organization. That's changed obviously, and there are good people across the board in all the key areas.'

Gatland had arranged for Duffy to play the summer of 1998 in New Zealand, but he was injured two weeks before his planned departure. After signing his first contract the following season, he became a regular in the Connacht line-up under Glenn Ross, starting all six Challenge Cup games in the second-row alongside Graham Heaslip. 'Following that summer, however, I was diagnosed with a suspected heart condition and about six months later I had to finish playing, unfortunately.'

That premature end to his career was tough to take, to put it mildly. 'I have probably only come to terms with it in the last 18 months, I'd say, genuinely. It was something that I probably would never have acknowledged before. I was born in the seventies, and it wasn't the kind of thing you talked through. You just got up and got on with it.

'I'd been involved with Connacht and national sides, and things were going well. I was only playing for four years at that stage and thought that I wasn't big enough, strong enough or fit enough. So I worked really hard that following summer [of 1999].'

He had bulked up; his strength and fitness had improved. He had never felt better. It was September 1999, but a supposedly routine medical with the Connacht doctor in UCG showed up a fairly irregular heartbeat.

'You live in a big bubble to be honest in this game. A lot of adulation goes with it, and you're basically paid to have some craic. It's a very privileged job, and I think the players who understand that the earliest have the best careers. But, yeah, it rocked me. It absolutely rocked me.

'I passed all the other tests. Actually, only just this season I've seen a cardiologist who made a different diagnosis, but the technology wasn't there at the time. What can you do? There is something there, but the medics don't believe it's as serious as was first thought.'

Duffy doesn't know whether he could have continued playing. But back then, at 20, that news changed his life completely. As well as playing for Ireland As, he had been part of a wider national training camp and, above all, he wanted to play for his country.

'That was top of the pile. I wanted to go to the [1999] World Cup. I'd played in a really strong Under-21s side, with Marcus Horan, Frankie Sheahan, Martin Cahill, Leo Cullen, Mick O'Driscoll, David Wallace and myself. Ciaran Scally and Tom Tierney were the 9s, ROG [Ronan O'Gara] was 10, Cian Mahony and Shane Horgan were in midfield. Melvin McNamara and Conor Kilroy were on the wings, with Tom Keating at full-back. A very, very strong team.

'Brian McLaughlin was coach, Philip Rainey was the manager, Dave Irwin was doc. Mark McDermott was helping with the forwards.

We were fortunate enough to win the Triple Crown before we got bullied in France for 20 minutes, but great memories.'

He decided to go back to college and completed a degree in business studies in GMIT. Then he worked in sales and marketing in Dublin for two years, before returning to Galway to work as a sales rep.

'After I retired, I couldn't watch a game for about three years. Even when Ireland played, I was pretty hung up on not watching them. But one day I got a phone call from Mick Grealish in OLBC, who asked me would I give a hand with my dad's old club. Straight away I got the bug, and I've loved it ever since.'

He began doing his Level 1 coaching with the IRFU, and a little over six months later a position as a regional development officer (RDO) in Connacht became vacant. 'I applied for it, did the interview, got the job, and I've never looked back.'

He coached the Connacht Under-18s, which led to an invitation to be assistant coach to Greg Lynch with the Irish Under-18 club side in 2004.

A year after marrying Orla in 2006, Duffy resolved to have a family home built in her village of Barna, and he left Connacht to set up his own sales and marketing business. 'Setting up a business was something I always wanted to do, and we were building a house at the time, so it was a busy time all round. I was fortunate that Allen Clarke was the IRFU high performance manager at the time and he got back involved with the 18s again for a season with Wayne Mitchell. That got me back on the horse, a position came up here in the academy (player development officer); I was interviewed and got it.'

He had missed coaching. 'I missed the people. I missed that environment. I'd had jobs that were far better rewarded financially, but that was never my driver. You wouldn't be as challenged, which was what I liked here. I also liked maybe being written off and proving them wrong, or perhaps more accurately proving myself right. When I had the opportunity to return, I felt very, very fortunate.'

His new role also meant coaching the Connacht Under-20s, and then the Connacht Eagles, as well as the Irish Under-18s with Nigel Carolan in 2008.

Not only was he coaching academy players but also senior professionals in need of game time, perhaps recovering from injury. 'It was a nice little introduction to those guys.'

He also found spending up to two weeks in camp for a tournament such as the FIRA (Under-18) European Championships an invaluable experience. 'You get to know what players are like off the field. You get a true measure of them, and I found that invaluable, just observing them work, as well as learning from the other coaches.'

It also enabled Duffy and Carolan to identify talents like Ultan Dillane and Sean O'Brien. Carolan had been pretty much a one-man show in the academy, an experience Duffy knew well from his initial stint as an RDO, and their working relationship contributed handsomely to Connacht's growth from the bottom up.

'He's ultra-professional,' says Duffy of Carolan. 'He's well liked, and he's on top of his brief in every facet, a smashing fella. There's bigger and better things up ahead for him. It's quite difficult to encapsulate what he's about. He's got an eye for talent, an eye for detail, he's a top coach and he's respected across the organization and the province and nationally as well, for his ability as a coach. I don't know how he manages to juggle the Irish Under-20s and the academy, but he manages to do so comfortably.

'As a province, we're reaping the rewards here. We have numerous players through every year and he's always tweaking things. Probably his biggest asset is that he trusts people. If they're able to do the job, he'll trust them to do it. I found working with the guy fantastic. A top coach, top man and probably one of the biggest assets in this organization.'

Away from the frontline, Duffy appeared to have a job for life, but that wasn't for him. 'I loved working with the academy and the younger players. You'd get a great, great buzz out of that and from being involved in the national team as well, but I always wanted to push on.'

There had been tempting offers from abroad – France, and a couple in England. 'But I'm really, really happy I stayed. We live nearby,' he says, in reference to Orla and their son Joseph, 'and you can't beat coaching with your own province.'

That opportunity arose when McFarland decided to move on to Glasgow. 'I was genuinely in two minds. Maybe I needed a break from here. The guys were a tight bunch here, so I wondered, "What can you bring to the party?" The usual doubts you'd have about yourself. But I applied.'

Three days before going on holiday, Duffy was interviewed in the Berkeley Court Hotel in Dublin, the panel consisting of Lam, David Nucifora, Willie Ruane and Barry Gavin.

While Duffy was on holiday in Lanzarote, Ruane texted him. 'I left the phone in the safe for a few days. It's nice to switch off. We had just finished the invites for the summer underage programme. I was worn out at the end of the season. I rang him and we met up when I got back, and thankfully he offered me the job.

'I had a really good working relationship with Dan, so it was just a matter of continuing what he'd started. But he'd been in the role a long time, which brings its own challenges.'

Duffy was acutely aware that several of the forwards had been around a long time and had become accustomed to working with McFarland. But constant one-on-ones with them, and Lam, helped. 'Pat will challenge me and I'll challenge Pat. He works as hard as any coach I've ever seen. He is constantly trying to push fellas. It's good, it keeps you on your toes, and it's nice to keep re-evaluating what you do, how you do it, who you do it with, and make sure you're improving all the time.'

On top of Duffy's relatively seamless transition, Connacht had a relatively settled playing squad, with much less turnover during the off-season than in the previous two.

Quinn Roux and John Cooney had also joined, initially on loan, during the 2014–15 season, before signing full-time. 'I think we were the first Irish team to bring in players on loan,' says Lam.

With Jake Heenan still a long-term casualty, Lam again dipped into the Auckland set-up by signing Nepia Fox-Matamua before the start of the 2015–16 season. A. J. MacGinty would later join, after the World Cup, for the remainder of the season. With such a settled squad on an upward curve, Connacht saw it as a season of opportunity. The

World Cup would effectively take up the first two months of the season; akin to chucking a boulder into a pool, there'd also be ripple effects beyond that.

'Because of how the fixtures were changed, we'd have two games before a three-week break, then another game and another week off, and then 16 games on the trot, which is unheard of,' says Lam. 'The most you'd normally ever have was ten in a row.

'Usually, when you have nine or ten in a row, you could manage to put out the strongest team every time, but we said, "Nah, the reality is no way. No way at all." We said this to the squad at the start of the season, that the same group cannot play for 16 games on the trot.

'Jimmy had done a statistical analysis of the forwards' playing time the previous season, and the difference between the tiers of players was too skewed. Too many guys had played a lot, others hadn't played that much, and we couldn't survive on that. We talked about our challenge as coaches. We had to get tier two and three closer to tier one, if not on games, then certainly on clarity and game planning.

'We put a lot of emphasis on the players learning and sharing the knowledge. We spent more time with players like the Peter Robbs, the Rory Paratas and the Ultan Dillanes, making sure all of them understood their roles. And they saw their window of opportunity, as we'd have to rotate the squad.'

Monday, 22 June – The first day of pre-season

Fitness testing for two days. Any players who passed the tests were afforded the rest of the week off, to come back on Monday, 29th. If they didn't, they continued pre-season for the rest of the week. That was the carrot, and the stick.

'The benchmarks were high, if not looking for world records,' says Tim Allnutt. 'There was a 1,300-metre run on the college track in Dangan. The players had their body fat tested, each having their own individual targets, and there were strength tests in the gym.

'It was more maintenance than anything, and they all love their bodies now, so they all do gym anyway, even when on holidays. The track run is always the difficult one, especially for the forwards.'

That's been fun to watch for the coaching and fitness staffs over the years. Some players would be smart enough to use their watches and pace themselves. Others might have tried to go too quickly too soon and hit the wall. There had been a small number of failures in previous pre-seasons, but not this time. Everyone passed. So back they came on 29 June.

The day started with an 8 a.m. meeting of coaches and management, followed by an admin meeting and then a full squad meeting.

Lam welcomed everybody, introducing new staff or explaining changes to the roles of existing staff. Pre-season goals were set by all the coaches and by the head of fitness, Paul Bunce. There were to be three sessions each day: for weights, for skills and for fitness.

'Every club has a pre-season, and every club thinks they train harder than every other club, but they're all pretty much the same,' says Allnutt. 'It's just how you shape your week, and to be honest our guys are bloody good at it at this stage.'

Allnutt had been encouraged by the 2014–15 campaign, despite its bitter finale. 'We'd had a real taste of success. It was our best-ever season. Everyone was gutted after the Gloucester defeat, but it showed there was a real hunger there. The boys would have had to put up with that disappointment all summer, so when they came back for pre-season it was still there. We talked about it on the first day back. We wanted to be better than that. We wanted to be at the top table.

'I still knew it would be tough to climb ahead of any of those six teams who'd finished above us, but we hadn't made many changes in our squad. For most of the lads it would be their third season working with Pat and the coaches, while others were in their second.

'From day one it was snappy. It was sharp. Pat and the coaching staff had put a lot of work into their prep. He had a clear vision of where we were going and the game plan, with tweaks here and there, a few little subtle changes, but the majority of it was the same.'

Lam had opted for three warm-up games and an internal hit-out in pre-season, playing Grenoble at home and Castres Olympique away. 'I love playing the French teams, because they are ready to go,' says Lam. 'Normally, we lose to the French teams, because their season starts sooner and it's our first hit-out.'

Connacht were well beaten by Grenoble on 7 August in their first pre-season friendly. As in the previous two pre-seasons, Connacht's next game was against Castres as part of a five-day mini-camp in Saint-Affrique, in the Aveyron in southern France – this is also part of an annual competition, the Challenge Vaquerin. Connacht travelled on the 12th, played Castres on the 14th and returned on the 16th. Despite missing many front-liners, Connacht lost a competitive game narrowly and were content with their week's work.

The day before travelling home, the tournament organizers brought the Connacht squad to a lakeside barbecue in glorious weather. No wonder Connacht keep going back.

'For whatever reason, they've really enjoyed having us there, and we really love going there,' says Allnutt, 'and it's good for us to have five days together in a pleasant environment with no distractions. We do a lot of goal-setting. At the end of this trip, they said, "Look, we'll leave you off for a couple of years." But we've been invited back again.'

The following Friday, 21 August, Connacht played their final warm-up game against Munster in Thomond Park, and much store was placed by the 28–12 win.

'They were strong, we were strong, and it was a big win for us,' says Lam. 'It broke the [Thomond Park] hoodoo. It may only have been pre-season, but the boys were celebrating. "Wow, we won at Thomond Park." So that was a good one for them to store away. Some big hits. Some big D. That was the big one. Bundee was on fire, and Nepia was on fire in his first game. We won the physical battle. That set a really good tone for us.'

'We'd never beaten them in Limerick in my time,' says Muldoon, 'but we scored a few tries and came away with a bit of confidence. We went into the season conscious that other teams were short a few players because of the World Cup, whereas we were not. So we needed to start well and win a few games.'

On 23 August, the Connacht squad went to Belmullet on the Mayo coast for another five-day camp, rounding off their pre-season with an internal match on the 28th before hosting a party with their season-ticket holders.

Friday, 4 September
Connacht 29 Dragons 23

Connacht won on the opening weekend for the fifth time in six seasons.

Tries by debutant Fox-Matamua and Danie Poolman, along with Jack Carty's boot, meant Connacht led all the way, but it was still 22–20 with five minutes remaining.

'It was a tight enough affair until Bundee put the foot on the throat, made that break and put Fionn [Carr] away for the try,' says Allnutt. 'We were hopeful that it would be a sign of things to come, but we've won that first game for so many years we weren't getting carried away, that's for sure. And we knew that Glasgow the following week, especially with Dan [McFarland] over there as the forwards coach, would be a tough proposition.'

'The Dragons are a team that we've traditionally done well against at home, and we thought it was a good opportunity,' says Muldoon. 'A few of us were chatting amongst ourselves. "If we can get a lot of wins from that block, we can give ourselves a head start. Then, when the World Cup was over, other teams might have a hangover and we could find ourselves at Christmas still near the top of the League."'

Job done. The squad flew to Glasgow on the Thursday night, returning on an 8 a.m. flight on the Saturday morning.

Friday, 11 September
Glasgow 33 Connacht 32

'That was a disaster,' says Muldoon. 'They scored one or two poxy tries and we were down 23–6 at half-time. Then John Cooney slipped trying to box-kick and fell over, and they scored off that. We came back with a flurry of tries, and they were clinging on for dear life. Their emotion at the end made us realize that was a big win for them. We were pissed off, but we took a bit of solace in that we were missing players, made a lot of mistakes but yet had the wherewithal to come back and score four tries. We took some confidence from that game.'

'I did the referees' report for the referees' assessor after that game, and 27 of their 33 points came off what I believed to be wrong calls,' says Lam. 'The Pro12 came back and said, "Yeah, agree with this, agree with that, got this wrong, agree with that, agree with that." But we had played well and came back strongly.'

'We were actually quite excited coming home,' says Allnutt. 'We knew then that we had a weapon up front. Rodney [Ah You] and Denis Buckley played really well that night. So we were disappointed not to have won, but from a ground where we hadn't had any luck before it wasn't a bad result.'

It also earned them two bonus points. The squad were given a week off and returned to camp two weeks ahead of their next game.

Saturday, 3 October
Connacht 36 Cardiff 31

Connacht coughed up an early intercept try before roaring back to lead 19–7 with tries by Kieran Marmion, Fox-Matamua (scoring his third try in three games off a line-out maul) and Danie Poolman. But Cardiff, as is their wont, were like a dog with a bone and came back to lead 24–19 early in the second half. Tries by Tiernan O'Halloran, off Jack Carty's crosskick, and Aly Muldowney after waves of pressure sealed a bonus-point win, albeit Cardiff rallied and Sam Hobbs' try earned them two bonus points.

'You can't shake those bloody guys off,' admits Lam. 'But that was a lot more comfortable than the score suggests.'

Friday, 16 October
Connacht 34 Zebre 15

With Ireland having helped to evict Italy from the World Cup in the pool stages, Zebre could welcome back 11 of their Azzurri squad, but on his 50th appearance Matt Healy scored the night's first try and Connacht secured a bonus point by half-time to win easing up.

Connacht's third win in four lifted them to third in the table.

They were enjoying the good autumn weather and dry tracks, scoring 17 tries and conceding 11. With the World Cup stars away, Connacht were making hay while the sun shone.

'A lot of people suggested that the World Cup gave us a real opportunity,' says Allnutt, 'but being expected to win creates its own pressure, which Connacht have never handled very well over the years. When you're expected to win, around Six Nations time and November internationals, we have often dropped games.

'It was an entertaining brand of rugby but probably not as clinical as we needed to be. There were concerns over our defence, over letting teams back into the game, but we were scoring freely and we were quite happy to keep doing that.'

Saturday, 24 October
Ospreys 16 Connacht 21

Again, Connacht travelled on the Friday and back on the Sunday morning.

A week after the World Cup quarter-finals, and the exits of both Wales and Ireland, the Ospreys were desperate for a second successive win. Steve Tandy was able to call on Eli Walker, Scott Otten, Paul James and Justin Tipuric after their World Cup exploits.

Tiernan O'Halloran captained Connacht for the first time as Muldoon was given a rare outing on the bench. Another Healy try, off a break by Marmion, gave Connacht the lead at half-time, before Bundee Aki scored off Craig Ronaldson's offload.

'That was a big win, because they'd just got back one or two of their internationals,' says Muldoon. 'I think that raised a few eyebrows as well. I'd be quite friendly with Steve Tandy because I played against him and we'd always have a chat afterwards. He admitted, "We were worried about this one and now we know why we were worried." And later in the year when they came to us in the Sportsground, he said, "Like I said to you earlier in the year, we were worried about you at the start of the season and it's come to fruition now." I think they had a poor season by their standards, but they'll be all right. They'll make a few signings.'

'We'd never beaten Ospreys in my time here,' says Lam, 'and never won at the Liberty Stadium. First time ever. So that was significant. Bundee scored a good try after Aly put Craig through a gap and then Craig popped it up for Bundee. Winning that one gave us real belief. The guys celebrated that one well.'

Not only had Connacht never won at the Liberty, but they'd beaten the Ospreys only once in 14 attempts over the previous seven seasons. Connacht had led 11–8 at the break, at which point the Irish referee Andrew Brace was taken ill and replaced for the second half by the Welsh assistant referee Sean Brickell. 'That's never easy for either team, but the boys actually finished real strong that day,' says Allnutt.

Aki also scooped one of his regular Man-of-the-Match awards with a trademark, all-action, try-scoring and match-winning performance. Allnutt recalls, 'He was up against Josh Matavesi and they know each other quite well, so they were bouncing off each other and for whatever reason there were a lot of verbals. That got Bundee fired up. It's the same when he plays against Ben Te'o, and they're "best buds" as well. You see them after the game and they're arm-in-arm, but Jeeze, the verbals! I think if I was playing against Bundee I'd keep my mouth shut.'

The win sent Connacht second.

Saturday, 31 October
Connacht 14 Edinburgh 9

Less than an hour after Nigel Owens signalled the finish to the 2015 World Cup, and thus not long after Richie McCaw had lifted the William Webb Ellis Trophy, Connacht kicked off against Edinburgh.

A tenth-minute try by O'Halloran, after a break by Healy, was the only try of the game. Two Carty penalties to pull two scores clear late on fell short and wide, leaving Connacht to survive a 15-phase attack to dig out an ugly win.

'It wasn't a bad crowd actually,' says Lam. 'We just took our lessons from the year before when they managed to choke tackle us and hold us up a lot. We lowered our body height in our carries and we won the breakdown really well in that game. Edinburgh helped us improve our breakdown.'

The Scots would do that to you! Edinburgh had also won four from five.

'That was real tough,' admits Allnutt, 'and what stood out from that game was their defence. They were a really sound defensive unit. We scored a good try through Matty [Healy]. It was a set play, from a line-out. Matty cut them open and Tiernan [O'Halloran] finished superbly. It was one of those games we had to dog it out. The conditions weren't great, but defensively we were very sound that night as well, which was pleasing.'

The win meant Connacht remained in second place, behind the Scarlets on points difference.

Friday, 6 November
Connacht 33 Treviso 19

Try-less in the first-half, Connacht were set in motion by Robbie Henshaw scoring in his seasonal debut after his return from the World Cup. Tom McCartney added the second off a cleverly worked line-out move but pulled his hamstring in doing so. Another searing finish by Healy left Connacht five minutes to secure a bonus point, but they fell short, instead allowing Treviso to score off a turnover.

Although it was Connacht's fifth win out of five at a well-attended Sportsground, Lam was less than amused. 'More comfortable than the scoreline suggested. We just weren't clinical enough. We could have won by more.'

Still, Connacht had made good on their promise to maximize the opportunity presented by the World Cup window.

But for the Glasgow defeat, they'd have been seven wins from seven. As it was, six wins out of seven and five on the spin had left them in a good place going into the opening weekend of the European competitions.

Connacht were top of the table.

15

Bundee Aki

Unlike Pat Lam and the countless others who blazed a trail from New Zealand to the northern hemisphere, Bundee Aki was both relatively young and inexperienced, having played just two years of Super Rugby before pitching up in Connacht.

It's hard to credit now, given he has become the standout player in the Guinness Pro12, but Aki struggled in his first season. With his partner, Kayla, and their two girls, Armani-Jade and Adrianna, back in New Zealand, he found life away from rugby hard going and he also had teething difficulties on the pitch.

'My first couple of months were quite tough. Super Rugby is a different brand of rugby. I settled in after a while in my first year, and then in the second year I started rolling, but that first year I struggled. I was trying to find my feet. My second year was a lot better, and I tried to take it to another level.'

Akin to Lam, Aki was born in Auckland to Samoan parents, Hercules and Sautia. He is the second oldest of seven, with four sisters, and two brothers. His older sister is Becka, and after Aki come Kine, Mary Anne, Bob, Sam and Irae.

His parents met and married in Samoa before moving to Auckland, where all seven kids were born. Hercules is a security guard and Sautia 'is at home looking after the family'.

Ask him his full name and he responds, with a loud laugh, 'Bundee

Aki.' But after a pause and another laugh, the truth is finally out. 'It's quite interesting actually, it's . . . Bundellu.'

He is named after the doctor who delivered him. 'I have met him a few times. He was our family doctor when I was growing up, but yeah, that normally never comes out, that's for sure!'

Throughout primary school, all his teachers called him by his full name, before rugby brought about the abbreviation, and immediately too.

'It was my first time at rugby training, and one of the coaches couldn't pronounce it. "Ah, nah, I've had enough of trying to call you. I can't pronounce it. I'll call you Bundee." He called me Bundee the whole time, and it stuck with me.'

This was his first coach in the local Weymouth club, where Aki began playing in South Auckland. There had been little rugby in his family before him, though he says, 'My dad's brother played a bit of rugby,' in reference to his Uncle Simi. 'I think he made New Zealand Colts as a half-back.'

Uncle Simi has always taken a big interest in Aki's career, ever since he began to play at about five years of age. 'I still talk to him now and then, although he loves his league nowadays.'

His father has also been a keen supporter since the early days. 'Dad loves the rugby. My dad has always been at my matches. Ever since I started, he's always been hard on me about rugby – always. Until this day, he hasn't stopped. Even if I think I have a good game, he'll think I could have played better,' he says, laughing again.

It's the usual story of a young boy in New Zealand. He began playing, barefoot of course, at five, progressing to his first pair of boots relatively young, at ten. And all, as he puts it, at 'the same club as the late Jonah Lomu!

'I didn't know him until I was older, but when I was at the club there were photos everywhere of him when he was young. Of course he was really good as a kid, and obviously he went on to be a legend.

'When I then played provincial rugby for Counties [Manukau RFC], where he also played, he was a legend there as well. He came into the club a few times when we won the Ranfurly Shield and the ITM

Championship Cup, the lower division. I met him a few times then. He was a really down-to-earth guy, a really humble, good guy. He was just hanging around in our changing-room most of the times when we were playing.'

Yet some of his earliest memories of rugby were not particularly fond ones. 'Bare feet, oranges at half-time – I used to love that. But I couldn't get over how parents used to yell on the sideline, thinking they were playing. Every time I played, I used to hate it. All the parents did it, including my mum and dad. It took me a while to get used to that. The boys in that team used to mock me all the time: "Hey, your cheerleaders are here again." And I'm like, "Yep, they're here." Ah, it was good craic at the same time.'

It helped that he quickly realized he might be quite good at this rugby lark and was enjoying it more than he first thought he would. 'It was something to do on the weekends. Normally after school I was just strolling around with the boys and doing whatever, but then every Saturday there was something to do, and all my friends started playing as well; it was quite cool.

'At around age ten or 11, I realized I actually quite liked playing rugby. I think what I most enjoyed about it was just seeing my friends every week. And then there was the food after the game!'

Lots and lots of good junk food, as he remembers it. 'Sausage rolls, meat pies, chicken pies, every kind of pie, fish and chips. It was great. I loved it. I used to go to the game just for the feed-up. They'd always give me food after the game, so that was fine with me.'

In that innately happy-go-lucky way of his, Aki describes his childhood as 'happy but a tough one, because my parents weren't the best off financially. We had no car, so every day I'd walk to school. It was a long walk. But there was always a group of us, and it was good to have friends to share school with.'

That was his primary school, Finlayson Park School, and at least when he progressed to his senior school at 13, Manurewa High School, it was a shorter walk, less than ten minutes, and with the same neighbourhood friends. There he started playing schools rugby.

'Our schools team was good, but it wasn't good enough to beat

Wesley College, who'd always be our main rivals, but that was the bigger rugby school. That's where Jonah Lomu, Sitiveni Sivivatu, Casey Laulala, Charles Piutau and those guys went to school. That's an all-boys school with great facilities, very rugby-orientated. We used to lose to them all the time, get a whipping sometimes, like 70-odd points. That was in my first year or two in high school. As I grew older, the margins closed, but I don't think my year ever beat their firsts.'

After school, Aki played with Manurewa Rugby Club for two years and then Patumahoe High. 'I jumped around a few clubs,' he admits. 'We won two championships at Patumahoe High.' From there he joined his last club, Karaka, although reckons he only played one game with them, as by then he'd begun to play provincial rugby for Counties Manukau.

This in turn led to New Zealand Under-20s trials. 'I got into all three camps, but then I had a kid at the age of 18 and took a year off rugby to work as a bank teller. I started working to raise my oldest [Armani-Jade].'

He admits he actually quite liked working in the bank, but noticed himself becoming quite 'edgy' whenever he tried to watch games or when rugby was discussed, as it is in pretty much every New Zealand workplace. 'I used to tell myself, "You're here to work, your rugby time is finished, you've got a family you need to look after now."'

Unbeknown to Aki, one of his best mates whom he grew up with, fellow Counties centre Tim Nanai-Williams, brother of another good mate, Nick Williams, recommended him to Tana Umaga, then coaching Counties.

'One day, as I was serving, I saw Tana. I thought he was just there for a normal everyday transaction. I said, "How are ya? How can I help you?"

'He said, "Oh, I'm here to see you."

'I was like, "Who? Me?"

' "Yeah, I'm here to see you."

'And I was like, "Oh, OK, what's this about?"'

They went into a room and began talking.

"'I've heard a few good stories about you. You're a pretty good footballer?'"

"'Aw yeah, it's been a while, though,'" said Aki.

'I was over 100 kg then. I was pretty fat,' he admits with a chuckle, looking back.

Umaga continued, "'I'm pretty interested in seeing how good you are and seeing how you play. I'm not going to promise anything. Just come along and train. If all goes well, all goes well.'"

Aki had a long think about Umaga's offer. 'I spoke to my partner Kayla. At that time, it was quite tough, because we were expecting a second baby.' They agreed he'd try to balance the two, so spoke to his boss about taking a little time off here or there to resume his rugby career. Nagging at Aki was the knowledge that he hadn't really given rugby what he calls 'a good crack'.

This was the tough year. Now living in West Auckland, he'd set his alarm for 5 a.m., drive 35 minutes to the Counties ground to train at 6 a.m., then drive another 35 minutes to work, do a full day and drive back to Counties or his club, Karaka, to train most evenings. That might not finish until 8.30 or so, meaning he usually returned home after 9 p.m.

'It was quite tough at that time, because I wasn't paid either for missing the hours at work or for rugby. Then I had a few ups and downs with my partner, just because it was so rough – especially when you leave at six in the morning and come home at night. But I knew I had to do the hard work. You can't go anywhere in life without the hard work.'

Umaga duly included Aki in his first-team squad in 2011, which went well enough on the pitch, with three tries in his nine appearances, four of them off the bench. But off the pitch, it was still hard going.

'The salary wasn't great, because in your first year playing provincially you start on a minimum salary. It was around 10k really for the whole year – a lot less than my earnings at work. But then in 2012 I found my feet.'

In 2012, he made his breakthrough with Counties Manukau,

playing 11 games, scoring six tries and being voted Player of the Year as they won promotion to the Premiership.

Then 2013 was a golden year. The Chiefs had won their first Super Rugby title the previous season and now went on to retain it, beating the Brumbies in the final on 3 August. Counties Manukau then won the 2013 Ranfurly Shield in a 27–24 win over Hawke's Bay on 7 September.

'It just all went well from there, really,' he says, seemingly as surprised as anyone.

He owes Tim Nanai-Williams, his Counties and Chiefs teammate, and Umaga plenty. 'I do. Tim knows that. I owe them heaps, and I tell him every day. I still keep in contact with him, and I still keep in contact with Tana. Those two gave me my chance to play rugby again, and I was quite fortunate to work with some good coaches too: Tana at Counties and then Wayne Smith and Dave Rennie at the Chiefs. Everything I've learned and know about rugby I learned from people like them.'

It's hard to believe it now, but initially he played as a scrum-half, or half-back as the Kiwis call it. 'But I could only pass one side, from right to left,' he admits, laughing again. 'I couldn't do the left to right, so I had to turn around and do the pass the other way,' he adds, and demonstrates by swivelling 360 degrees.

'People used to mock me all the time at school. So slowly, as I put on the weight, I moved out, first to winger, but I was too slow for that, so I moved in to centre. And that's when Tana took me under his wing and started teaching me how to play centre. I learned heaps from him.'

No better man to teach him about playing at centre.

If Aki were to relocate anywhere, certainly in Ireland, Connacht was perhaps a natural fit. Nowadays he beats his chest where the Connacht crest is, and he did the same with Counties. As Pat Lam says, for Aki rugby is family. It's a cause, which demands loyalty and passion. Counties are a source and expression of pride for many in South Auckland, as the area has had a reputation, angrily decried as stereotypical, for being home to the toughest streets.

'Counties will always be my club back home,' he says proudly. 'I grew up with them. That's the area I grew up in, yeah, South Auckland. A lot of Pacific Islanders are there anyway, as are a lot of country boys. We never used to get looked at by other selectors and coaches when we were there. I see Counties as really similar to Connacht.

'All we needed was a breakthrough, and once we got it, now obviously Counties is doing well. But if I ever go back home and play ITM, I don't think I'd ever go anywhere else except Counties.

'I think it took us over 50 years to win the Ranfurly Shield. We'd four goes in three years to try and win it, and we lost all by a fair number of points. Then we went to Hawke's Bay in 2013. We were behind the whole game. They had a couple of good Super Rugby players as well. We were down by four points in the last minute when we managed to sneak in a try at the very end. Great memories. We got back to the airport to be met by thousands of people, crying and emotional, because they'd never seen the Ranfurly Shield before. So we had three parades, because South Auckland is quite big! We had one in Manukau, then one in Papakura and then our main one in Pukekohe. I couldn't believe how many turned up at all three.'

In his first Super Rugby campaign with the Chiefs, Aki started a dozen games, played in three more off the bench and scored five tries as they defended the title they'd first won a year before.

'In that first year, I was actually very surprised with the number of games I played. I thought it would be my year to learn, and I learned a whole heap. But I was actually quite fortunate to play due to injuries. I wasn't even meant to play the first game of the season, but I started with Tim [Nanai-Williams] in midfield.'

His first match was against Ma'a Nonu and the Highlanders in Otago. 'It was a cracker of a game, and we won, but I was shocked at how fast it was. The pace of the game was at another level. It was so open because of their roof, which made for open rugby. But I was really happy with how it went and how we won, playing against the best. He [Ma'a Nonu] was the best centre in the world at the time.'

Aki tends to be inspired by coming up against the best midfielders. The bigger the name, the more it galvanizes him. 'We clashed into each other, but I actually think I did really well. You're always nervous when you come up against a player like that because you've been watching him since you were a kid. You think, "Wow, he's a good player."

'He's a huge man too, and that year I was actually quite small. Me and Tim were probably the smallest midfielders in the competition. But we actually did really well. It was quite nerve-racking going into the quarters, the semis and then the final.'

As a rookie, he resigned himself to not being in the starting line-up for the final against the Brumbies at home in Hamilton, and was glad for a spot on the bench.

'The Brumbies were a good side, and they were whipping us in the first half, but the coaches had a bit of faith in me and chucked me on, and I did well.

'I'm pretty proud, and I'm grateful to have had the chance to do things that no one thought I could. I never thought I'd win an ITM Championship Cup, let alone the Ranfurly Shield, and then to win the Super Rugby final – I'm probably the luckiest person on earth.'

His second season with the Chiefs was harder. Aki underwent surgery on his shoulder, delaying his start to their campaign and limiting him to eight games (scoring four more tries), and the Chiefs lost in the quarter-finals. 'It was quite tough trying to do "a three-peat", but I enjoyed it, and they wanted to keep me on.

'I was chucked in at the deep end. The reason I transitioned so well into Super Rugby was because of the players around me. Obviously the coaches really helped me out, but having the likes of Craig Clarke, Aaron Cruden, Tawera Kerr-Barlow, Richard Kahui, Robbie Robinson, Liam Messam, Sam Cane and Brodie Retallick made it so easy. Heaps of great players. All I had to do was just make sure I turn up and do my job properly.

'Craig Clarke is one of the greatest captains I've ever had. I just wish I could have played a lot more with him. I'm happy I played with him for two years, but I was quite gutted when I joined Connacht that he wasn't there any more. He's a great leader.'

So why leave New Zealand?

'Well, at the time I was looking at what was best for my family.

Where would I be if I stayed? They did want me to stay, but I was still fighting for a position at centre and Sonny Bill Williams was coming back in. I was trying to be realistic, to find out where I'd be rostered, and what would happen if I went somewhere else in New Zealand. I might not get as much game time as I did in my first year. There were a lot of things going through my head, and family-wise I had to think about what was best for us financially as well.'

Kayla had stuck with him and backed him through the difficult years. At 24, he was also conscious that rugby offered him a relatively short window.

He sounded out his coaches. 'They all wanted me to stay, but I made sure I put everything else aside and just thought about myself and my family.'

Aki asked his agent what else might be out there in the northern hemisphere. There was interest in France and England, as well as from Leinster and Munster in Ireland.

'I only knew stories of Munster, Leinster and a bit of Ulster. I didn't really know of Connacht at all. Mils Muliaina was with the Chiefs in my last year there, and we talked one day. I don't know how he knew that Connacht had offered me a contract, but he asked me, "Have you signed your contract yet?"

' "What contract?"

'And he's like, "Don't lie – your contract for Connacht."

' "How do you know?"

' "Because I'm going there," he said.

' "Ah no way."

'He's like, "Yeah, I am."

'That made it a lot easier for me to join Connacht. I knew straight away then that I had my mate to come over with.'

Muliaina joining Connacht, in addition to Clarke before him, were major factors in Aki's eyebrow-raising choice at the time. Clarke told Aki nothing but good things about Connacht: what a nice city Galway was and how Connacht were building. And, of course, Lam was selling his vision. Aki had never met Lam, but was intrigued merely by speaking to him on the phone.

'He's a persuasive person, that's for sure! But I think the biggest reason why I chose Connacht was because I knew Mils was coming here. I thought, "At least my first year will go all right. At least I've got someone there to help me out." I knew Mils had been overseas before and he would know what to do. It was difficult to find my feet in that first year, but Mils was like a mentor for me.'

Aki took an instant liking to Galway and its people, and to this end was helped by Muliaina too, for it was with him that, fittingly, Aki went to his first bar in Galway, An Púcán. 'Everybody said hello and came up and introduced themselves,' he says.

No, the problem wasn't Galway or its people or supporters. 'The most difficult part was the brand of rugby and trying to adjust myself from running rugby to a lot of confrontational rugby that's played here. I had to get used to the weather too, but the weather wasn't the main factor, it was just about finding my feet on the pitch.

'When I first came here, my family only stayed for five days and then went back home. It was quite difficult to adjust to standing on your own two feet, as back home I was spoon-fed. I could always rely on my family and my parents. I had to become more self-sufficient and it took a while.'

As ever, though, this memory of his initial time with Connacht is delivered with an engaging smile. 'I was living on my own and had a three-bedroom house to myself. It was quite quiet,' he adds, now laughing. 'So my first year was quite tough.'

With Counties and the Chiefs, he had become a little spoiled by success, and while Connacht had their best season in 2014–15, they still lost more matches than they won in the League. He wasn't used to this. 'I was used to a winning environment, and I was always happy. Coming here, I was a little shell-shocked.'

He found that the losses lingered longer than the wins, as did missing out on their stated goal of European Champions Cup rugby. 'I couldn't take coming seventh. I couldn't take it at all. So I was asking myself, "Am I at the right place? I'm here to win. I'm not here to come seventh." But then I thought, "I'll just see how I go in the second year", and the second year changed everything.'

It transpired that everyone else shared his acute sense of disappointment at missing out on the Champions Cup, and as a result there was a changed mindset from pre-season onwards.

'If you want to win a championship, you've got to believe you can be a champion, and you've got to act like a champion, walk like a champion, do things like a champion. And that's good. We got stuck into each other, and we started to become comfortable in the brand of rugby we began to play in pre-season and in the early games.'

He noticed more scuffles in training – and loved it. This was more like the Chiefs, he thought, and for him a turning point was their second round defeat to Glasgow.

'After we won the first game against the Dragons, in our second game we were getting a whipping in Glasgow. We were getting smoked in the first half, and somehow we came back and lost by a point. And that was against the champions. The boys started to believe in themselves more, we started winning and the boys grew.

It's quite cool how confidence can help you so much. That's all they needed. Once you start getting a winning culture, you start forgetting how to lose. Now all they knew was how to win.'

It was Aki's extraordinary finish against Munster that sealed a first win at Thomond Park in almost three decades. 'I was just picking up off the fruits of Robbie,' he says in reference to Henshaw's footwork and offload. The way Aki punched his chest, it looked like he knew the significance of it all. He didn't.

'I found out at the end of the game. I didn't realize how much it meant, but I enjoyed every moment of it. That was another turning point. We started making our own history and our own stories, and that's what you want to do.'

Connacht and Bundee were only starting.

16

Krasnoyarsk

Prior to the win over Treviso, Lam had notified the squad by email that the week's schedule would begin with a meeting that Friday night in the Sportsground. There he told them they'd be training at 6 p.m. to begin acclimatizing for their opening European Challenge Cup against Enisei in Krasnoyarsk, Siberia, the following Saturday.

Lam was not only taking no chances, he was not taking Enisei lightly either.

'This is where my experience of Super Rugby really helped, because for a New Zealand team so much preparation was required before a trip to South Africa. Before the Treviso game, I had been working with Paul Bunce. The boys knew that we'd be heading off to play in Krasnoyarsk, in minus 30 degrees, the next Tuesday.'

Lam addressed the squad: 'Right, fellas, I've talked about preparation and planning, but there's not many opportunities to practise mental toughness like this one. We're about to go to a place where none of us have ever been before. The conditions will be freezing. There are a lot of different challenges. It is what it is, but how we prepare is the key.'

Lam recalls, 'I used all the clichés. And I said, "We have a choice. Things aren't going to be perfect. Things are going to be tough. We can complain about it or we can get hold of it and use it for mental toughness, as something that will build you as individuals, as rugby players and as a team." And I couldn't have planned it any better,' he says, laughing. 'Everything went right until the end, and then everything went wrong.'

Initially, John Muldoon had been of a mind to skip the trip. 'A couple of weeks beforehand, Pat told me about his plans for Russia and asked if I wanted to be part of it. And I thought about it, and I knew I'd never be in Siberia again. I went back to Pat: "I want to go." And I talked to Aly and one or two others. "Do you know what, I kind of want to go," I said. I think I helped to convince some of the older lads that this could be, perhaps, a good trip. And we were conscious of the fact that it was their [Enisei's] first ever game in a European competition.'

Tuesday, 10 November

Four days before the game, the squad assembled in the Sportsground for a team photo at 3.10 p.m., in their home kit. Along with their passports, the squad were advised to bring snacks and two-prong adaptors. They then travelled to Shannon airport for their ten-and-a-half-hour haul via Moscow to Siberia, arriving in Krasnoyarsk at 11.30 a.m. on Wednesday.

They were transferred by bus to the Hilton Garden Inn Hotel and, after check-in and lunch, had a team meeting before an indoor training session at a gym. 'We just did a walk-through, just to get the trip out of our legs, at a local gym,' says Allnutt. 'Actually, it was more like a warehouse with a basketball court, which was shared with a wrestling club.

'The kids ranged in age from about three to 13, and watching them train was unbelievable. They must have been aspiring Olympic wrestlers. They went about their work with military precision, so sharp; the boys got a real kick out of that experience, quite unlike anything you'd see on a normal training day.'

The squad watched on agog. Not a bad way to start proceedings either. Basic facilities and freezing temperatures weren't deterring these young Siberian wrestlers, which also helped to put Connacht's week in perspective.

The squad returned to the Hilton Garden Inn Hotel at around

4.30, with a team meeting scheduled for 5.45 p.m. – as much to break up the evening as anything else – before dinner at 6 p.m. Not for the first time in this long week, that still left plenty of time to fill. But they'd factored that into their planning too.

'We just didn't want to treat it like an ordinary trip,' says Allnutt. 'That's why we tried to give ourselves as much time as possible over there.

'In the evenings, we had team quizzes and unit meetings. We tried to keep each other busy. During the days, the boys could go to a shopping centre nearby for a coffee. But then again you couldn't go too far because of the cold. It was just dangerously cold to be fair. At night it would be minus 30, no problem, and the locals advised us not to go walking too far because you'd bloody freeze in no time. To be honest, there was a lot of rest on that trip. The boys were catching up on sleep.'

Thursday and Friday were the longest days. On the Thursday, after lunch and a team meeting at 2.45 p.m., they departed for a training session.

The outdoor session was adjacent to the gymnasium/warehouse they'd been to the day before. At first sighting, Allnutt thought the rugby pitch resembled an ashtray more than a pitch.

'They used it for different things. I don't know what type of grass it was, but I've never seen anything like it. It was really dusty, and there was no green on it at all. But out the back there was the Astro area, and that's where they put us. That was set up for soccer.'

The temperature was minus 20.

'It was just so, so cold,' remembers Allnutt. 'Dave Ellis thought he was having a heart attack. Our masseur brought him back to the doctor at the hotel. Dave had never experienced cold like it in his life, and he started to get a pain in his chest. It was that cold. If you were just standing around, which I was, you just got so cold so quickly. It's something I'd never experienced before.'

In an apartment block overlooking the training area, Allnutt noticed a bike hanging out on the 13th floor. 'They obviously had no balcony or room inside for it, so the bike was hung on a piece of wire attached to the window.

'The old cars and trucks were like a step back in time. You just don't see them any more, except in old movies, and that was cool.'

The hotel food was good. 'They said it would be western-style food. It wasn't like we would normally get, but it was close to it, and the hotel staff were fantastic. The club loved having us there in their home town. It was a big thing for them, and we embraced it. We were breaking new ground in Europe. We'd played in that Challenge Cup for many years and we've been to some pretty cool places, but this one was just amazing.'

The mornings were spent on walking tours around town, and the numbers expanded by the day. Muldoon recalls, 'Me and some of the lads agreed, "Ah, damn it, I'll never be back here again, let's go and embrace it." Some of the lads wouldn't even leave the hotel because of the cold. But myself, Aly and Denis [Buckley] went walking the first morning. James Crombie, the photographer from Inpho, met us in the lobby on the Wednesday morning and asked what we were doing. "Oh, we're going for a walk."

'"Do you mind if I come with you and take a few pictures?"

'"Yeah, yeah, work away."

'He took loads of pictures, and me with my beard frozen. Typically, the young lads saw some of these photos on social media, and the following morning half the squad were in the lobby waiting for us.'

By Friday morning, most of the squad were in the lobby, wearing scarves: '"Are you going for a walk?" And, "Is James [Crombie] coming?" All they wanted was a few photos to chuck up on Instagram or whatever.'

On the Friday morning, some took a trip to a local market. 'The trip to the market was something special,' says Duffy, although not without its consequences. 'I decided to walk back to the hotel because I thought it was a nice day. It was only 20 or 25 minutes, but I almost froze to death on the way back. Most of the guys took taxis, but I said, "No, I fancy a walk." But the temperature dropped, and I ended up actually jogging, I was that cold.'

Friday was structured almost identically to Thursday, with a 2.45 p.m. team meeting preceding the 3 p.m. departure for training, which this time was the Captain's Run at the match venue, the Central Stadium, a vast ground with a running track where Ireland had beaten Russia in a World Cup qualifier in 2002.

'The Captain's Run itself was great,' says Allnutt. 'We saw the stadium, but it was all about getting used to the temperatures, really.

'Most of the time there were clear blue skies that took the sting out of the cold a little. The day before was really cold as there'd been no sun. But by night-time, it was horrendous! So, to be honest, most of the lads didn't leave the hotel that often.'

Saturday, 14 November – Match day

As is the custom for all away matches, Lam insisted on an early-morning run for himself and the management. And at 7.30 a.m. local time, no exceptions were made for Siberia, even in winter.

Hence they were first at breakfast at 8 a.m., with the players all following in due course. At 11.30, the squad had their usual unit meetings before lunch. After the team meeting at 1.05, they took the half-hour bus journey to the Central Stadium for the 3 p.m. kick-off.

On arrival at the ground, they found an army of volunteers shovelling snow off the pitch and repainting the lines. 'It was going back to the sixties,' says Allnutt, 'with some of their equipment. It was quite amusing to see. But I watched their team warm-up, and they were as cold as we were. They wouldn't have played in such conditions too often before either, if at all.'

Needless to say, in temperatures of minus 20 degrees or worse, Enisei were playing out of season. In addition, they'd normally have their home games in Sochi, which is relatively warmer and where they would host the other teams in the group – Brive and Newcastle.

Watching Enisei warm-up, so to speak, Allnutt couldn't stop smiling at one of their wingers. A huge lad, he was shivering violently and almost frozen to the spot. This was not a day for any player, in any position, but certainly not wingers. 'I sort of thought then, "Well, if they're going to struggle, then hopefully we can hang in there."'

Duffy looks back. 'When we got the fixtures, we knew Enisei would have two games in Sochi, and I said, "I bet you we get the one in Krasnoyarsk." And sure enough we did. On the plus side, I'd never have gone there had we not been drawn against Enisei. We'd played them here with the Eagles a number of times and at first I thought, "This is going to be a pain in the ass." But it was a new adventure, especially from a coaching perspective. [At one point it looked as though] the hookers were throwing potatoes. I was in the stands thinking, "What's wrong?" But down on pitchside, the boys told us the air was so cold it deflated the balls.'

The crowd was about 2,500, and a band played during the match. 'Bizarre stuff,' says Duffy. 'There must have been 50 plugs coming out of one cable. Laptops crashed during the game. You couldn't recall anything, and you realize that computers have become your crutches during games; you normally check something as many times as you like. So it was back to old-school coaching: spot something, confront what you see, try and fix it.'

'It was tough,' says Muldoon. 'I've never played in cold remotely like it. I remember at one point I looked at Aly and he went, "Jaysus, I thought I was bad", nodding to one of their players. I looked across at their number 6. He was shivering and trying to blow on his hands. He was worse than us!'

It wasn't much fun on the sidelines either. 'When the balls deflated, Marty [Joyce – the kit and logistics manager] struggled to pump them up because of the cold,' says Allnutt. 'When trying to write the sub cards, the pens froze. The water bottles also froze. We had hand warmers, but if you walked outside they too would just freeze straight away.

'They were the most extreme conditions I've ever known,' admits Allnutt. 'In the second half, I think it went as low as minus 23 or minus 24. Despite their underground heating, the pitch was beginning to freeze by the end.'

Allnutt has rarely admired a Connacht team so much, not least for 'the courage they showed to go back out after half-time.

'I think there's a video of Niyi [Adeolokun] in the changing-room. He couldn't hold his hot drink. It was spilling all over him. Some just couldn't control the cups in their hands.'

Connacht had led 6–0 at half-time through two penalties on his debut by A. J. MacGinty. In the second half, their scrum cranked up the pressure, paving the way for Adeolokun to score the first try, before Muldoon and Darragh Leader scored either side of the hour. Aki had a big hand in all three, and although Connacht conceded two late consolation scores to the spirited Russians, a try by Rory Parata sealed a bonus-point win with five minutes to go.

Dave Ellis's playing and coaching career has usually tended to take him to warmer climes and certainly never anywhere like Siberia. 'That trip will always stay in my mind. We took a lot of kids on that trip, and they fronted up. The Russians fronted up too. We looked at them. We knew that we were better than them, but on their home ground, in the freezing damn cold, it would be difficult. The rugby balls froze, for God's sake. They had to bloody keep them in wraps on the side of the pitch. I was running out with the water, like I always do, but the water in the drinks bottles froze! It was crazy. Hell of an experience.

'I got caught in a few cold places in Canada, and in the Rockies a couple of times, but nothing like that.'

Straight after the match, Enisei hosted a post-match meal at a local restaurant, complete with speeches and presentations to mark their first game in European competition. The squad then clambered aboard their coach for the half-hour drive to the airport. Everyone was on time. They arrived at Krasnoyarsk airport at 7.30 p.m. for their flight at 9 p.m. But this is where things became interesting!

The check-in was routine, and the bags were sent through. In the departures lounge, Lam and Allnutt chatted together.

'That was an unforgettable trip,' said Lam. 'Everything has just gone like clockwork.'

Allnutt concurred. 'Aw, mate, it was brilliant.'

They reminisced about the trip some more, before Lam went off for a quick interview with a journalist. A while later, Allnutt looked at the information screen, which flashed that word dreaded by all airport travellers: 'Delayed'. 'Uh-oh,' thought Allnutt. 'Here we go.'

When Lam came back, Allnutt informed him, 'Pat, I think we're delayed.'

Right: George Naoupu tackled by Thierry Dusautoir during Connacht's landmark win against the four-time champions Toulouse in the Heineken Cup, December 2013.

Below: Michael Swift and John Muldoon celebrate a famous victory.

Bottom: Thumbs up from coach Pat Lam after the match.

Left: (*L–R*) Aly Muldowney, Finlay Bealham, John Muldoon, George Naoupu and Ian Porter out for a walk around a hard-frozen Krasnoyarsk, November 2015.

Below: Bundee Aki breaking through the Enisei line.

Right: A. J. MacGinty shivers with the cold after the game.

Below: Keeping the cold at bay as the game reaches its final stages: (*L–R*) Finlay Bealham, Bundee Aki, Shane Delahunt, Ian Porter, John Muldoon, Denis Buckley and Aly Muldowney.

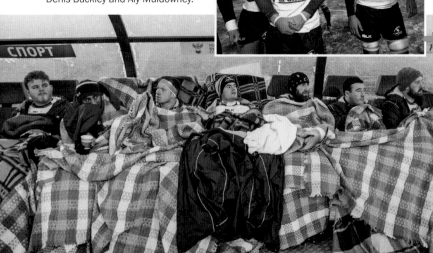

Above: Connacht's five, Ireland v Italy, RBS 6 Nations 2016: (*L–R*) Kieran Marmion, Nathan White, Finlay Bealham, Ultan Dillane and Robbie Henshaw.

Below: Launching Connacht Rugby Vision and Strategy 2016–20 at the Aviva Stadium: (*L–R*) Domestic Rugby Manager Eric Elwood, Connacht Rugby Academy Manager Nigel Carolan, CEO Willie Ruane and Head Coach Pat Lam.

Above: Glasgow forwards coach Dan McFarland with Connacht's skills coach Dave Ellis.

Above: Jake Heenan drives into the tackle from Glasgow's D'Arcy Rae during the 2016 Pro12 semi-final.

Above: John Muldoon celebrates as Niyi Adeolokun runs in for a try, 2016 Pro12 semi-final.

Right: Aly Muldowney celebrates the semi-final win at the Sportsground with his son Arlan.

Above: Ultan Dillane drives past Leinster's Dave Kearney and Richard Strauss during the 2016 Pro12 final at Murrayfield.

Right: Tiernan O'Halloran evades Leinster's Rob Kearney on his try-scoring run.

Below: Bundee Aki holds off Leinster's Richard Strauss during the 2016 Pro12 final in Edinburgh.

Right: Tom McCartney tears past Leinster's Johnny Sexton.

Below: Niyi Adeolokun gets past Eoin Reddan and dives over the try line to score.

Bottom: Matt Healy celebrates his try.

Above: Sweet victory: (*L–R*) Tiernan O'Halloran and Ronan Loughney celebrate the moment.

Right: A delighted John Muldoon and Eric Elwood after the game.

Below: Belting out 'The Fields'. Connacht: Pro12 Champions 2016.

Above: The team behind the team: (*L–R*) Dave Ellis, Andre Bell, Pat Lam, Tim Allnutt, Willie Ruane, Jimmy Duffy and Conor McPhillips in the dressing room after the game, 28 May 2016.

Below: The Homecoming. Coach and captain, Pat Lam and John Muldoon, celebrate with a huge crowd in Galway – *'We have a title to defend!'*

'Delayed?' Lam looked up at the screen as well.

One hour became two hours. By now, all were also aware of the Paris atrocities of the day before, in which terrorists had murdered 130 people.

'I think it was 11.30 when we were told to get our bags and go back into town,' recalls Allnutt. 'We were frantically trying to find a hotel. The Hilton, where we'd been staying, was booked out that night, but thanks to the airport staff another one was found, as well as four minibuses to take us all into town.'

Welcome back to the cold they thought they'd left behind.

'I was in the last of the minibuses,' says Allnutt, 'and it was after midnight when we reached the hotel. There was no food available for us at that time, so we had a team meeting about what we knew, what we'd heard and what we hadn't heard. All we could do was head to our rooms and sit tight until we heard something.'

'We'd been told that a part in the plane had broken,' says Duffy, 'but the part in question was to come from Paris, and this was the day after the bombings there. We did the review that night, in the hotel at 1.30 a.m., to get that out of the way.'

'At the dinner, we'd had a few beers and a singsong with the Russians,' recalls Muldoon. 'I said to the lads, "Jeeze, this week would have been capped off with a great night out, but anyway, it's done. We're going home tonight, so we can't go out." We had a couple of beers in the airport and were about to take our sleeping tablets for the long haul home. But then I realized there might be a problem. Is that the captain and the air hostesses leaving the airport? There's something wrong here. I went over to Pat.

'He said, "Yeah, we have the feeling that there's something wrong as well." So I went back to the lads. "Order another drink there." Before we knew it, we were all bundled out of the airport. So we went out that night for a couple of drinks – a good old night with the lads, including a couple of vodkas, which didn't help the head too much. Some of us were fairly shook the following day.'

On Sunday morning, they still had no idea when or how they would be able to leave Krasnoyarsk.

Muldoon recalls, 'On Sunday morning, Pat called us together. "Look, lads, this is not looking good. I need a bit of positivity out of you." But by that stage our view was that this had been a great trip and to hell with it. "It is what it is." '

They spent most of Sunday in their new hotel, with still no word or hint of any possible departure date or time.

Their new hotel was grand, but when the Hilton Garden Inn Hotel became available at 6 p.m., the management decided to transfer there en bloc – as much for something to do as for familiarity. By nightfall, still no word.

'A guy called Vincent [Prébandier] from the EPCR [European Professional Club Rugby] was with us, and it was his event basically,' says Allnutt. 'He and I were just putting pressure on the airline, trying to find out about the aircraft. On Monday morning, we were told we wouldn't be getting that aircraft any more, and that furthermore we'd have to split into groups.

'Your worst nightmare as a manager is having to split up your group, as you no longer control everything. It was a difficult decision, and myself and Pat talked long and hard about what to do. In the end, we decided to split into three groups, and it was pretty random how we did it. We chose different guys to lead each group.'

The party consisted of 25 players, 13 management, two officials, a translator, an official from the tournament organizers (EPCR), and travelling media. The party of 42 could at least be divided equally into three groups.

The squad had to take three different flights from Krasnoyarsk to Moscow. From there, one group would fly home to Galway via Amsterdam, another to Ireland via London, and a third would stay in Moscow for a direct flight to Shannon on the Tuesday.

A serious problem arose in Moscow.

'Our visas had expired,' says Allnutt. 'We had flagged this before we left Krasnoyarsk and been told it would be sorted. But it hadn't. As our group leader, I was taken away into a room by three Moscow officials. They wanted to know why we were breaking the law, coming into their country without sufficient visas.

'They had built a profile on me. They took my laptop and my phone to find out if we were legit. They asked me a lot of questions, and to be honest it wasn't great. After about an hour to an hour and a half with them, I was let out to rejoin the rest of the lads.

'Then it was about trying to get our visas renewed so that we could actually fly out. One of the officials said that we had to pay everything by cash, so we had a whipround. Then we had all our forms to fill in so that we could fly out that night. It really did come down to the last minute before some of the group were allowed to leave.

'Pat was part of our group, for instance, and by the time he got through security, he boarded the flight to London with me, literally with a minute to spare. It was an unbelievable experience, but we just rolled with it. Everyone handled it so well, including the journalists who were travelling with us. Everyone just took it in their stride, no bitching or freaking out. We just worked together in what was a very stressful situation. A lot of it was out of our control, and we just wanted to get out of there.'

According to Muldoon, it was in Moscow when Bundee Aki did as much as anyone to maintain spirits. 'I'll take my hat off to Bundee. At one point we were standing in the middle of Moscow airport, everyone scratching their heads, being told we wouldn't be going because our visas had expired. Tim had admitted, "This could take hours."' And then Bundee came along with this massive tray of coffees. He was like, "Coffee? Coffee? Coffee? Coffee?" And all the lads grabbed one. "Oh, thanks, Bundee." Next he comes around with a massive tray of croissants and pastries. He'd gone to the shop himself and bought them for all the lads. I'd had a run-in or two with him at the start for being late to training, but he is kind-hearted and he's always one of the lads.

'When I got home, I told Lorna, "Do you know who I have a lot of respect for after the weekend?" She asked, "Who?" I said, "Bundee. He was brilliant on tour, constantly keeping the lads' spirits up when everything was going against us, buying coffees and doing whatever else."

'In the airport, we played a stupid game called Prudo and were laughing and messing. Bundee had music playing. Anybody walking by looked at us a little perplexed. We must have looked like a group of drunken lads coming back from a tour or a stag.'

Still and all, they had to eat as well.

'Tim's card had maxed out helping to pay for the visas,' says Muldoon. 'We were playing cards and messing and chatting and said, "Right, we'll go for food." I asked Tim, "What will I do?" And he said, "Just chuck it all on your credit card." So I went back to the lads and said, "Come on, lads, I'll buy everyone food." I thought, "To hell with it, I'll buy steak for everyone."

'Afterwards Tim said, "Did you pay for dinner?"

' "Yeah."

'And he said, "You'll get it back. Do whatever you want. Get whatever you want. Get coffees."

'So I bought coffees for the different groups, because we all knew we had to stay awake. A few lads did take a kip on tables or whatever, but there was nowhere really to sleep anyway.'

'To hear that plane take off was a relief for everybody,' says Allnutt.

'Our group stayed in a hotel in London by Heathrow airport on the Monday night. One group went to Amsterdam and stayed overnight in a hotel by the airport, and the other group stayed in Moscow. They had a great time, going into Red Square for a look around. Everyone made the best of a bad situation.'

The Moscow group was composed almost entirely of management and media, amongst them the logistics manager Marty Joyce, the masseur Robbie Fox, press officer Louise Creedon and journalists John Fallon and Linley MacKenzie.

Duffy was amongst those who returned home via Amsterdam, each group sharing pictures from their three locations via WhatsApp. The Amsterdam group also included Dave Heffernan, Jack Carty, Andre Bell, Jason Harris-Wright. They arrived in Amsterdam late on Monday night.

'We went into town for a few beers,' says Duffy. 'The Amsterdam 12, I think we ended up calling ourselves. We went into town, had a look around and popped back soon after as we were flying out early again in the morning, which was great. It was such a relief to get home.

'Everything was a challenge in one regard or another, but I'm absolutely 100 per cent delighted to have been part of it. It was an epic trip in the end, absolutely an epic, and it worked out. It could have gone so wrong, but in fairness to the lads, they made that trip, as did the people over there. We were lucky. We had a lovely hotel, which all added to the journey of the year.'

They'd left on a Tuesday and returned home the following Tuesday.

'Our group didn't get back until 7 p.m. on Tuesday, when we were supposed to be back in Ireland at twelve on the Saturday night,' says Muldoon. 'But it was funny, because we used it as a joke. "The road home from Russia." We tried to keep ourselves entertained. It was just a bit of craic. I think that's when the likes of Peter Robb and James Connolly felt more involved in the squad.

'And it was a great trip. I don't think anyone would speak badly of it. If you asked me on the Sunday when my hangover was killing me, I might have said something different, but looking back, no. It was one of the great trips.'

'Like I said, I couldn't have planned it any better,' says Lam. 'Everything went right until we were due to fly home, and then everything went wrong, so much so that some of the boys thought that somehow I'd deliberately changed the plans!

'I was just so proud of the guys. Every challenge presented to us that week was met with the right attitude, and that whole trip brought us closer together. It made us tough and strong, and put us in a great place for the rest of the season. Newcastle and Brive both went to Sochi. They got the easy option going to Sochi, and they both lost to Enisei. They had shorter flights and played in normal temperatures but obviously just rocked in and didn't do as much preparation.

'That win would effectively get us through, because everyone won their home games, but we'd won in Krasnoyarsk.'

17

2015–16 – Low Points, Checkpoints and Turning Points

After their exhausting trip to Siberia and back, the squad were given Wednesday off. The coaches came in that morning, however, to plan for the Brive match the following Saturday at the Sportsground. Jimmy Duffy had settled in well but knew this would be their biggest challenge of the season to date, in his domain at any rate.

'Up front especially, Brive are seriously strong. They have a massive pack and they love to maul, absolutely love to maul. One of our goals as coaches from the start was not to concede any mauls if we could, or as few as possible, and the count was pretty low – four or five in the Pro12.

'But Brive are big boys, a club with a history of forward play. That was a real tough battle up front, which was great, because it set the tone for the rest of the season. Edinburgh as well, three weeks before, were a massive mauling unit. It was good to be genuinely challenged up front. What you put down on paper, and what you do, can be vastly different. But the boys backed up what they said they'd do. That Brive game was a massively physical battle.'

Connacht won 21–17, to leave themselves with two wins out of two in the Challenge Cup, and on nine points. The win came at a cost, though, with their new Kiwi flanker Nepia Fox-Matamua sidelined for the rest of the season.

John Muldoon was rested, as were Aly Muldowney and Tom McCartney, with Jason Harris-Wright, Ben Marshall and Eoin McKeon all starting. 'We had to have faith in everybody,' says Duffy, 'and the lads did really well. And Brive came to play. They stuck in the game right to the end. There were lots of sore bodies afterwards.'

'Brive were probably the biggest team we played all season,' says Lam. 'So that was an important game, to learn that we can handle big teams as long as we play our game. They tried to beat us up physically, and we stood up to them physically.'

This fixture also proved a turning point in another way, according to Lam.

'After that Brive game, we completely changed the way we were dealing with referees. We had been in their faces, complaining. In our review, we decided that we'd have a "next job" mentality – to concentrate on moving on and forget about the referee.'

A week later, Connacht travelled to Thomond Park, where they hadn't beaten Munster in a competitive game since 1986. While McCartney was still sidelined, having pulled his hamstring in the act of scoring his first try against Treviso three weeks before, Muldowney and Muldoon returned.

At the Monday coaches' meeting following the win over Brive, they considered juggling their back-row options in the absence of Fox-Matamua and their other Kiwi open-side, Jake Heenan.

'We debated moving Muldoon and McKeon. But I'd been really impressed with James Connolly and in that discussion said, "No, I want to play James." There were a few looks. "Are you sure, Pat?" I said, "Yeah, let's back the kid." He had shown me a real doggedness. He'd also have Muldoon beside him, with Eoghan Masterson at 8.'

Muldoon's return was one of nine changes. A. J. MacGinty made his first League start, Henshaw reverted to full-back, with O'Halloran on the wing and Aki shifted to outside centre, with Craig Ronaldson on his inside.

'I did that because Robbie had just come back, so it was far easier to integrate him there,' says Lam. 'Craig was our goal-kicker at that stage. A. J. MacGinty hadn't been with us for long.'

In the event, MacGinty suffered severe bruising, which would sideline him for three weeks, and was replaced early in the second half by Jack Carty.

The pack featured two academy players, 21-year-old hooker Shane Delahunt, in just his third start for the province, and the debutant Connolly (22), as well as two first-year graduates of their academy, Ultan Dillane and Masterson. Another academy player, the 20-year-old Galway born and reared and Roscrea educated Sean O'Brien, would make his debut off the bench before the hour mark. It would be the first of 20 appearances for the former Ireland Under-19 and Under-20 captain.

Delahunt is a product of Kilkenny College who came through the Leinster underage set-up and Irish Under-19s as a prop. He was then converted to hooker, whereupon his career stalled. Released a year later by Leinster, he was given a trial and then an academy contract by the eagle-eyed Nigel Carolan. A month after this Munster game, both Delahunt and Connolly signed their first professional contracts for the 2016–17 season; O'Brien and Peter Robb followed suit in January.

'That game highlighted the importance of bringing tier-two and tier-three players up to speed. "Here's our structure, know your job." That reinforced it for everybody. Tom and Heff [Dave Heffernan] were out, yet Shane Delahunt went in and did a bloody good job, as did James. And what did they do? They just ran the system, ran the process, which cemented them into our team.'

By his own admission, it took Lam three attempts to incorporate the correct number of academy players into training sessions with the senior squad.

'In my first year, I didn't know anybody, and I was shocked that academy players were available for selection. "What?" Because in New Zealand, it's totally different. A young player has to wait for injuries. So I said, "Everyone has to train." But we were low on staff; Nigel was low on staff. So although I'd got Jimmy involved, I quickly realized that with so many players, it brought some of our training standards down in that first year.

'In the second season, I managed to get Dave [Ellis] in, and we kept everyone separate, only calling in players from the academy if we needed replacements. Then, before my third year, I went through the academy and identified who, realistically, could play for the senior team and where, potentially, there might be holes in the squad.'

Accordingly, nine of the 19 academy players trained fully with the senior squad from pre-season onwards, others being upgraded during the season.

With Henshaw away at the World Cup, Rory Parata had made his debut in the seasonal opener against the Dragons and, in his third year in the Connacht academy and having just turned 21, played in 16 of Connacht's first 18 games (nine from the start) before injury intervened.

Born in Sydney to an Irish mother and New Zealand father, his family had moved to Ireland when he was nine; he'd come through Rockwell College and the Munster Under-18s before switching to Connacht at Under-19s and joining their academy.

Lam says, 'Although Robbie was away, I wasn't sure Rory would make it. He has plenty of talent but wasn't putting all the work in when I first arrived. But he came back this season in great nick. He did a lot of work, his skin folds came down, and so he now had the physique, the fitness and the conditioning to supplement the talent. He had a great start to the season before he was injured.'

Saturday, 28 November
Munster 12 Connacht 18

An in-and-out raid; Connacht travelling by coach for lunch in the Clarion Hotel.

They took the game to Munster for much of the night and led from the moment Ronaldson kicked an 11th-minute penalty, extending the lead soon after through a Tiernan O'Halloran try.

However, the momentum appeared to shift decisively towards Munster in the 65th minute when referee Ben Whitehouse yellow-carded Muldoon for impeding Ian Keatley and also awarded a penalty try. Leading 13–12, Connacht had to withstand ten minutes of pressure without their captain.

That they did, though, and Aki sealed the win with a wondrous finish at the corner flag from an offload by Henshaw.

It wasn't just the finish that gave Lam so much satisfaction. 'I go right back to the scrum. That showed how far our mentality had come. We'd conceded a penalty try, and Mul had been sinbinned. We were still leading by a point when Mul returned for a scrum on our own 22.

'Mul picked off the base and then we went wide, and Matt Healy kicked it because their winger came up. We re-gathered the ball, went through phase play, played our system, went that way, came back, went that way, came back, went back there, Robbie offloaded – boom. Try! It was straight off the training park. I have training footage of that play off a scrum, us playing this way, and everyone executing their roles. We'd worked our way from the 22 to score in the corner.'

The away dressing-room fairly buzzed afterwards.

'Yeah, there was a lot of singing,' says Lam. 'We have our song. We sing "The Fields Of Athenry" as soon as we win. And there were a lot of good speeches, a lot of good chats. That was a big moment in the history of Connacht rugby.'

Jimmy Duffy recalls, 'We had won the pre-season game there, and they had some big guns playing. For the League game in Thomond, we didn't get carried away, but we genuinely believed that we'd do the business. It wasn't anything that Munster had or hadn't done. We had started to take the focus off others and on to ourselves, and I think that has been the biggest change in this organization. For a long time, you can rely on hard times and crutches, but they're excuses. You have to change your mindset. "It's an opportunity. What do we need to do to make this happen?"'

So instead of being weighed down by history, they embraced the opportunity to make it.

To put the callowness of the team further into perspective, Dillane, Buckley, Connolly, Masterson and Finlay Bealham had all been in the Corinthians pack for the wins over Shannon and away to Blackrock two years previously.

Dillane's roots and unlikely route into rugby are almost the stuff of folklore, but then again it was perhaps his natural calling, for he is actually a cousin of that famed Irish lock from Kerry, Moss Keane.

Dillane was born in Paris to an Irish mum, and his father comes from the Ivory Coast. When he was seven, his mum, Ellen, moved back to her native Tralee and famously bribed him and his older brother Cian with €5 to attend a training session in Tralee Rugby Club. He has described it as 'the best fiver she ever spent'.

His mother has remained central to her boys' rugby careers, augmenting her own nursing in the Bon Secours Hospital in Tralee with other jobs.

'She's a super mom,' says Jay Galvin, who was the club's director of rugby when the Dillanes first pitched up. 'She travelled the highways and the byways with Ultan in his younger days, to training and to games, to Munster games and Irish trials, and everything else.'

Like Galvin, everyone who encountered Dillane on his unlikely journey from Paris via Tralee and Galway to the Irish team talks about his humble, grounded and good-humoured personality. Here is a product of the club game, an immensely talented athlete who strives for self-improvement, all the while growing into his body and the game. It has only ever seemed a matter of when rather than if.

Through his exploits with Tralee in their underage ranks, Dillane played for the Munster Youths in the 2010–11 season. Duffy was then assistant coach to the Irish Youths (clubs) Under-18 team. The head coach Greg Lynch asked Duffy to run the rule over a Youths 'interpro' between Connacht and Munster in Dooradoyle.

'That was the first time I saw Ultan play, and I immediately thought, "Wow, who is this kid?" He was tall and gangly at the time but had a burst of energy constantly through the game. He had a lot to learn, but the way he threw himself about the field was something impressive.

'He was about 6 ft 5 in. at the time, and I spoke to Greg after the game and said, "Look, we need to get this kid up to Dublin and have a look at him." Needless to say, he made the squad that year.'

In the Irish Youths' first away win over their French counterparts, Dillane scored a barnstorming try with a galloping run from about 30 metres. He played in the Irish Under-19s again the following season, at the end of which Munster offered him a sub-academy contract. Duffy and Nigel Carolan had been keeping a close eye on him and offered Dillane a place in their full academy and, along with his brother Cian, places in NUIG while also putting them into Corinthians in 2012.

It's hard to believe now that bulking up was a priority for Dillane. 'Ultan always had a bit more to do in terms of his physical development. That's something he would initially have struggled with – his [lack of] weight,' says Duffy. 'He worked very, very hard with the S&C guys, and all of a sudden he kicked on. He's 6 ft 6 in. and 115 kg, but he's only going to get better and stronger.'

Midway into his third season with the Connacht academy, 2014–15, Dillane made his debut as a second-half replacement against Leinster at the RDS Arena, started in the 13–10 defeat away to Ulster and then came on again in the New Year's Day win at home to Munster. His first senior contract swiftly followed.

As with that New Year's Day win over Munster, Dillane was especially fired up for that first start of the season at Thomond Park in November.

'That was the night Ultan came of age,' says Duffy. 'Eoghan was bloody good, and Sean O'Brien was good too off the bench.

'Munster mauled us over the line, which was a real pain in the ass, to be honest. We defended the first one, but the touch judge called it an illegal takeout, so they got a second shot and we blew it, which was disappointing. There were a few sharp words on the Monday.'

Of Connolly, Duffy says, 'He has a big future. Putting his X factor in a box, it's his surge, his carrying ability. He is quite similar to David Wallace in that regard. You think you have him and all of a sudden he's gone again. I've huge time for James, and he's another that's learning fast. His attention to detail has gone through the roof; he goes around with a notebook now, asking questions and challenging himself.'

The win extended their lead over Munster, now down to third, to four points, with the Scarlets second but still two points adrift. But there were no wild celebrations on the journey home that night.

'We just took stock of what was coming up,' says Allnutt. 'We knew we were coming into a really important stage of the season, so we weren't getting carried away. It was a case of getting the bodies healed, as we had Cardiff away six days later.'

Friday, 4 December
Cardiff 20 Connacht 16

Connacht's storming of Thomond Park extended their winning sequence to eight matches. But six nights later they lost in Cardiff.

Lam made eight changes in personnel, most of them enforced, with one-time Ulster scrum-half Ian Porter making what would prove to be his only League start of the season. Muldoon made his 200th League appearance, but this is a luckless venue for Connacht.

'We had a massive injury crisis, but we were going quite well until half-time when we led 13–10,' says Lam. 'Ian Porter did his ankle, Marmo came on and was concussed straight away, so Matt Healy went into half-back with 39 minutes to go; then Quinn Roux had to be taken off with a bad head injury. We got stung badly in that game. Déjà vu.'

Beating Munster in Thomond Park had been a landmark win for this Connacht team, but in retrospect perhaps some took a little too much comfort from the result.

'I think maybe we started to believe in ourselves too much,' says Duffy. 'I felt a little complacency had crept in that week. We went over to Cardiff and lost, and I was pretty cross that night, to be honest. I don't think I slept afterwards. We had opportunities, and we had chances. You can't start looking at referees or officials for decisions that you may or may not be given.'

Connacht had scored one try off a maul but missed two others. In the Monday review, they decided there were to be no excuses. Given these chances, they simply had to take them.

Friday, 11 December
Connacht 25 Newcastle 10

Time to juggle. Facing into their tenth game of this 16-week bloc, the defeat to Cardiff had come at an additional cost, with Eoin McKeon and Roux suffering elbow and ankle injuries, while both scrum-halves, Marmion and Porter, along with Ronaldson, were also sidelined.

Lam made a dozen changes to his starting line-up, resting Aki, Muldoon and others, with just Muldowney, captain for the night, Carty and O'Halloran retained, but the latter pulled up in the warm-up and Healy changed position again, playing at full-back for the first time for Connacht.

Connacht led all the way from the first of Carty's six penalties before a late try by the returning Danie Poolman sealed the win.

'It was a physical game, but we came away with a very good win to keep that [European] journey on track,' says Lam.

Sunday, 20 December
Newcastle 29 Connacht 5

The management decided to fly to Newcastle on the Friday, two days before the game, as the flight on the Saturday morning was so early it would have meant an overnight stay in Dublin on the Friday anyway.

Such are the vagaries of travelling from the west. 'That can't be underestimated,' says Allnutt, speaking from many years of bitter experience. 'When you go to Italy, the trek to and from Dublin at either end really adds to travel time. Then you've got to round them all up, get on the bus, and stop on the way home for food, and it's another three hours by the time you get home. It can be a nightmare. The boys have coped with it for years, but for younger or newer players it takes a little adjusting.'

They stayed in the Marriott in Gosforth Park, near the racecourse, but there was no sampling of Newcastle's famous nightlife. The management went into town for a meal on the Saturday night but had an early finish, what with their 7.30 a.m. run the next morning.

So severe was Connacht's injury crisis at this juncture – all told 23 players were ruled out of this game – that they travelled with just 22 players. As he knew they would be facing Ulster at home a week later, Lam made another eight changes in personnel and several positional switches, as the captaincy passed to the long-serving George Naoupu.

Conán O'Donnell, their first-year academy prop from Sligo, made his first start. 'As always, it's around now when the season and the injuries take their toll,' says Lam from bitter experience. 'And we lost Danie Poolman [who started at full-back] early on in that game.'

Drawing 5–5 at half-time, Connacht went down to four second-half tries, two of them penalty tries, to compound a yellow card for Eoghan Masterson.

'In my view, Ben Whitehouse had a poor game that night,' maintains Lam. 'We scored in the opening minute, and he wrongly disallowed it. He awarded a penalty try to them with another wrong call and yellow-carded Eoghan Masterson. We started that game tremendously well, but it just blew away from us. We came away from that game barely intact. It was a day when everything went against us, and we just had to let that one go.'

The afternoon kick-off at least meant they could fly out of Newcastle that night to Dublin and take a bus home, returning to the Sportsground at almost 2 a.m.

Saturday, 26 December – St Stephen's Day
Connacht 3 Ulster 10

The squad trained on Christmas Eve to afford everyone Christmas Day off, about the only day of the year when the gates to the Sportsground stay locked.

'But the boys can't really blob out with the full Christmas dinner,' says Allnutt, who had even more sympathy for Ulster. 'The previous season we had to charter a plane [to Belfast], and you can't travel on Christmas Day because nothing is open to have food. It's a tough fixture, especially as there's a fair distance between us and Belfast.'

Lam rang the changes again, 12 in personnel, with front-line players Muldowney, Muldoon, Marmion and Aki all returning, and an outside three of Healy, Adeolokun and O'Halloran.

Connacht had only beaten Ulster once in their previous 18 attempts, and a dogged arm wrestle was settled by Nick Williams' 76th-minute try.

'There was a real sense that we blew that one,' recalls Lam. 'We knew we had to start really well, and we did. But we dropped the ball near the line and did all but score. It was a missed opportunity, but the mindset had been very good. It was 3–3 with 20 to go, and we missed a couple of kicks before Nick Williams barrelled over. It was similar to the previous year when we lost 13–10 at their ground – again we played well but missed opportunities.'

'That was tough, because we felt we'd done enough, but they scored late,' recalls Duffy. 'Five or six minutes in, we had a maul opportunity in the corner when we nearly went in from 25 metres, but one of their players joined on the wrong side, and they snaffled it. The backs had a couple of cracks, and it was a real disappointment.'

As it was Connacht's first defeat of the season at the Sportsground, for the first time there was no singing of 'The Fields' in a disconsolate home dressing-room.

'That was one positive, I suppose, that we didn't hear some of the boys singing!' quips Allnutt. 'Some of them are bloody good, but some of them can't hold a tune to save themselves. Nah, we love that song, and it's all part of the motivation for acquiring victories. Over the years, we didn't get to sing it a hell of a lot, so not being able to do so that day must have stuck with the boys.'

Friday, 1 January
Leinster 13 Connacht 0

The squad travelled by coach to Dublin on New Year's Day and, as usual when playing Leinster, had an early lunch in the Herbert Park Hotel. 'Dave McSharry's father is one of the owners, and we normally go there, prepare for the game, have our meetings and lunch, and then walk over to the RDS,' says Lam.

Leinster had first use of a strong wind on an utterly miserable, rain-lashed, howling night in the RDS, but Connacht restricted them to one Johnny Sexton penalty, withstanding several kicks to the corner by the home side. However, a highly contentious try awarded to Josh van der Flier by the officials when there appeared no clear evidence of a touchdown, and a late Ian Madigan penalty, meant Connacht returned west pointless.

'Conditions weren't great, and we didn't handle their high-ball game well at all,' admits Lam. 'We were right in that game until the decision, and we should have come out of it with at least a bonus point.'

'We did superbly well into that wind to keep them out,' says Duffy, 'and we thought, "We'll have a real crack here." But then we just didn't execute well. It was a good lesson for us. We didn't deserve to win. We were admirable and brave in the first half, but that doesn't win you matches unfortunately. That was a tough loss.'

Of some comfort was the return of Jake Heenan from a career-threatening injury for his first game of the season.

Sunday, 10 January
Scarlets 21 Connacht 19

Same old, same old.

'That was a killer blow, that one,' says Lam. Connacht started brightly, but Eoghan Masterson's touchdown was ruled out for a knock-on, one of two disallowed by the TMO that night. Even then, a scorching 80-metre finish by Healy helped them into a 10–0 lead. Connacht fell behind, before leading 19–18 through a penalty by Carty.

'Then we gave away a silly penalty with two minutes remaining,' says Lam in reference to the tip tackle which also earned Ronan Loughney a yellow card. 'That was a frustrating game, but I think many of the things we did in the back half of the campaign came from that difficult part of the season.'

'In the changing-room, we were angry,' says Allnutt, 'not with the way we played, but you're gutted to drop points. Away wins are so important, and we felt that we played well enough that day to win. It was a tough trip home that night.'

This fourth League defeat in succession since the win in Thomond Park in November dropped Connacht to fourth in the table, with Ulster and Munster three points behind, having played a game less.

Saturday, 16 January
Brive 21 Connacht 18

Returning to their Challenge Cup campaign, the squad left the Sportsground at 4 p.m. on the Thursday and stayed at the Carlton Hotel at Dublin airport for a 9.45 a.m. flight the next day.

After lunch at a hotel in Lyon, they took a bus to Brive. 'That took about five hours, because it was snowing on the way and the roads were brutal,' says Allnutt. 'We had to break it in half and have another stop at a service station, for the lads to get tea and coffee.'

By the time they reached their hotel in Brive, it was 7.30 p.m. After a 27-and-a-half-hour trip, they deferred their visit to the Stade Amédée-Domenech until the following morning.

'Yeah, not great,' remembers Lam, 'but it was nothing compared to Russia. After that, we could take any trip on the chin.'

Although Connacht played poorly, a try by Muldoon appeared to have rescued a draw. But for the second week running, a penalty in the last minute, this time by Thomas Laranjeira, condemned Connacht to their fifth defeat in a row, albeit four of them had been away.

Another blight on the night for the coaches was seeing the players begin to bitch at each other on the pitch. They flew home the next day, and at their squad review on the following Monday morning, a few grievances were aired and dealt with.

'That was possibly the real turning point of the season,' says Lam. 'A lot of players didn't play well at all. It was a game we should have won. But what we couldn't help noticing was how many back-to-back mistakes we were making. I sat with some of the leadership boys and said, "Fellas, what is going on here?" Everyone was getting frustrated and having a crack at each other.

'So it was a good checkpoint in the season to say that although we challenge each other during the week [in training], in a game we cannot bring back minute seven if a mistake has been made; we have to move on to minute eight. We were going from one mistake to the next, sometimes in the same play. So from that game on, we placed a real emphasis on a "next-job mentality".'

'It was refreshing,' says Duffy. 'It's my first year, but there's a lot of honesty in the group. That's one of Pat's best traits. If something needs to be addressed, it is addressed. He's bloody good at that, and it's good for the organization.'

Saturday, 23 January
Connacht 47 Enisei 5

A no-win-yet-must-win scenario, and a welcome win at that. Connacht needed a bonus point to have any hope of reaching the Challenge Cup quarter-finals again. O'Halloran, Healy, Buckley and Poolman scored tries to secure the five match points by half-time, and Newcastle's late win at home to Brive meant they were the only Irish side to reach the knockout stages of either Euro competition.

They would be away to Grenoble in the quarter-finals, but the change in mentality, shown by the determination to pursue a bonus-point win from the off, was another lesson for Lam.

'It was good to get back on the winning horse, but we knew we had to get five points, so we trained and prepared accordingly that week. Because of that game, I then realized we had to target the four tries for the rest of the season. We put that pressure on ourselves from then on. We were still in the top four, but because of those earlier losses we knew we'd have to chase bonus points, so we really cranked it up. We changed our mindset in the way we trained and the way we did things.'

'It doesn't take long to accumulate a run of losses,' says Duffy. 'But I think everybody trusted what we were doing or trying to achieve. Then we had the Enisei game here. It was only Enisei, but it was a win. It was job done. Right, next job.

'At no stage during that period did anyone here panic, players or coaches. "No, we'll get there. We'll get there." Coming out of that losing run was probably the most pleasing thing for me this season.'

Saturday, 30 January
Connacht 30 Scarlets 17

After the loss away to Brive and then beating Enisei at home, Connacht welcomed the Scarlets to the Sportsground. Connacht had lost four consecutive League games. It was also the last of their punishing bloc of 16 games in a row.

In the context of a 22-game League campaign, it doesn't strike you as a stand-out fixture, but on days like this leagues can be won, or certainly lost. After four Pro12 defeats in succession since that win over Munster, their season was in danger of unravelling. Some of the older hands had been through this before.

'The Scarlets at home was huge,' Muldoon stresses. 'We'd hit a losing run, and that was when everyone began thinking, "Aha, here we go again." Then we beat the Scarlets at home with a bonus-point try. The scrum was big, and we knew then we had a break of a week to recharge. We had momentum again.'

'It was the manner in which we did it,' says Duffy. 'The boys made a statement that day up front, and the whole team literally cut loose. Our scrum was strong and we scored off three mauls, which was brilliant, but it was also because of our threats elsewhere. They could see Robbie and Bundee in midfield, and they were worried about Niyi and Matt as well. That could take out their 7 off the back of a line-out. Pat always emphasizes it. If we're scoring in one area, it's because there are threats elsewhere. But we'd had two wins back to back and then a bit of a break, which was great.'

Not only had Connacht arrested their slide but by dint of accruing five points and sending the Scarlets home empty-handed, they moved up to second place behind the Welsh region on points difference. Admittedly, only four points covered the top six, and Connacht's three Irish rivals could all overtake them with their game in hand.

But Muldoon was aware that opportunity had knocked again. 'We all knew we then had Dragons, Zebre, Ospreys at home and Edinburgh away in the international break for the Six Nations. We told ourselves that three or four wins here would mean that other teams would welcome back their internationals, look at the results and the table, and wonder, "What the heck have Connacht just done?"'

Going into the Six Nations window, Connacht had four games to make another charge.

18

Never Die Wondering
(Jake Heenan)

On New Year's Day, halfway through the 2015–16 season, Jake Heenan played for Connacht against Leinster in the RDS. It was his first game in nine months, and only his sixth since February 2014, during his first season with the province.

He could possibly have played a few weeks earlier, but he wanted to be sure of his fitness. 'Named to start against Leinster in the RDS was pretty intimidating,' he says, smiling.

The squad travelled on match-day, basing themselves in the Herbert Park Hotel as usual, before walking across Anglesea Road to the RDS for the 5 p.m. kick-off on an utterly foul night.

'I was nervous but was really grateful to be starting and to have the backing from Pat. During those times when you doubt your abilities, it's so important to have someone like him backing you. And the conditions suited me to a T. Wet game, lots of collisions. Ideal for me to get back into it.'

Johnny Sexton kicked off, John Muldoon carried the ball into the first ruck, and from the recycle Kieran Marmion passed to Heenan.

'First ruck, I got to carry into Jack McGrath or one of those boys; put on a bit of footwork, try to find a bit of a hole. Great! Thirty seconds into the match, I'd had contact. Into it.'

His head ached afterwards. 'I was a bit rusty, so I was running into everything bolt upright and at one stage collided with Dave Kearney.' But Heenan's shoulder was pain-free. He was back.

He was taken off with Connacht losing 10–0, and it would finish 13–0. A grim night for the province, but Heenan is not ashamed to admit he was close to elated.

'I hate to say it, but I couldn't get enough. When I walked off that field and we were 10–0 down, I gave Dave Ellis a big hug. Mate, I couldn't have been happier.

'Dave and I had worked very closely together. What I really like about working with him is that we seem to coach one another almost. He'll never tell me how to do anything without first asking me how I want to do it. So, every time I've come back from injury he'll suggest a way he thinks it should be done. We'll find something together that works for me, and that's why I've been able to keep improving, because we trust each other. We've become quite close.'

Heenan's journey from boyhood in New Zealand to the west of Ireland echoes that of many others from the southern hemisphere, even that of Ellis himself to a degree, though of course with subtle differences.

Heenan was born and reared in Whangarei, a pretty town on the northern coast of New Zealand's North Island. 'It was just me, my dad [Hugh] and older brother [Ben]. We had a small farmhouse outside town. About 300 acres, I think. It was mostly beef farming when we were younger, and then Dad got into horses as we were getting older.'

His parents broke up when he was very young. His English mother relocated to Auckland and remarried, as would his dad later.

'I never experienced the break-up. I was too young. So it was just the three lads, and I had a great time. We went everywhere on the farm with Dad. We had a really good childhood. Went to school [Whangarei High School] in town, and because we were near the coast we went fishing and diving regularly. We were fortunate to be outdoors so much, and there was a lot of back-yard rugby with my older brother. Typical, I guess.'

He was three years old when pictured in his first team photograph with the local Marist club, alongside his brother, then six, although

Heenan is not sure how much rugby he played. Typically too, he played barefoot and reckons he purchased his first pair of boots at about 12 years of age.

'I remember one day I refused to play because of the frost. I was crying on the sideline because the frost hurt my feet so much. Dad was refereeing, and when I finally summoned the courage to run on he said, "No, game's over." So I also remember my first game with boots, when I was about 12. I was running around pulling up my socks the whole time. But, no, it was all good. All the kids played. It was cool. We'd spend every Saturday playing rugby from 8.30 or 9.00 in the morning until just after midday. Hundreds and hundreds of kids.'

If his dad wasn't refereeing, he was coaching. He also played for Marist Old Boys, and on trips to Guernsey and Scotland combined playing rugby with some sheep shearing.

His parents having both remarried, Heenan now has a younger sister Taila on his mum's side, and two younger brothers, Garth (13) and Thane (8) on his dad's. He describes his full brother Ben as, simply, 'my best mate', adding, 'He's scaffolding north of Perth at a gas plant.' Both his brother and father have been to Galway, his dad for the month of October 2015 when, alas, Heenan was sidelined.

His school rugby went well, but at 15 he left home and went to live with his grandmother, Jill.

'She was great. I couldn't have done what I did without her. She gave me a home in town. She could be pretty tough, but she fed me, and she looked after me. She was always there, and she was a wonderful grandmother. She still lives in the same house in Whangarei. I'd never sent a postcard in my life, but I send her postcards.'

For a while, though, while living with his grandmother, Heenan admits he lost his way a tad, skipping school to go fishing and diving. Rugby, in a way, kept him on the straight and narrow, as it were.

'The year before, a load of boys were picked up by the Blues Under-18s, and I thought, "That's awesome. Imagine that!" So I stayed in school for another year, to give rugby a go, really.' However, when he told his grandmother he was going back to school in order to pursue his rugby ambitions, she was aghast. 'Why not get a real job?' she asked him.

But schools rugby served its purpose, earning him a trial in Auckland. Remarkably, he'd played at prop until he was about 14, then converted to a lock cum 6, and was picked in an Auckland underage trial as a number 8. Then, fatefully, Pat Lam was one of the coaches that day and moved him to open-side during the game.

'I'd never played 7 before, but then I was picked for the Auckland Blues Under-18s at 7. I was pretty shaky at first, because I hadn't played at that level before, but I played better in the second game.' The second was against the Hurricanes in the final, which the Blues won.

Amid a general shortage of 7s, he then made the New Zealand Schools team. He hadn't even known of its existence. 'You didn't really hear about it up north, and I don't think anyone from Whangarei had made that team in a long time. And I'm the first to admit I was extremely lucky, the way everything fell into place.'

The NZ Schools side played Otago and Tonga as warm-ups for the big one against Australia, which they won, in Dunedin in 2010. 'We beat them fairly well. It was really fast, and I was playing against bigger guys. It was awesome. On the back of that, I moved to Auckland when I made their academy.'

Heenan had two and a half years there, making the Auckland Under-20s and then captaining the NZ Under-20s at the Junior World Cup in South Africa in 2012. But he was on the bench for both the semi-final and final, when they lost to the hosts.

He admits his rival, Hugh Blake, was playing well. 'He's now playing for Scotland Sevens and Glasgow Warriors. It was disappointing, but you don't let something like that spoil an amazing tournament. To play national age-grade rugby was pretty special.'

Although he made the Auckland Under-20s again the following season, he couldn't crack the Auckland ITM Cup team, whereupon Lam called offering him a chance to join Connacht in May 2013. Heenan was 21.

'In all honesty, I didn't really want to move. I was happy.' His ambition was to play for Auckland, the Blues and one day the All Blacks, and moreover Derren Witcombe had asked him to join Heenan's home province of Northland. As he's qualified to play for England through his mum, there was also interest from there.

'But the way I figured it, worst-case scenario, I'd have three years' professional rugby, working really hard on my craft and my body, and become a much better professional.

'The other bonus was travel. Because of rugby, you miss out on your European OE [overseas expedition]. I never had much money anyway, so I saw it as an opportunity to see some of the world and enjoy a bit of football.'

His dad was supportive of what was a brave move for a 21 year old.

'Pat also made it really personal. It wasn't me and an agent; it was me and him. It was never really about the money for me. I couldn't really demand much, because I didn't have the CV, so it was more about the rugby and the life. And knowing Pat, it would be a good brand of rugby.'

He'd also known of Connacht through a childhood friend from Whangarei whom he played alongside at school, Isaac O'Grady. His father hailed from Mayo, and O'Grady played for the Connacht Under-20s with Robbie Henshaw and Kieran Marmion on the team that won the Interpros.

'Isaac gave me a Connacht shirt, which I wore all the time. I actually have a photo of me fishing in that shirt and a pair of Galwegians shorts back in 2011 or 2012. Isaac told me about the nightlife and plenty of really cool bars. So I had some knowledge of Connacht.'

Heenan arrived in June 2013.

'There'd been a big shift in their game, but it wasn't a big transition for me because it was the same kind of rugby I'd been playing back home. I was also aware of the culture Pat was trying to instil. I moved in with a couple of good boys, Conor Finn and James Rael.'

Heenan was a replacement in Connacht's first two games, at home to Zebre and away to Cardiff. The flight home from Cardiff was overbooked, and as Heenan and Parks were last in line they had to take a bus to Birmingham, a flight to Dublin and made it home the next day to Galway. 'That was my first away game.'

When Willie Falloon was injured, Heenan was pitched straight into the team in round three at home to Ulster, and went on to start 11 games in succession. Despite a run of defeats, he was enjoying playing pro rugby week to week, and was named Connacht's Player of the Month for October.

'It was tough after games, and coming in some Mondays was pretty bleak, but, mate, I really loved the rugby. I could run around and hit anything I wanted, and I was making plenty of carries.'

There was also the highlight of that win in Toulouse. 'I was rattling off their names before the game. I was pretty star-struck. Thierry Dusautoir! I was a huge admirer of his.

'Two years previously, Dusautoir had been International Player of the Year. They also had Hosea Gear. I remember tackling him. I swear I had him tackled and he just ran off! It was so cool playing in a big stadium and against one of the giants of European rugby. To win that was amazing. When Kieran [Marmion] scored, I think I pushed him over. It should have been me who scored it. He took that one.'

Two weeks later, Heenan injured his shoulder against the Dragons. Rested for three games, he had surgery booked for his shoulder on the Tuesday after an upcoming run of three games against Saracens, Glasgow and Edinburgh. That, however, wasn't his main problem on that horrendous day away to Saracens.

'I remember being really hyped up. I really wanted to make a physical impact, but my collisions were very average. I learned a big lesson that day. When I'm relaxed, I'm not only a lot better but I'm a lot more physical. That was a big learning for me in what was all around a pretty shitty day at the office.'

In other words, he had been too pumped up for his own good.

Before the Edinburgh game a few weeks later, he knew he was having his shoulder reconstructed the following Tuesday. After that game, his season was thus done. It had a strangely liberating effect. Edinburgh's kick-off literally came straight to him. Bring it on.

'I don't try to run over people, certainly not Edinburgh with their big South African forwards. But I remember picking the two biggest boys I could find and running at them as fast as I could. "Damn it. I'm done. Let's have a bit of fun." I shifted a rib or something, and it hurt. But it was a great way to get into the game. I'll never forget that one.' He played the full 80 too.

His first Connacht season had been cut short, but it wasn't the end of his world. Heenan was assured that his shoulder would be stronger and he'd be back for the start of the 2014–15 season. He knew he had to mature physically and saw this break as his opportunity. However, as he entered the contact stage of his recovery in the 2014 pre-season, he felt his shoulder wasn't right.

'During an internal game in pre-season, the physio called me aside. "Mate, your shoulder's not right, it's lax and it's loose. It's not good." This was after six months of supposedly getting it right, except it wasn't.'

Nonetheless, he played through the internal game quite comfortably. Falloon had played the other warm-up games, and in the week of the League opener at home to the Dragons, Lam called Heenan into his office.

'He asked me straight out, "Are you good for it? For a start, are you good for it?" And I didn't think about it. "Yeah, of course." I remember walking out of his office thinking, "Willie has been playing really well. I've played nothing. I'm not right for this." But I backed myself, and actually I went on to have a really good game. Then in the 78th minute, I popped it again. That was me out until midway through the season.'

After further surgery, Heenan didn't play again until the Scarlets, away, on 15 February. That was the first of four consecutive games, culminating in the 18–17 defeat away to Cardiff, when his shoulder popped yet again.

'That was my darkest day in rugby,' he admits. 'I'd need surgery again. I remember thinking, "I'm done. I've had enough of this." George Naoupu was my roommate in the hotel, and if you ever want a man when you're on the edge, George is that man. He packed my bag and sorted everything for me. I was lucky to have him around that night and the next day.'

Heenan's injury was diagnosed as a muscle tear. He rehabbed it for a month but came to the realization that it was not improving. So he underwent his third shoulder operation in May of 2015.

His first operation had been to put his shoulder ligaments back into place. The second was a 'Latarjet', a procedure used to treat recurring shoulder dislocations caused by bone loss, and the third was to re-attach his subscapularis muscle, which had ripped off his bone. Heenan is all too familiar with these terminologies.

'The surgeon, Lennard Funk, in Manchester, who'd performed the second surgery, told me, "Look, if you want to take your time, I'll back you." I said, "No, we'll give it a go." And he advised me there was a 30 per cent chance that I wouldn't return to play again.

'The big concern was that the tendon was too damaged and that he would need to take a tendon off my pec, just to have a functioning shoulder, never mind a shoulder to play rugby. But the tendon was fully intact. It just needed to be put back. Essentially, he chipped into the bone, put a screw into the bone with a bunch of wires, and then wired the muscle on to the bone. Mate, he uses the same tools as a builder. He sent me the video. It's hammer-and-chisel sort of stuff.'

The surgery was a success, and within a few days Heenan heard with relief the words: 'You're going to be all right.'

It would still be a long road back. He went on holiday and returned resolving to learn from past recuperations.

'I've spent a lot of time with the shoulder injury, and, yeah, I had to rock in a bit earlier than the rest of the boys. But I was being paid to come in each morning, exercise to stay fit with my mates, and then watch a pitch session. As I improved, I started throwing a ball around.

'I was still travelling whenever I had the chance. I still had all my mates. I was still able to work out in the gym. After my first surgery, I made the 10k bike trial my baby. I picked up a bit of study. There were so many positives going on. Yes, it was a long slow process, but Pat was very accommodating, and the S&C staff and the physios were great. They took it slowly, made sure everything was right.'

He'd learned from his first two operations not to rush his

recovery. Where before his approach had been to return and make a difference as soon as possible, this time he realized he wanted to prolong his career as a rugby player.

'The goal I set myself was to play ten games in the season. It wasn't about being the best. I just wanted to keep playing. So that approach helped me. We took it really slowly, got everything right. It will never be 100 per cent, but I'm really happy with where it is now.'

Cue the comeback against Leinster at the RDS. Heenan was back at last, doing something which at Connacht, for the first time in his life, has earned him a decent income and allowed him to focus on his rugby as a true professional.

'Speaking of the Monday blues, I love getting in on a Monday and all the aspects of the job. The other thing I really love is travelling. Any time we get more than three days off I look on Skyscanner for the cheapest flight to somewhere. I love Europe. I've been to Amsterdam with the boys – my first away trip – to Tenerife with Niyi. I went to Prague with Finlay and Niyi, and spent time travelling around France.'

He has a dog called Brody, which he reckons is a cross between a Jack Russell and a collie. He now shares a house with Adeolokun and says he hasn't had a bad day in Galway since he arrived. 'Through the winter, there are plenty of places to eat and drink. The friendliness of the people makes it very easy to live here, and the supporters are great. When I first saw the Sportsground, I thought, "I've played at club grounds which looked similar to this." But I'll never forget my first night coming out here, with "I'm Shipping Up To Boston" by the Dropkick Murphys playing and the noise of the crowd. It was unbelievable. It's a great stadium to play in. I've looked back at my first start against Ulster, and coming on to the pitch I had a smile from ear to ear.'

Unlike many players, Heenan has not been reticent about declaring his ambition to emulate his role model, Richie McCaw, as the best number 7 in the world. He attributes this to when he was advised by the Northland Academy manager that he would be better off focusing on his studies, as they didn't envisage his becoming a professional rugby player.

'I went home and cried that night, but Dad straightened me out. I started studying sports psychology and met some sports psychologists. I really enjoyed that sort of thing.'

He'd always looked up to McCaw and Muhammad Ali. 'Perhaps Muhammad Ali is an extreme example, but I suppose the big thing for me was their courage. When John Kirwan had just been appointed the Blues coach, after Pat left, I met with a psychologist who'd also become a good mate and said in passing, "I'd love to sit down with John Kirwan and tell him what I want to achieve." He answered, "Well, give him a call." We talked about it some more and he said, "Well, your potential will only go as far as your courage allows it." That stuck with me, so I rang John Kirwan's secretary and met with him.

'I played in the Blues' development side and, although I didn't go on to play for the Blues, that was really good for me. It is uncomfortable, even now, to say I can be the best 7 in the world. It's not a natural feeling, but I've found from experience that the braver I can be in these situations, the greater dividend it pays.'

Accordingly, on his wall at home in Galway, underneath the words 'Have a Go' is the goal: 'Best number 7 in the world'. He also has a few others around it, the largest of them being: 'I know where I'm going and I know the truth, and I don't have to be what you want me to be. I'm free to be what I want' – Muhammad Ali.

'I think those words came from his religious beliefs, which I probably admire more than his sporting achievements, but he believed in himself.'

Heenan's desire to live by those words also means he'll have fewer regrets.

'If I never achieve anything more than I've achieved right now, I'll be a happy man because I've never shied away from it. I've always backed myself, so I don't think I'll ever die wondering.'

19

The 2015–16 run-in

After Heenan's return against the Scarlets, the Connacht players and management alike were delighted to have a blank weekend, their first since early October. Jimmy Duffy, for one, admits he was simply 'shattered'. Everyone was given the week off. But there was a problem. The Dragons away fixture, scheduled for the Friday week after the Scarlets game, was then brought forward by 24 hours. Nevertheless, Lam decided to stick to his word and not bring any player back before the Monday.

This gave them a two-day build-up before another long travel day on the Wednesday. But that bloc of 16 games in succession meant the preparation was now as much mental as physical. Relatively refreshed, they also had their revised match-day target. Four tries.

Thursday, 11 February
Dragons 21 Connacht 26

Despite first-half tries by Matt Healy, taking a sharp line off Aly Muldowney's inside pass as first receiver, and a well-executed backline move finished by O'Halloran, Connacht trailed 21–14 entering the last quarter. But a try off their potent maul by Masterson and Aki's close-range finish earned a five-point haul.

'We actually scored four good tries that night,' says Lam. 'But like every game against the Dragons, we clock off and let them back in. They're a gritty team, always difficult to shake off.'

'We didn't play brilliantly,' says Duffy. 'It was touch and go, but we were clinical at the right times. We won ugly that night. But to win with a bonus point while not playing to your potential is a real positive, and we said as much in the changing-room afterwards.'

They also rejoined Ulster at the top of the table, trailing them on points difference.

Saturday, 20 February
Zebre 34 Connacht 51

In a mad-cap game at the Stadio Sergio Lanfranchi, Healy's third try sealed a bonus point by the 47th minute, but it wasn't until Adeolokun scored his second in the 66th minute that Connacht effectively sealed a six tries to four romp in the Parma sun.

'The attack was on fire, but the transition to defence was terrible,' admits Lam.

'A rollercoaster,' says Duffy. 'Everybody came to play that day, but nobody came to defend! As Pat calls them, "coach killers"!'

'Poor Eoghan Masterson suffered a bad injury in that game,' he continues. The 22-year-old from Portlaoise, where he cut his teeth, played for the Leinster Youths team and then captained an Irish Youths team featuring Dillane. Eligible for Scotland through his father, Masterson played for the Scottish Under-20s in the World Cup after playing for the Irish Under-20s in the Six Nations. He then approached Carolan seeking a trial, which gives an indication of his ambition.

He trained for a few weeks without a contract, impressing Carolan, Duffy and Lam sufficiently to earn a place in the academy. But a bad knee injury in that Zebre game would require two operations and rule him out for the remainder of the season, though he had been a near regular until then.

'He'd been brilliant for us until that point,' says Duffy. 'It was tough on him, but he's got a huge future too. A bright guy and a future leader, I'd imagine.

'A big boy, 6 ft 4 in., 110 kg, and a massive aptitude and potential to improve. He's a driven young man and brilliant in 'the jackal'. He was winning one or two turnovers per game. He works his backside off and he can also play at 6, 7 and 8.'

This sent Connacht two points clear of Leinster at the top of the table, and with Ulster surprisingly losing at home to the Scarlets the following Sunday, they stayed there entering round 16.

Saturday, 27 February
Connacht 30 Ospreys 22

The Ospreys, boosted by Rhys Webb's return after a long lay-off, travelled to Galway intent on revenge and, like Connacht, also chasing their fourth win in a row.

Connacht led a high-quality game from Aki's try in the first minute, when he finished powerfully from Healy's offload. MacGinty did likewise from Adeolokun's pass out of the tackle, before Healy himself finished brilliantly in the 51st minute for his fifth try in three games. But Connacht were grateful to the officials wrongly ruling out Sam Davies' finish for a double movement before Ronaldson pushed the home side two scores clear.

What's more, Connacht had won without Muldoon. It was the only League game in two seasons in which their skipper did not feature, and ultimately he would start in all but two of the other 45 matches. Over the course of the season, he'd play over 1,000 minutes. 'We had to give Mul a rest,' says Lam. Tom McCartney captained the team.

'I'd watched Tom play before, but I didn't think he'd be so good,' admits Muldoon. 'Bundee is Bundee, and rightly he gets so much credit, but Tom's been phenomenal for us over the last two years. He sits beside me in the changing-room, and we've got on well since day one. He plays every week and never puts in a bad shift.'

Muldoon himself would be Connacht's Forward of the Year. For Duffy, Muldoon is a coach's dream.

'His most endearing characteristic is his honesty. There are no secrets with that man, but you need that to be successful. He's played some of the best rugby of his career this season. And it's special because he's from here and he's soldiered so long through good and bad times. He embodies everything that is good about the organization. He's a top player, a top man and respected by everybody here.

'His game time, for a back-rower, is off the charts, especially in such an attritional position, but there's something special there. You only meet a few people like that in your career, and I'm fortunate to have worked with him this season. Like Brian O'Driscoll, Paul O'Connell in Munster and Rory Best up north, he's our warrior, definitely.'

But winning without Muldoon was significant too, admits Duffy. 'Similar to Aly, they're core guys to the team, and it's important to win when they're not there, because you can't rely too heavily on some players. It's that old "nobody is irreplaceable" thing.' Even if some, such as Muldoon, are more irreplaceable than others.

The game also marked George Naoupu's last start in a Connacht jersey. After a season with Connacht in 2009–10, Naoupu then joined Japanese side Kobelco Steelers for the 2010–11 season before returning and for the next two seasons was simply – pound for pound – Connacht's best player.

His influence waned a tad in his last two seasons but he never grumbled. 'Great fella,' says Duffy. 'First time here, he was a huge crowd favourite and then went to Japan before re-signing. He's well respected by the coaches and players, and one of his best characteristics is his positivity. If he wasn't involved, he never let any disappointment show. He was good with the young lads and a good support to the senior leaders, whether in or out of the team. He's been a huge asset to the club and a crowd favourite. They absolutely love the guy here, absolutely adore him.'

Although they fell short of another bonus point, Connacht's first double over the Ospreys since 2004 cemented their place atop the table. With one eye on finishing in the top six, by denying the Ospreys even a bonus point Connacht extended their advantage over the Welsh region, who'd drop to eighth by the end of that round, to 16 points. Next up were Edinburgh, in fifth place and 12 points off Connacht.

Friday, 4 March
Edinburgh 23 Connacht 28

After their one-point win over the Scarlets the previous week, Alan Solomons and his Edinburgh team had targeted this potential double over Connacht as a significant stepping stone towards their own top-six ambitions.

But Connacht were on fire, creating a host of try-scoring chances and clinically converting four set-piece attacking platforms into tries by A. J. MacGinty, Jake Heenan, Aki and Eoin McKeon for a bonus-point win. The sole blemish on their night's work was allowing Edinburgh a bonus point with the game's last kick.

Muldoon, restored for this game, recalls, 'After beating Scarlets, Dragons, Zebre and the Ospreys, that was a huge win for us in Edinburgh. Huge! We didn't play perfectly but, as I said in the dressing-room afterwards, there was absolutely no panic at all on the pitch. Everyone just did their stuff, no bitching and no moaning. We scored four tries against Edinburgh, who at the time were going really well, and they walked off deflated.

'Afterwards, one or two of them said, "You're the best team we've played all year." That was nice to hear. We'd Leinster next in three weeks' time in Galway after the Six Nations. But we also knew we could play better than we did.

'I said to the lads, "Fellas, that's a big win for us. We've scored four tries here, which is a graveyard for us, and the f***ing great thing is we actually could have played better and scored more tries." And everyone thought the same.'

'Another learning for us that night,' says Lam, 'which we'd use in the Leinster game; when we kicked to them, they counter-attacked very well. It flagged to us that we needed to think about how we exited and not give other teams a chance to run back at us.'

From now on, come hell or high water, Connacht would keep the ball rather than kick it; no heed would be given to criticisms of their 'exit strategy' thereafter.

This sixth win in a row (five of them with bonus points), with the last five in the League, opened up a 16-point gap between Connacht, still in first, and sixth-placed Edinburgh. Effectively, this was the night Connacht announced they were here to stay by securing a top-six place and qualification for the European Champions Cup. Connacht now had bigger targets to aim for.

It made for a satisfying review on the Monday before they were granted a week off, as the Six Nations finale meant a three-week gap before Leinster's visit.

But, for once, not all the squad were then on holiday. The next weekend, for the first time in the province's history, five Connacht players played for Ireland in the same match. Robbie Henshaw, whose anticipated move to Leinster at the end of the season had been confirmed midway through the Six Nations, started in the win over Italy, while Nathan White, Finlay Bealham, Ultan Dillane and Kieran Marmion were all brought on as replacements. The five finished the match and were photographed together.

As bulk suppliers to Joe Schmidt's squads, Leinster are used to welcoming back a raft of internationals after the November window or Six Nations. But welcoming back a quintet of Irish internationals from the Six Nations was more new ground for Connacht.

'It showed how tangible that goal is for the other players,' says Duffy. 'It makes it achievable. That was the most pleasing thing for us as a coaching group. I think every Irish player in any of the provincial set-ups should realize how close they actually are. A couple of injuries and all of a sudden you're into that team and at the next level.'

Nothing Duffy or any of the other coaches might say to their academy players could replicate the impact of those five players returning from the Six Nations.

'Ultan lives with Eoghan Masterson and James Connolly, so those two lads are then thinking, "I want that too." They wanted it anyway, but now they'll want it that bit more.'

And that filters all the way down to the other academy players, given recent graduates Dillane and Bealham were only in their first and second seasons as professionals. Indeed, prior to the 2015–16 season, Bealham had only started one Pro12 game and Dillane a mere three.

Bealham's example is further inspiration for academy props such as Saba Meunargia, of Georgian origin, who has played for the Irish Under-18s and 19s; so too Jamie Dever, a product of Mayo and the Westport club, and Conán O'Donnell, one of their latest batch from Sligo along with Irish Under-20s lock Cillian Gallagher. 'They're all pushing each other, and the mentor system seems to be working,' says Duffy.

After Ireland's concluding Six Nations win over Scotland, Connacht's Irish quintet returned to training on the Tuesday before the Leinster game. 'It was a massive buzz for everybody,' reflects Lam. 'It had received a lot of media attention, and all the boys were talking about it.'

Lam formally invited all five of them to the front of the room at the team meeting. 'It was a big, big moment, and it was a good week, because we'd talked about this being where we wanted to be. Who would have thought before the Six Nations that Connacht against Leinster would be No. 1 v No. 2 – a top-of-the-table clash? If we had beaten Leinster before, it was usually a case of taking them by surprise. But there was no room for excuses with this one. If we were to have serious ambitions, this was the type of game you want to play. This was as close to a test as the League can throw up. There was huge media attention, we were playing the best in the country, with points on offer. It was a great learning experience for the guys.'

Connacht went into this summit meeting as the League's leading try scorers, but with the credo that attack was the best form of defence, it was inevitable that tries had been conceded.

'We spent the first five months of the season working so hard on our attack that we did shag all D [defence],' says Muldoon. 'Come Six Nations time, everyone knew our attacking game. It just needed little tweaks here and there, so then it was time to focus on our D. Up to then, we were making a habit of scoring four tries and conceding three.'

At the bottom of their Honours Board, Connacht's tries for and against are updated each week. As Lam was speaking at one meeting during the Six Nations, Muldoon noted the rather high tally – on both counts.

'I very rarely stop listening to Pat or whoever is talking, but I remember thinking, "Jeeze, we've scored 50 and conceded 35 or whatever. We've no notion of winning a league if we keep doing that." As Pat called the meeting to a halt, I got out my phone and checked Leinster's stats. They'd only conceded 14 tries or something. I thought, "We ain't gonna win nothing like this." I started dropping it into conversation with some of the lads. It's funny, as then it starts rippling through the squad.

'I then spoke with Pat about it. "If we are going to win a championship, we've got to stop leaking so many tries."

'Pat said, "Oh, it's funny you should mention that. Willie [Ruane] was on to me as well about that. What's your thoughts on it?"

'I said, "There's nothing wrong with our D. It's the time we're spending on it."

'He said, "Yeah, we've been talking about this in the management meetings."

'The final straw was the Zebre game,' recalls Muldoon of that 51–34 win in Parma. 'We scored six and conceded four. Pat was like, "Yeah, let's start doing more here."'

It was just a tweak. Connacht began devoting 20 minutes or so more to their defence each Tuesday. They still leaked tries against the Ospreys and Edinburgh, before having a timely three weeks to hone their defence before the Leinster game.

Saturday, 26 March
Connacht 7 Leinster 6

The extended capacity of 7,300 had long since been a sell-out as Connacht, sitting proudly atop the table, welcomed Leinster for a Saturday teatime fixture. Nigel Owens and the Sky cameras were there too. Connacht were dining with the League's glitterati.

Lam restored Marmion and White to the starting line-up, easing Bealham and Henshaw back on the bench, while affording Dillane a week off. Hence, despite the Leinster midfield of Ben Te'o and Garry Ringrose, Lam gave Peter Robb his first League start and retained another academy player, Sean O'Brien, in the back-row.

Leo Cullen restored a dozen of his Six Nations contingent. Fergus McFadden, Cian Healy, Richardt Strauss, Rhys Ruddock and Ian Madigan started, while half the starting Irish pack – Jack McGrath, Mike Ross, Devin Toner and Jamie Heaslip – were included on their decidedly heavyweight, all-international bench, along with Eoin Reddan, Sean Cronin, Noel Reid and Zane Kirchner.

Leinster won the toss and gave Connacht first use of the Atlantic wind, blowing in, as ever, from the Bohermore end.

Leinster opted for orthodox exit strategies whereas, true to their vow, Connacht counter-attacked with the wind and in the second half eschewed kicking into it by passing, running and recycling, then passing, running and recycling some more.

So, when Luke McGrath's box-kick almost boomeranged, Robb fielded the ball and Tiernan O'Halloran counter-attacked. The ball was recycled and moved wide to Niyi Adeolokun. The winger's previously non-existent kicking game, honed by Dave Ellis and Andre Bell on the training ground, saw him chip ahead for Marmion to win the touchdown inches before the dead-ball line at the College Road end.

'That came from our counter-attacking structure,' says Lam, 'and "Niysi" put in a good kick. He'd been practising that a lot. When Niysi first arrived, he couldn't kick; his improvement over the second half of the campaign was straight off his work on the training ground with Andre and Dave. And it gave him a lot of confidence.'

The Sportsground went wild.

'At half-time, we talked about backing our fitness, that if we all shared the workload – that is, everyone carries, everyone cleans out – we could do this,' says Lam. 'There was a real sense of "Let's go for it".'

Even so, a 7–0 buffer appeared insufficient as they ran into the second-half wind, all the more so when Madigan's second penalty trimmed the lead to a point just past the hour and Leinster unloaded that bench.

'When they unloaded their bench, we just went up another gear,' says Lam.

Muldoon recalls, 'We knew that we gave them a bloody hard game in the RDS, and we were very disappointed with our second half. We also knew they'd come down all guns blazing.

'I knew it would be a tight game and that a small little thing could win or lose it. But during the game I realized our lads were mentally on their money. We made a few errors, but I knew it wasn't through lack of effort, and I sensed the lads weren't going to let Leinster over the line.'

It came down to the last play, a five-metre scrum to Leinster at the College Road end. Leinster's one area of clear supremacy had been their scrum. 'The only thing that worried me was the possibility of a scrum penalty,' says Muldoon. 'That was my only fear. I knew if we got the ball out of the scrum, they wouldn't cross our line. And unless it was a pretty obvious scrum penalty, Nigel [Owens] wasn't going to give it.'

Indeed, as Leinster held the ball in the scrum, Owens was not for deciding the game with a penalty. Nor would he let Connacht run down the clock with re-set scrums. This would be a Nigel Owens endgame.

Thus, when Dominic Ryan carried hard and Eoin McKeon made his 23rd tackle of the game, Aki did enough to dislodge the ball for Muldoon to complete the game's final turnover. Caolin Blade hoofed the ball over the crowd behind the goal and into the front car park. Cue delirium.

Connacht had defiantly kept tackling through a nerve-shredding final quarter. Lam said to the media afterwards, 'Rugby's more than a game. It's about life. You build relationships, you go through things together and you build and create memories.'

This was old-school. But it was also a reward, as Lam saw it, for their systems and structures, and their passing game. 'I think we broke a record in that game by throwing over 280 passes. It was massive, not just the win but the confidence it gave us in our game.'

Connacht were also four points clear at the top of the table.

Friday, 1 April
Ulster 18 Connacht 10

The auguries were not good for Connacht. The last time they'd won in Belfast, Seán Lemass had just completed his first year as Taoiseach, John F. Kennedy and Richard Nixon had just conducted the first presidential televised debate, Alfred Hitchcock's *Pyscho* was in the cinema, Floyd Patterson became the unified heavyweight champion of the world and, eh, Burnley were champions of the Football League.

It was November 1960 to be precise.

A. J. MacGinty's shoulder injury against Leinster meant he joined Carty and Ronaldson on the sidelines, and so Lam gave Shane O'Leary – a Cork-born centre cum out-half who'd played with Young Munster and come through the Munster underage ranks – his first League start at 10. Through his mum's lineage, O'Leary had played for the Canadian Under-20s and then for a season with Grenoble before pitching up at Connacht. Robbie Henshaw was now the out-half back-up!

Ulster welcomed back their Six Nations leading lights, Rory Best, Andrew Trimble and Jared Payne, with Iain Henderson making his first start since December, and led 11–0 after Best scored off a huge rumbling maul. But Connacht were rewarded for some typically ambitious rugby with a superbly worked try for Blade. 'A cracking try straight off the training ground,' says Lam.

They then withstood Ulster's late pursuit of a bonus point when reduced to 13 men by yellow cards for O'Leary and O'Brien. 'That performance underlined our character,' says Lam.

'We lost, but in a way we got more out of that game than some of our wins,' says Muldoon. 'We walked away with a lot of kudos. With 20 minutes to go, I felt, "This is going to test us now." We had a man in the bin and then a few minutes later another one. "This is going to test us even more now." They tried to pummel us up front, without much change. Walking off, I felt we'd turned a corner.

'In the dressing-room, I spoke to the boys: "I haven't said this too often when we've lost, but, lads, I'm ****ing proud of everyone in here. Don't underestimate what fear that's put in others watching it. They'll have wondered, 'How did Ulster not score more?'" And ultimately that's the way all the press and the pundits saw it. That was the story of the game, how Connacht defended and held Ulster out with 13 men.'

Saturday, 9 April
European Challenge Cup quarter-final
Grenoble 33 Connacht 32

With the carrot of a home semi-final for the winners, and Connacht three games away from their first trophy, Lam and co. decided not to hold back. But with Grenoble three games away from their first major trophy since their sole Bouclier de Brennus in 1954, and adrift of the top six, nor did Bernard Jackman.

Hence both coaches declared fairly strong hands. When Heenan turned his ankle again in training before their latest long haul, via Geneva, McKeon reverted to open-side and Muldoon switched to number 8, with O'Brien coming in at blindside.

Bealham and Dillane made their first starts since the Six Nations, while Marmion, Henshaw and Danie Poolman also returned. Lam's boldest move of all was to shift Healy for only his second game at full-back.

Overlooked by the Alps, two like-minded teams ran the ball from everywhere. A French terrestrial TV audience were introduced to Connacht's brand of running rugby. 'The theme that night was, "Let's show the people in France what we can do",' says Lam.

A lovely, modern, 20,000 all-seater stadium. Cracking atmosphere. Superb playing surface. And a contender for game of the season.

Healy was simply sensational. Twice he made pacy incisions through the Grenoble backline, leaving players trailing in his wake like sketches from a comic book, to lay on two tries for Adeolokun. Healy's daring counter-attack led to Henshaw scoring off a pinpoint crosskick by O'Leary, and for his own try in the second half, Healy burned the 17-times capped Springbok full-back Gio Aplon to score untouched from 30 metres.

In all, he carried for 123 metres (from just six carries), beat four defenders and accounted for four of Connacht's eleven line breaks.

Even by half-time, French journalists wanted to know about Healy. '*Qui est l'arrière?*' Who the hell was this Connacht full-back? Why hasn't he played for Ireland? They could scarcely believe it was only the second time in his career that Healy had worn the number 15 shirt.

It had been the same in the home dressing-room at full-time, according to Jackman. 'All of our French players were saying, "Who's that guy, Matt Healy?" He hadn't played much at full-back, and we said beforehand we could target that. He targeted us!'

Connacht had leads of 19–3 and 29–16 in either half. The way they saw it in their review, 'We went into our shells,' says Lam. The first lead had begun to evaporate after O'Leary opted for a daring crosskick towards Adeolokun inside their own 22, which prompted criticism aplenty from pundits. Lam still isn't having any of that.

'No, I was really pleased, really pleased. It was on. He had a look and made a decision. The execution didn't happen, but it was the right decision. We say "What's on?", rather than play what's in front of you. If he'd executed correctly, Niysi was in the right place and we were gone.'

'Matt was awesome that night,' says Duffy. 'We're all huge fans, but that night he was just on fire, absolutely on fire. He broke the line, was quick, explosive and constantly involved. And when he decided to go, wow, he went, and it was awesome to see.'

It was also the night Adeolokun caught fire as well. Until then, he'd been playing consistently well. He'd bulked up, improved his aerial work and, according to Lam, had become as good at ball presentation in the tackle as anybody. But until that night, he'd only scored three tries in 13 games, against Enisei and Zebre. Like a striker ending a barren spell, thereafter he couldn't miss.

'People forget, he's only a couple of years in the professional game, and he's just getting better,' Duffy points out. 'He's adding little subtleties to his game, and he's so exciting to watch. He's accurate in defence, and he's a good kick-chaser. He's continually improving his game. The kids are screaming at him here. They love him. That's what you want.'

There was also a truly gobsmacking moment involving Dillane, which would give a hint as to his new, post-Six Nations level of performance for the run-in.

'We got pinched on a line-out and they rumbled us 20 to 30 metres on our own ball, which is a killer. Ultan stopped that maul on his own. We showed it as a highlight on the Monday-morning review. He made such an effort to get back and then minced it single-handedly. It was phenomenal.'

At Monday's team meeting, that won their Effort King of the Week!

'We wanted to be pushing for silverware on both fronts,' says Duffy. 'We really did. There was a really sombre mood in that dressing-room, and personally I was just really annoyed that we didn't close it out. But I think it fuelled our desire.'

Muldoon: 'That was hard to take. It was a great rugby match. Just the result was the only thing. We should have won. The two weeks before that probably took a little bit out of us.'

It may well have been a blessing in disguise too. Now, like all their title rivals, Connacht would have two idle weekends in the seasonal run-in rather than competing on two fronts.

'Absolutely,' agrees Muldoon. 'When Pat pulled me aside about ten minutes after the game, I said to him, "That's the best thing that's happened to us." And he said, "I agree, Mul. We don't have the squad." I said, "I'm absolutely gutted. But I still think that's the best thing that's ever happened to us."'

Saturday, 16 April
Connacht 35 Munster 14

Another near 8,000 sell-out. 'We were on a roll now,' says Lam. 'We'd become the hottest ticket in town. Everyone was looking for tickets. Every home game on that run-in was an unbelievable occasion.'

And another crisis, or at any rate a mini-crisis.

Going into round 20, Connacht trailed Leinster on points

difference, but bonus-point wins for Leinster, Glasgow and Ulster had upped the ante. Defeat would see Connacht slip to third, with the breath of the chasing teams on their necks too.

Munster came into this game ten points adrift but in sixth place, only one point ahead of Edinburgh in seventh and five points off the top four. They were in win-or-bust territory.

Munster came to play too. Tries by Simon Zebo and Mike Sherry, off a maul, had them 14–6 ahead after 35 minutes. After the defeats to Ulster and Grenoble, the atmosphere in the Sportsground was almost defeatist.

'You could hear the groans in the ground,' recalls Muldoon.

'Munster had owned the ball, but there was genuinely no panic, and the boys stuck to the game plan,' says Duffy. 'We got our hands back on the ball, began to put some phases together and scored a try.'

The game hinged on two sinbins for Munster. For the first, James Cronin saw yellow after an inordinate number of scrum collapses, much to the annoyance of Anthony Foley.

In Cronin's absence, Aki picked up a stray ball, broke through the red line and Bealham's transfer enabled Adeolokun to score. Aki then broke 50 metres upfield from the restart and when Connacht laid siege to the Munster try line, Billy Holland was also sinbinned for lying all over the ball. Munster were down to 13 men and, although the 40 minutes were almost up, Muldoon, home team and crowd alike scented blood.

'Although it was almost the last play of the half, we went to the corner again and mauled over.' That made it 20–14, after a 14-point swing in four minutes just before half-time.

Muldoon recalls, 'We had been down 14–3, but no one panicked and running in off the pitch at half-time I was thinking, "This is over." Munster had gone from 14–3 up and throwing the ball in the air, to being gobsmacked at half-time. You could hear them giving out to each other. Our crowd were going mental again. That was another defining moment in the season.'

'Half-time was good,' recalls Duffy. 'The fellas were feeling really energized. We were very clear in what we had to do. The boys were brilliant and closed out the game.'

Bealham, of all people, sealed the bonus point with the fourth try. 'My first meat pie for Connacht,' he declared in the dressing-room.

'He actually dislocated his jaw in scoring and popped it back in,' laughs Duffy.

The win felt seismic. Connacht had completed their first ever seasonal double over Munster with their biggest ever win over their southern neighbours, relegating them to seventh place and in an almighty dogfight for a top-six place.

Not only had Connacht rejoined Leinster at the top of the table, they had mathematically secured a top-six place to ensure European Champions Cup rugby for the next season. 'That's that box ticked,' said Lam to the media afterwards. 'Now we have to get Connacht into the semi-finals.' One more win in their last two games would ensure that. Win both and they would have a home semi-final.

Friday, 29 April
Treviso 22 Connacht 21

Despite a weekend's respite – thanks to their Challenge Cup exit – Lam shuffled his deck, making ten changes from the team which had beaten Munster. Healy, Aki, Marmion and Dillane all put their feet up at home, and with Muldoon joining Henshaw, MacGinty and Muldowney on the bench, McCartney captained the side again.

Connacht started in trademark fashion, playing with width and leading 14–0 inside 15 minutes through early tries by Fionn Carr and Rory Parata. But they lost their way and, though they regained the lead in the second half through a superbly worked try by Robb, the Treviso scrum repeatedly turned the screw for Jayden Hayward to eventually win it with the last kick of the game.

A little ominously, Glasgow overtook Connacht that night with a 70–10 win over Zebre, their ninth League win in a row before the two sides would meet a week later at the Sportsground on the final Saturday.

So although the losing bonus point had secured a top-four place and qualification for the semi-finals, the general reaction was that Connacht had blown it.

But all it meant was that Connacht went into the last weekend two points behind Glasgow rather than one ahead of the Scots. So, neither that defeat, nor Ulster's 30–6 rout of Leinster the next day, effectively changed the equation. On the presumption that Leinster would beat Treviso at home on the final Saturday afternoon of the regular season, Connacht still faced a shoot-out with Glasgow to earn a home semi-final.

Going into the game, Muldoon and the management knew that a win without a bonus point against Treviso wouldn't really change the equation much. Nearing the end therefore, with three tries scored and leading 21–19, they went for the fourth.

'We went for a risky-ish maul on the halfway line,' says Muldoon. 'When I say risky, a maul is the least risky thing you can do when you have the ball on the halfway line. We decided to do a play that we'd done all season and repped, I'd say, 1,000 times. And we passed the ball forward off the first phase.

'Afterwards, Pat said to me, "That was a risky play." And I said, "Is it? We've done it 1,000 times this season, easily, and I've never seen us throw it forward." Pat said, "Yeah, OK. I agree."'

Nor, like the Grenoble defeat, was it the worst thing that could have happened. 'It also kept some lads grounded, I think,' says Muldoon, 'and it probably helped us before playing Glasgow. It was always going to be easy for us to motivate ourselves for that one, especially the pack, with Dan [McFarland] now being the Glasgow forwards coach.'

'We had that Treviso game in full control,' reflects Lam. 'The boys decided to go for the bonus point, and I admired that, but it was a frustrating game. And it cost us finishing in first place; that cost us top dog at the end of the [22-game] round robin.'

Lam would have liked that. But then again, he'd rather win the trophy.

Saturday, 7 May
Connacht 14 Glasgow 7

The 'quarter-final', as Muldoon and the players called it, and akin to a knockout match even though their place in the semi-finals was already secured.

The squad's training load was deliberately kept light that week. 'It was all around our mental prep and getting our detail right,' says Lam, 'so we had a lot less physical output. It was more about clarity. It was our last home game, and a chance to get a home semi-final, which is what we wanted. The build-up was perfect, actually. The weather forecast wasn't great, so it would call for a massive team effort physically.'

The prize was huge, namely a home semi-final, most likely against the same opponents two weeks later. In Pro12 semi-finals, the home sides tend to win; since the introduction of play-offs in the 2009–10 season, the twelve home sides had won every time.

Glasgow were on a nine-match winning streak going back to February, and had won their last eight meetings with Connacht, dating back to the Sportsground in February 2011. Almost exactly 12 months previously, Glasgow had won 31–13 in Galway en route to their first title.

Connacht had lost only once at the Sportsground all season, but they'd never won in Scotstoun, where Glasgow had won 20 of their last 21 Pro12 games – the one exception being the season's opening-night defeat to the Scarlets in the absence of their sizeable World Cup squad.

As Muldoon had deduced, whatever chance they had of beating Glasgow at home in the semis, it was considerably better than having to do so in Scotstoun.

Lam restored all his big guns – Muldoon, Aki, Henshaw, Healy, MacGinty, Marmion and Dillane – making nine changes from the Treviso defeat. Marmion and O'Halloran would each make their 100th appearance for the province.

In teeming rain, the Sportsground heaved with another near 8,000 sell-out. After Aki's typically powerful first-half finish off MacGinty's flat carry and offload had been cancelled out by a Gordon Reid try, the game then pivoted on a 51st-minute red card for the Glasgow prop Sila Puafisi.

At 7–7, Muldoon opted to kick to the corner rather than take a shot at goal. 'It's backfired on me before, and it had done so just a week before, but I felt we had momentum. There are times in games when a team has a psychological advantage and have to press it home. At another time, if they had the momentum, I'd have told our kicker, "Take that kick." But we'd just had an onslaught on their line, and I felt we were banging on the door.'

The mauls were held up, but the unrelenting pressure told. Cometh the hour, literally, O'Halloran used his formative Gaelic football skills to rise, gather and score off O'Leary's pinpoint crosskick.

Aki, Connacht's heart-on-the-sleeve cult hero cum human wrecking ball, was serenaded from the pitch when hobbling off late on to familiar chants of 'Aaa-ki, Aaa-ki'. That night, unsurprisingly, he scooped both the Connacht Players' Player of the Year and Supporters' Player of the Year awards.

For his part, MacGinty was proving himself something of a one-season wonder, the 26 year old arriving after the World Cup, ultimately playing 13 League games, starting nine of them, before moving on to Sale.

'I saw him play for the USA against Samoa and heard he was Irish,' says Lam. 'I knew we were short, because [Marnitz] Boshoff couldn't come at that stage, so we grabbed the opportunity and he took his chance. A great kid. Great kid.'

MacGinty made ten carries (only Henshaw and Aki made more) and two clean breaks, beating eight defenders and offloading for Aki's try. 'We took the inside options a lot against Glasgow because they were flying up,' says Lam, 'and A. J. and Kieran made good breaks.'

As it was their last regular game of the season at home, the players stayed on the pitch to acknowledge the home supporters, and then formed a huddle with the management for Lam to present their departing players with autographed jerseys.

As well as MacGinty and Henshaw, Carr, Jason Harris-Wright, Rodney Ah You, Muldowney, Naoupu, Conor Finn, Api Pewhairangi and Ian Porter were all moving on.

'We always do that after our last home game,' says Lam. 'As always, John Muldoon spoke really well. It's always a sad moment, but the beauty about it now was that we would have one more game at home.'

Muldoon: 'The best thing about that match was that we were on top, then they had a man sent off, and the pressure came on us to win. We didn't win by that much, but did just enough. In the dressing-room, everyone was delighted to be in a home semi-final but disappointed with how we had played.'

Saturday, 21 May – Guinness Pro12 semi-final
Connacht 16 Glasgow 11

For the biggest game in Connacht's history, with the prize of an even bigger one to follow, Lam made just one change, restoring McKeon to the back-row.

This was Connacht's first semi-final in the League, and hence their preparations were a little more focused on their opponents than usual.

'Have they got anything else?'

'What will they come at us with?'

Recalls Lam, 'We knew they'd think things might have been different if they hadn't had to play the last half hour with 14 men, but we were in a good place mentally and felt we could have the edge physically. So we lightened the training load again and let the psychology of it take care of itself. By this stage, the boys were just lifted by the crowd. Motivation wasn't a problem. It was just making sure we could channel all that emotion, because we knew if we won the physical battle, the rest would come. That was the key.'

Indeed, with the help of their 16th man, Connacht produced perhaps their best performance of the season to date. Adeolokun was the match-winner, gathering Aki's deft grubber on the run and using his footwork to leave three opponents trailing before sprinting away from 50 metres. He and McKeon also had tries overruled by the TMO in what ought to have been a more comfortable win before that nail-biting endgame.

'I was crook as a dog for the semi,' admits Heenan. 'I was throwing up all Thursday night and came in on Friday for the Captain's Run. My brother had just arrived in Galway, so it would be the first game he'd see me play since I was fifteen. I mulled it over and over, and said, "Damn it, I'm not telling anyone for the moment."

'I got through the Captain's Run and felt all right. Then I woke up on the day of the game and thought I was going to die. I was in a really, really bad way at home. But there wasn't a chance I was going to miss that game, and I felt better when I got to the Sportsground. At the end of the day, it might be uncomfortable or whatever, but it's not incapacitating. Once into the game, I got on with it. It wasn't my best game ever, but I did my job, made my tackles. So I was all right.'

Reaching the final meant his brother would stay around for another week and make the trek to Edinburgh.

'We felt we could have a real go in the semi,' says Duffy. 'In the semis, all bets are off. It's open season, but I was chuffed for the players and John Mul in particular. I think that was an awesome night for him. There was a lot of emotion around. Everybody was waiting for us to fall out of that top four or six all season. And it hadn't happened. I remember speaking to Mul that night and him being immensely proud, and we were immensely proud of him.'

But that night, Duffy learned that his uncle, Noel, had passed away.

'We were close and he was a lifelong Connacht fan as well. I was on a high from the game and hung around in the Sportsground, just having a MiWadi and chatting to people, before I hopped in the car. But I hadn't seen my mum and dad that night, and they are always at the home games, particularly since I got season tickets for them, and I thought that was unusual. Then I had a missed call and rang my mum back.

'"Are you home?" she asked.'

'"Not yet,"' said Duffy. It was 11.30 p.m.

She said to call her back when he arrived home.

'I knew then there was something up. My dad had gone to Dublin. He and my uncle were very close, but my uncle had had a transplant a couple of weeks back and he'd been ill for about two or three years. He died at about eleven o'clock that night, which was tough.

'My uncle had been in St Vincent's [University Hospital] for much of the last three years, and my dad went up to see him pretty much every week, and I visited him whenever I was in Dublin. He was a good man, a good sporting man. He loved his sport, loved West Ham and loved Connacht. They were his two teams.'

His uncle's removal would be on the Tuesday, with the funeral on the Wednesday morning. For Duffy, the week of the final would be particularly emotional.

20
Connacht's Cutting Edge –
The Three Amigos

Niyi Adeolokun's match-winning try in the semi-finals was his fifth in five games. Going into the final, their then uncapped back three of Healy, O'Halloran and Adeolokun were all in razor-sharp form and had 19 League tries from a combined tally of 55 games in the season.

This compared to two tries from 23 combined League starts between Leinster's Rob and Dave Kearney, along with Luke Fitzgerald, a testimony as much to Connacht's brand of game as to their trio's finishing skills.

Adeolokun was born and reared in Ibadan, the third largest area in Nigeria, after Lagos and Kano, with a population of 3.5 million. When he was ten his mother Rebecca took him and his brother Laurence with her to Dublin, in 2001. She wanted to pursue better work opportunities, and in one of several parallels with Ultan Dillane's story, became a nurse in St James's Hospital.

Adeolokun re-visited Ibadan in June 2015 for the first time in 14 years. 'I remembered glimpses of it, but it was an eye-opener. I enjoyed it. It is congested, and parts of it are quite old, but parts of it are quite nice as well.

'It's a lovely city, and it was great to meet up with cousins and uncles and aunts and nephews also. Some parts hadn't changed at all, and it brought back flashbacks of my childhood. I won't be able to go back this summer, but I plan on going back more regularly.'

Growing up there, he recalls that his parents moved around quite a bit, as his mum searched for work. 'We lived a lot with my grandma, who had a restaurant. I remembered we mainly did stuff ourselves and played football and other sports late into the evening, and then my uncle would get angry and call us in. But we had nothing to worry about and just enjoyed ourselves.' Ironically, his Uncle Solomon has since been over to Ireland and watched Adeolokun play for Connacht.

On arriving in a strange new country, sport was Adeolokun's main way of making friends and settling into his new life. Initially, while at De La Salle Churchtown, Gaelic football and dreams of playing for the Dubs held sway. But Adeolokun's coach at De La Salle, Lorcan Balfe, contacted Leinster, and Adeolokun trained with the Leinster Under-19s in the summer of 2009 after leaving school. A week before the Interpros, though, he was cut from the squad, and it hurt him deeply, although he's the first to admit he was a little too laidback for his own good then.

'I was surprised how much it hurt me. I suddenly realized how much I wanted to play rugby and be a professional rugby player.'

Adeolokun resolved to fight his way back into the Leinster system and, with the help of Tony Smeeth, relaunched his career as a prolific try-scoring winger at Trinity before Smeeth put together a video to send to various contacts, including Carolan.

At times, Adeolokun does allow himself to pause and reflect on his unlikely journey. 'When I was in Dublin, I wanted to play for Leinster obviously, and when that didn't happen I didn't think I was going to get a chance to play professional rugby.

'So in the position I'm in right now, I do look back and think, "Yeah, I'm very lucky to be where I am." I'm very grateful that Pat gave me the chance to be here. When I first arrived, I found it difficult. Galway is completely different from Dublin, but I quickly came to love it. The people are good, and in the last week and a half here the sun has been shining every day and the atmosphere around the town has been buzzing.

'I'm absolutely honoured to be a part of this. None of us have been in this situation before, even the likes of Muls.'

Similarly, Healy had been let go by Leinster at 20 years of age. Reared in Ranelagh, and a product of Gonzaga, Healy had been released from their sub-academy after returning from the 2009 Junior World Cup with the Irish Under-20s.

Likewise too, he rebuilt his career at club level, in his case with Lansdowne. Coming up to a Division Two promotion game back in January 2010, Lansdowne were to play Trinity at their then home of the RDS. Brian O'Riordan, the ex-UCD and Leinster scrum-half, was their first-choice 9, and so the first-team coaches, Willie Clancy and Stephen Rooney, persuaded their then back-up scrum-half, Healy, to try playing on the wing. Lansdowne won 17–12 to virtually seal their runaway promotion, and Healy scored two tries, thereby sealing his re-invention as a winger, and the rest, as they say, is history. Healy had three prolific seasons with Lansdowne, mostly on the wing, as they progressed to the club's first league title under Mike Ruddock in the 2012–13 season with a team that also featured another current Connacht teammate, Craig Ronaldson.

Through contacts at Lansdowne, he was put in touch with the ex-Irish left-winger turned IRUPA CEO and then agent Niall Woods, who sounded out English clubs, and Eric Elwood, a former Lansdowne player. That was at the start of the 2012–13 season, when injuries contributed to Healy playing mostly in the British & Irish Cup as well as for Lansdowne, while making three appearances for Connacht. Over the next three seasons, Healy established himself as Connacht's best finisher.

A turning point came in the summer of 2014 when Lam sought out the sports psychologist Enda McNulty to talk to Healy. 'After my first year under Pat, we sat down at the end of the season, and it was more a confidence issue that I wanted to fix. Confidence on the ball and backing myself. So he got in touch with Enda, who gave me some time in Dublin, and that started a new approach to training. He highlighted different ways you can approach your training rather than just leaving it to the main sessions with the coaches.

'Let's say you wanted to work on handling or passing, you might get two or three reps [repetitions] in squad training, whereas if you spend ten minutes on your own you might do 100 reps. That shaped my approach to training. I started making little schedules for myself on a weekly basis, and setting goals and objectives. That designated individual practice was massive for me. Over that summer, those skills came on in leaps and bounds. I became a different player and that carried into the following season.'

Healy also hails the emphasis on skills of the other coaches at Connacht, Andre Bell and Dave Ellis, his partner for those skills sessions, and Conor McPhillips, video analyst cum backs coach, as well as Lam, of course. 'Back then, I was still a very raw winger. I didn't understand positional play or defensive positions. Pat talked me through what he wanted from his wingers.'

Come the final against Leinster, Healy had scored nine tries over the course of the League campaign, to add to his ten from the previous two seasons, as well as ten tries in Europe.

'I think Matt has unbelievable gifts,' says Lam. 'There's no doubt he's got the X factor. The key is the effort and time he has put into his game, through his preparation during the week. He has some serious firepower, and the best is still to come from him as an all-round rugby player.'

O'Halloran, the Clifden-born local boy made good, has had to serve his time, mostly as a winger, while Gavin Duffy and to some extent Robbie Henshaw occupied his favoured position of full-back.

After a few injury-blighted years, O'Halloran had played 21 of Connacht's 23 League games before the final, scoring five tries to add to one in the Challenge Cup.

'Tiernan has matured this season and become a leader,' says Lam of his 24-year-old full-back. 'He came here as a winger, but he's always been telling me he's a full-back. Like Matt and Niyi, and all the players, Tiernan knows he can't take his skills for granted; they have to keep putting the work in.

'He also came here at a young age and was one of the lads, but now he's one of the leaders of the team. He's a local, has great family support, and he's been a big part of this season's success; and he's going to continue to be that as a big leader for Connacht rugby.'

21

Nigel Carolan

Nothing gives Nigel Carolan more pleasure than seeing graduates of the Connacht underage pathway and academy grow as people and players, then play professionally, particularly for Connacht, and most of all for Ireland. That's the ultimate goal. Of the quintet who broke new ground for the province by playing for Ireland in the Six Nations win over Italy, four of them fall into this category – Finlay Bealham, Ultan Dillane, Kieran Marmion and Robbie Henshaw.

That's almost as many players as Connacht's academy had in its entirety back in 2004 when it was originally set up by the IRFU, with Carolan its first and thus far only manager. The academy also has more off-field staff now than they had players then. In 2004, the academy had six players – Ronan Loughney, Danny Riordan (who played for Connacht, Leinster and Munster, and is still playing club rugby with Old Belvedere), Eamonn Bracken, Mike Diffley, Tim Richardson and Colin Finnerty. Carolan has a picture of them on the wall in his office.

In total, 35 graduates of the Connacht academy have progressed to professional contracts, and in the 2015–16 season, 21 of the Connacht senior squad were graduates of the academy.

Back then, he had one full-time assistant, fitness coach Antoine Mobian, from Strasbourg, who currently works at Setanta College and with the German rugby team. Now there are ten, with 20 players contracted in the academy for the 2016–17 season. Connacht and their academy have come a long way.

With Carolan now part of the Sportsground furniture himself, it's ironic to think that there was absolutely no rugby whatsoever in his family tree. His dad, Mick, had been a soldier from Drogheda, who was stationed in Renmore, and married Anne, who is from Loughrea, rearing Nigel and his older brother Glen.

'Dad played everything but rugby. He was a Gaelic goalie, he played basketball, volleyball, soccer, everything. He had very little interest in rugby but would occasionally go and watch a game, but he was never affiliated with any rugby clubs.'

A neighbour in Renmore, Al Corcoran, who delivered cooking oil to the various restaurants around Galway, also used his Hiace van to take his rugby-playing sons and their friends to rugby matches in Corinthians. Carolan's brother hopped aboard one morning, and soon after so did Carolan.

'When you think about it, you wouldn't get away with it now, but he used to drive around Renmore every Saturday morning to round up all the kids and take us to Corinthians. He'd have about nine or ten of us. We'd hop in the back of the van and sit on oil drums.'

Carolan was late to rugby, at about 14, having played Gaelic and soccer until then. Six years later, Carolan was playing for Connacht against Australia at the Sportsground.

It was a rapid rise. Carolan was always naturally fit, trained hard and enjoyed the physicality of the game. 'I made a lot of good friends in Corinthians, and they're still my mates. We enjoyed training and playing together, and because we enjoyed it we actually did well as a young team. We won all our leagues and cups all the way up, and I got recognition from there in development squads and so forth.'

This included emulating Eric Elwood by playing for the Irish Under-21s, a relatively rare achievement for young Connacht players at the time. Before playing for Connacht, he'd only ever been to the Sportsground once to support them, when they played the All Blacks in November 1989.

Carolan made his debut for Connacht against the Scottish

Borders in the 1995–96 season under Eddie O'Sullivan at the age of 20. He would go on to become a regular in Warren Gatland's second season, 1997–98, playing in all three Interpros and in their run to the Challenge Cup quarter-finals.

'I'm not surprised Warren has done so well as a coach. I try to emulate him in some of the aspects that he would have instilled in us as a coach. He had an innate ability to bring out the best in every player.

'Even though he had a very quiet demeanour and wouldn't have been the most outspoken of coaches then, he still had a way of communicating and interacting with all the players which drew the maximum out of them. He was very good at instilling cohesion in the team. He encouraged us to go out socially and enjoy each other's company, so much so that he had a group of coaches in another corner of the bar doing the same thing. That team became a very tight-knit group, and so really played for each other.'

Reflecting on his own playing career, Carolan says, 'I probably did as well as I could for what I had. I started off as a centre and ended up on the wing. I wasn't the fastest, and I had a limited kicking game but I was a reasonable defender and brave in the tackle. I was also at the end of a couple of plays, either with Eric on a dummy switch line or a pass from Willie Ruane or Mervyn Murphy, but I knew I was limited in terms of where I was going to go.'

However, during the 2000–01 season he was forced to retire with a neck injury. 'It happened during a high-ball exercise we were doing on the main pitch in the Sportsground,' he recalls. 'I landed on my hand and then the elbow of another player came down on top of my head. I damaged nerves in my joints, and I struggled to lift my arms for six months.'

Those first few months were the toughest. He still watched games and still wished he could be playing, but while it was a cruel way for his playing career to end prematurely, Carolan admits he was already drifting away from the pro game at that stage, having spent the summer of 2000 in South Africa. 'I'd kind of had enough of pro rugby at that stage and I'd started to look beyond it.'

Having graduated with a degree in marketing from GMIT in 1996, he went back to college to do a Higher Diploma in systems analysis at NUIG. 'I knew that rugby wasn't going to be a long-term prospect for me, and I thought I was going to be a web designer or an Internet geek,' he admits. 'But the IT industry took a bit of a slump in 2001.'

After his injury, he had travelled to Australia with his then girlfriend Siobhan – they have since married and have two kids, Milly (six) and Ben (four). 'I had a job lined up there. We were all set to stay and settle down in Australia, but at the last minute a low-level IT job fell through, so we finished our travels and came back.'

Before going to Australia, the then Connacht provincial development manager, Tommy Conneely, had notified Carolan that a job as a rugby development officer with the province was coming up. Carolan was keener to travel to Australia and pursue a job in IT, but upon his return that industry was still in a slump, and when the same job in Connacht came up again, he was more interested.

'It became a little more appealing the second time around. Tommy must have seen something. He had tapped me on the shoulder before I left and asked me if I'd be interested in it, but I wanted to travel. When it came back up again, he said, "This could be your last chance. I think you should consider this." I did, and I haven't looked back since. It was an extremely rewarding job.'

So, in February 2002, Carolan became an employee of the IRFU as a rugby development officer with the Connacht Branch, and when the IRFU regionalized their academy into the four provinces, Carolan was appointed as Connacht's first academy manager. 'Having the opportunity to work with players and develop them by maximizing their potential can be hugely rewarding.'

Allowing for his Aussie odyssey, Carolan has effectively 21 years without a break in the Connacht set-up.

'I'm a bit of an institution around here now,' says Carolan self-mockingly when reminded of this. 'Only Eric has been here longer, and in cumulative years I may have him by a year.'

The last dozen of those 21 years have been as the Connacht academy manager, but all has changed, changed utterly, since Connacht and Carolan moved from the branch's old offices in the Lisburn Industrial Estate to the Sportsground in 2004, where they had two rooms.

Back then, all the playing, coaching and administrative staff were housed in one building, since when a stand-alone gym has been built along with a smaller-scale AstroTurf pitch.

Where before Carolan was one of a staff of two, now there are ten. Ambrose Conboy and Mossie Lawlor are the elite development officers, Andrew Murphy and Michael Devane are the two S&C coaches, Rachel Wyer and Orla Armstrong are the physiotherapists, Jim Herring is the performance analyst, Laura Mahony is the academy's nutritionist while Colm Tucker runs the junior academy, and Aidan O'Flynn is a part-time employee in charge of personal development with the players. They are also helped by Deirdre Lyons of IRUPA.

'We have a wraparound service that every player needs,' says Carolan. 'All bases are covered. I'm only the jack of all trades, but we have experts in every area. It just means that whatever the players' requirements are, we have a specialist in that area to ensure that they are developing.'

Carolan and co. start identifying players from around the age of 14 onwards, as part of what the IRFU call a National Talent Squad (NTS). 'We try to accelerate their development by resourcing them earlier. We try to see them twice a week, so that they're in the gym twice and get two skills sessions with our staff in season.'

With the smallest playing base of the four provinces, Connacht have also been adept at identifying players from outside.

'Because of the geography and cultural nature of Connacht, rugby is not our first sport, so we recognize that we need to keep the door open for good prospects in other provinces who maybe aren't being picked up for whatever reason. It could be that there isn't enough space or they're not deemed good enough at a given time.'

The first player Connacht brought into their academy from the other provinces was Mick Kearney, then 20, from the Leinster Youths' set-up. James Connolly, from Naas, Rory Moloney, from Abbeyleix, and Peter Robb, a Dubliner who went to Blackrock, all followed from the Leinster underage set-up into the academy. Marmion was identified while playing for the Irish Exiles, a system designed for Irish qualified players based abroad, at 19. Dillane and Bealham were brought in from Munster and Ulster at the ages of 18 and 19.

'The likes of Ultan Dillane and Finlay Bealham are not deemed to be the most talented players when they come in first, but they certainly have the character, the drive, the dedication and the willingness to learn that far exceeds talent at the end of the day, and it's easily resourced talent; that is, it's easy to pinpoint the areas they need to work on and resource that.

'Others might be very good rugby players and might be very good at drills, but if they don't have the right attitude or they're not committed to doing their extras, it's very hard to make them realize what's required. Sometimes it might take a kick in the arse or an arm around the shoulder to try to make them work in the areas they're not so good at. Every player is a project, and every player is different, and as such you have to apply a different programme and recipe for every player.'

The key to a good academy? 'I think adaptability,' says Carolan. 'We do it slightly differently every year. You have to be flexible. You've got to cater to the players' needs, to tap into their ability, but more importantly ensure that it's their plan and they are actually driving it. That's the culture that we want to create in the academy. It is about hard work, and there are no guarantees, but they will be resourced and we do adapt in when and how we do sessions. Ultimately they must recognize what their shortcomings are and ensure that they are addressing them.'

In other words, guide them rather than spoon-feed them.

'I still love it, and I still find it very enjoyable, but I'm not sure it's a job for life. At some stage, I'll have to look at where I go, but if I do, I'll make sure that I leave this place in really good stead.'

22

The Final Week – Monday

No rest for the finalists. For all but two teams from the four countries which participate in the Pro12 – namely Ireland, Wales, Scotland and Italy – the season was over. Not so Connacht or Leinster. The Connacht management team met, as usual, at 8 a.m. on Monday morning in the Sportsground. Pat Lam thanked everyone for their contributions to the semi-final win and undertook a quick review of the week and the match. As ever, he asked what they'd done well and what they could do better. Everyone was given a chance to speak, before Lam himself expressed his prime message of the day and thus the week.

'I want this week to be a celebration. Everything is going to be based on enjoying ourselves by working hard. Everything.'

He added, 'Keep an eye out for any negativity. If a player comes to you complaining he's tired, just give him a boost. Everyone just take it to a final standard this week.' He wanted the entire management to be alive and alert.

Lam explains, 'I always say that the management are the role models for the players. It's like parenting, and it's very hard for me to tell the children to be tidy if I'm a mess! The management set the standards, and at that meeting everybody has a chance to speak. That has started our week from day one of week one of year one.'

After that, the coaches met at 8.15 for half an hour. Lam was joined by Jimmy Duffy, Dave Ellis, Andre Bell and Conor McPhillips. In essence, they went through and confirmed the game plan for the final. They'd had the advantage of watching Leinster beat Ulster 30–18 in the first semi-final the previous Friday night.

'The coaches' meeting,' according to Lam, 'is all about saying, "OK, what do we think? What do you think? What are we going to do on our attack shape? Anything we want to change? What about our defence, given what they do?" Bang. Done. We formulate our game plan.'

At 8.45, Lam expanded the meeting for what he has entitled 'Connacht's Alignment Group'. He calls it that because it's a strategy group that also involves the senior players. Necessity being the mother of invention, it had grown through the season to about 10 or 12 players due in large part to injuries. Thus, all the 8s (Muldoon and Eoin McKeon), 9s (Kieran Marmion, John Cooney, Caolin Blade and Ian Porter) and 10s (A. J. MacGinty, Jack Carty and Shane O'Leary) attended, along with hooker Tom McCartney, centre Robbie Henshaw and full-back Tiernan O'Halloran. Hence, when MacGinty had to step in for Carty, or one of the other scrum-halves for Marmion, they were au fait with the Alignment Group's thinking.

They began, as normal, by reviewing the Glasgow semi-final, and primarily the decisions that were made on the field, whether opting to take a penalty at goal or going to the corner, exiting from their half, options in attack and so forth. Lam prompted the review of specific moments with clips that he showed on their video screen, and then came the questions.

'OK, what were you thinking here?'

'Was there a better option?'

Rather than passing verdict, Lam does this to challenge their thinking and understand it better.

Then Lam outlined the game plan and asked if there was anything the players would change and modified it accordingly.

That done, at 9.30 a.m. the coaches and the entire squad came together for a team meeting. As normal, this began on a light-hearted note with a joke from one of the squad's court jesters, the 24-year-old Australian-born prop Finlay Bealham. He'd arrived in the summer of 2014, having spent the previous four years in Ulster, as his grandmother hails from Fermanagh.

Lam called him to the front of the room to teach the squad some chat-up lines, with John Cooney chosen to 'play' the girl.

Bealham: 'Are you from Google?'

Cooney: 'No, why?'

Bealham: 'Because I've been searching for you all my life!'

Cue groans and/or laughter, depending on taste.

Lam then set the scene for the week, repeating his mantra about it being a celebration.

'We have earned the right to be in this final. I've looked at the forecast. Unbelievable. It's going to be perfect for us. And that pitch. We all know Edinburgh. Murrayfield is a magnificent international stadium. And Nigel Owens is the referee. We are going there to play international-standard rugby and play our game. All right?'

That was the 'Outcome', which is how he likes to set the tone of the meeting, which in turn brings him back to the process of achieving that outcome.

'So, what do we need to do to be able to play international-standard rugby in a magnificent international stadium?'

They had to train like an international team all week. They understood. They knew.

Following the players' input, each of the management team – administration, strength and conditioning, physios, medical staff – was asked for their say. Team manager Tim Allnutt began by outlining their travel and hotel arrangements. The squad would travel to Edinburgh from Knock airport on Thursday afternoon and, due to hotel demand compounded by the Edinburgh Marathon that weekend, would have to switch hotels on Friday morning before flying home after the final on Saturday night.

Three La-Z-Boy sofas were then brought to the front of the room. As usual, the Players' Player of the previous week was selected – all of the squad having sent a WhatsApp to Allnutt with their vote. The top three were announced in reverse order. Each was given a La-Z-Boy sofa. Allnutt had also collated the weekly tally for the Players' Player of the Season.

Lam then conducted a review of the semi-final win, highlighting aspects or moments from the game on the video screen, freeze-framing clips and asking questions.

'Where were we trying to attack? Is it on?'

'Yeah.'

'OK, so why did it break down?'

'Execution.'

Next up was the Honours Board, with players being recognized as 'Defence King' (most effective tackler), 'Breakdown King' (most effective at clearing out rucks), '50/50 King' (whoever won the most 50–50 balls in the air or on the ground) and 'Effort King' of the week. For this, either the coaches put up some clips or it is opened up to the squad.

There's also the 'Truck King', for what they call the YAC (Yards After Contact) if a player breaks the opposition defensive line. Bundee Aki has a tendency to lord this one, although A. J. MacGinty was deemed the Truck King for one carry into contact against Glasgow.

The meeting would normally have ended there, but Lam broke with custom by naming the starting team, as he had done for the semi-final, rather than waiting until the Tuesday. Lam's primary objective before leaving the Sportsground on a Monday is to ensure that everyone knows the game plan, how they're going to attack and defend, so that the coaches assume more command for the remainder of the week. The sooner the squad have the big picture, the better.

Clarity is key, and it was to further facilitate this clarity for the semi-final and final that Lam named the starting team on the Monday. Normally the lights are dimmed and player profiles are shown on the video screen from one to 15, to the backdrop of the Dropkick Murphys 'Shipping Up To Boston', the track to which both the Irish and Connacht teams run out at home matches.

On this Monday, however, Lam had the entire squad form a circle with their chairs and called up all the players in each of the 15 positions in turn. So he began: 'I want all the hookers to stand up and come forward.' There were four of them, Tom McCartney, Jason Harris-Wright, Dave Heffernan and Shane Delahunt.

Lam spoke of the quality they had in this position and the

contribution all had made during the season. Delahunt began the season in his third and final year in the Connacht academy and had turned 22 only in February. Due to injuries to more senior players, however, he had played in four League games and had started the historic win over Munster in Thomond Park in November. Lam reminded everyone of Delahunt's superb performance. Harris-Wright had played only six minutes of the return meeting at home to Munster in a season blighted by injury, but Lam spoke of his perseverance and his contribution over the previous four years.

'The guy who's going to represent all of you hookers this week is Tom McCartney.'

No surprise there, as the ex-Auckland Blues recruit had been one of Connacht's rocks over the season, but Lam was reminding everyone that this was truly a squad effort, as well as reminding McCartney of his privileged position.

Next, Lam called up the props, with the exception of the injured and absent Nathan White and Denis Buckley, who was having surgery that morning. So Lam spoke about their contribution as well before declaring, 'The player who will represent us at loose-head prop this week will be Ronan Loughney.'

'That was a nice touch,' says Loughney. 'The academy players had been so important, and as Mul and a few of us would say, "It's all in or not in at all."'

Denis Buckley had been the first-choice loose-head for the season but sustained an ankle fracture in training which ruled him out of the last four games. Yet although it seemed certain Loughney would start the final, his fourth game in a row in Buckley's absence, he couldn't help but feel relieved.

He knows all about life as a sub. Prior to the two Glasgow games, he'd started only one of his previous dozen League games that season, against Cardiff in December. Of his previous 141 League games, 88 had been as a replacement. For J. P. Cooney, the final would be his 20th League game for Connacht, and his 20th off the bench, so when the younger man came up to Loughney towards the end of the season bemoaning his lack of game time, the older man had sympathy for him.

'It's much more difficult to play from the bench than to start, especially in a pressure game like that,' says Loughney. 'You make one mistake and it's amplified because it happens in a shorter window on the pitch. If you start a game and you make a mistake, you usually have time to make up for it. And when you're starting, you do a lot more reps, so you are better prepared. You have a little more confidence, and you're a little more at ease. Whereas as a sub you're doing more mental reps. It's different. It's tougher. Denis's misfortune was my opportunity.'

And so Lam continued, all the way through to Tiernan O'Halloran at 15.

Looking back, Lam admits, 'It was funny, because it was almost a spur-of-the-moment thing. I just wanted to do it differently for this occasion, and it was more to emphasize that the guy going out there is the fortunate one. He is the lucky one, but he's playing on behalf of the others in his position. But it wasn't until I saw them all standing up that I realized, "Jeez, we've got some quality here. We've got some guys who've done some serious work to get us here."'

The squad went out to their AstroTurf pitch behind the main building and walked through a few plays they intended to alter for the final against Leinster.

Then it was over to Paul Bunce and the strength and conditioning team, as players opted for massage, weights and/or pool work before lunch. There was massage for all of the starting 15 in the afternoon. Recovery and rest were the priority. For Lam, the remainder of Monday was about paperwork.

'I always like to stay ahead on these things because on Tuesdays myself and Tim meet up with Willie Ruane to go over admin stuff, so I like to prepare for that.'

Winning continues on Tuesday.

23

The Final Week – Tuesday

John Muldoon drove from his home to the Sportsground, arriving shortly after 8.45, parked his car, walked back to the main entrance and into the Connacht changing-room. Strapping was optional before morning weights, then forwards' and backs' unit meetings and, for Muldoon, the weekly media duties at 12.15.

He'd noticed that Monday training had been 'a little bit nervier' than normal. Players had got things wrong. Some had had a go at each other. Still, he thought, they'd get it right by the end of the week.

'There were about 15 players in the dressing-room when I walked in. The lads were bouncing around the place, practising some Samoan song that Bundee has adapted for Connacht. I don't know where it came from. It's the song that has been put up on video. I thought to myself, "You wouldn't think it's the week of a big final." There was a real calm, and I thought, "Jaysus, we could be all right here."'

'Tuesday is a massive day,' says Lam. The forwards and backs do weights at different times, interspersed with Duffy's meeting with the forwards and Bell's meeting with the backs. His own morning begins with a senior leadership meeting in the offices upstairs with Willie Ruane, Niamh Hoyne (head of finance), Karl Boyle (head of operations), Tim Allnutt, Nigel Carolan and Eric Elwood.

That meeting started at 9.15 a.m. and finished at 10.20. In an initiative introduced by Ruane, the chairperson is rotated and everyone comes away with a clear understanding of what they are all doing each week.

The ticketing issue had dominated the previous week. This meeting centred on flights and hiring a charter plane for the return journey, organized by Boyle and Allnutt. Since the full-time whistle in the semi-final, they'd been working on the cost and size of the plane.

They'd settled upon a 130-seater plane, of which 46 seats were being reserved for those who had played in the League that season, thus omitting four members of the academy who had not played.

'When the academy boys come in, it has to be earned,' says Lam. 'They have to earn everything, a message I try to get out from day one: that it's a privilege to be training with the senior team. They might not have the same gear or a suit. If a player is given everything without earning it, you're sending out the wrong messages. So we decided that the full professional squad would travel along with the academy boys who had started training from day one. There were another four guys who had joined at different times during the season but hadn't yet played.'

These four were Cormac Brennan, Rory Moloney, Saba Meunargia and Ciaran Gaffney. That decision was conveyed to the squad. Within an hour of training finishing, Muldoon knocked on Lam's door.

'Pat, we've had a discussion amongst the players, and we'd like those four lads to go, and the boys are going to chip in.'

'Sweet,' said Lam. 'Well done. I like it. Good.'

In the meantime, Lam had observed Jimmy Duffy train the forwards and Andre Bell the backs. As the coaches need to know the replacements for the final, Lam then announced the make-up of the bench.

As with the starting team, the bench was unchanged, meaning no place for their naturalized South African lock Quinn Roux, even though he would go on to make his debut for Ireland against the Springboks the following month.

'You need to have another line-out caller on the bench, and Aly

Muldowney and Andrew Browne call the line-outs,' explains Lam. 'Quinn and Ultan don't yet. Jimmy's working on them, but effectively Ultan and Quinn are competing for their place.

'Jack Carty was a tough one [to leave out] too. Who would have thought, at the start of the season, that Shane O'Leary would be in our final match-day squad? But if you asked what our strongest team was at the start of the season, it was far from what we ended up with. But that's what happens in rugby, and that's why I always encourage players to keep working.' Leaving out Craig Ronaldson was also tough, but, like Carty and others, he just ran out of time.

In this decision-making process, Lam stresses to the players that he never mixes selections and relationships. It was partly with this in mind that he introduced the Connacht handshake every morning.

'It used to bug me as a player that the coach would be my best mate when he picked me, and then would blank me when he didn't. That's the beauty of having the handshakes every morning. I know players are disappointed, but my relationship is one thing and my selection is another, based on a thorough process. I don't like to mix it. So I'll still say "Good morning" and treat all the players exactly the same. How they deal with it is their problem.'

Lam then joined Muldoon for their 12.30 media session, after which Allnutt thrust a sandwich into his hand. The players left for lunch before a 1.20 p.m. team meeting in advance of the main training session on the main pitch at 2 p.m.

The meeting centred on their defensive review and the fundamentals about contact, during which Ellis, Duffy and McPhillips demonstrated their drills on the video screen. McPhillips had focused on Leinster's attack, and the on-field session would highlight key things learned from the last time Connacht played Leinster.

It had been widely reported that Leinster's performance against Ulster had been their best of the season, and publicly Lam was happy to go along with that. Privately, though, he placed an onus on his 10–12–13, MacGinty, Aki and Henshaw, to deny Leinster's playmakers time and space, which in his view Ulster had also done.

'Everyone said how well they played, and they did, but as with Finn Russell and Glasgow, players always look good with time and space. When you take time and space away from them, you don't just affect the ball carrier, you affect the timing and rhythm of the whole team.

'Johnny Sexton and Garry Ringrose had looked particularly good, but they'd had time. If you take away even one second, or a couple of metres, not only do you affect them but also those around them. So one key was to ensure A. J., Bundee and Robbie [Henshaw] pushed up hard. My system on defence is pretty organized and, similar to attack, makes the most of the talent we've got. An "in your face" defence is what those boys have.'

On the main pitch at the Sportsground, a group of 15 went with McPhillips to mimic the Leinster attack, and the rest stayed with Lam for a defensive drill. They then moved on to Ellis and Duffy for footwork and clear-out drills, before Lam brought them all together to run a drill on their defensive shape, both to counter Leinster's phase play and set plays.

Every session is videoed from high and close angles, mimicking a match, so they can move on quickly from one drill to the next. If there's a mistake, rather than discuss it on the training ground, this way it can be reviewed more accurately later. A full-scale game follows, which is as much as anything a blow-out. Akin to Joe Schmidt signing off an Irish session, Lam will use his whistle to transition from defence to attack and vice versa, in sets of two and three minutes, and with input from Bunce.

They then moved on to 'fundamentals' – specific drills with two-minute rotations that they've been doing all season. McPhillips worked on the first part of the contact and the clean out, Ellis on the tackles, and then Jimmy and Bell work on the 'plus-ones', i.e. the support players.

'These drills,' says Lam, 'are our bread and butter.'

They finished the session with exit drills, i.e. exits from their own territory, before a squad huddle and ten minutes of individualized skills.

The session had lasted for about an hour. It was now 3 p.m. Some players lingered on the pitch, mostly the kickers and Aki, who never wants to go home.

At about 3.15, the coaches assembled for a meeting along the corridor from the changing-room. This began with an update from head physio Garrett Coughlan regarding any niggles or injuries. Bunce talked about the training load and provided feedback on how the weights session went and any red flags or warning signs concerning players, before the coaches reviewed the training session.

Lam asked for feedback.

'Andre, tell me, are the boys sharp?'

'Yeah, everyone is. There's a really good feeling.'

Bell went through a couple of things he was happy with.

'Jimmy?'

'Yeah, good. A couple of the guys were maybe a little bit grumpy, but generally, yeah, I'm really happy.'

That confirmed to Lam how well he felt the session had gone. They talked about Thursday's session and what needed to be done.

'Let's just do what we normally do,' said Duffy, to uniform agreement.

'So,' says Lam, 'everything was cool.'

That night, Eric Elwood had 'a bit of news' for his wife Tara and their three children. For weeks, he had had a strong feeling Connacht were on to something and at the very least were going to reach the final, but he didn't want to tempt fate.

'I'm not an arrogant guy in any way. There were so many times I wanted to press the button for the flights just in case, because I had a good feeling. I've watched a lot of rugby and I said, "I'm telling you, Tara", but it's not in me. I couldn't do it.'

First thing at the Sportsground on Monday morning, Elwood booked the trip for himself and his family: a drive to Belfast on Thursday for the Friday-morning ferry to Scotland, a drive to Edinburgh, two nights in an Edinburgh hotel, the return ferry to Belfast and the drive back down to Galway on Sunday night.

He then had to spend the rest of that day and Tuesday in Dublin, during which Tara said to him over the phone, 'You can't go without Callum.'

'I had it booked, but I couldn't tell her because I wanted to tell her face to face. I wanted that "we're going to Disneyland" family moment.'

He drove home from Dublin on the Tuesday night, sat his family down and said, 'Bit of news. I want to tell you something . . . about this Pro12 final . . . we're all going!'

Cue the screams. Not only Callum and the girls, but Tara went wild too.

'They were leaping around the kitchen. To see their faces was fantastic.'

24

The Final Week – Wednesday and Thursday

Wednesday, as usual, was a down day for the players, although, like the coaches, some come to the Sportsground to do kicking practice with Andre Bell or skills work with Dave Ellis. Thursday was unusual in that it was a travel day, and the squad met up at 9 a.m.

Lam showed clips to start the review of Tuesday's training session, as ever beginning with 'good clips' followed by 'work-ons'. From there the squad went to the AstroTurf training pitch and jogged through some plays from scrums or line-outs on specific areas of the pitch. They always have a preordained sequence.

The forwards and backs broke up for line-outs and strike plays. On Tuesday, Duffy had asked Muldoon and other team leaders what they wanted to do in Thursday's forwards session. Everybody looked at each other. 'The same as we always do,' came the reply.

So the forwards did some mauling, then defended mauls, before Lam approached and suggested cutting back on contact. 'Everyone stood back initially,' recalls Muldoon, 'but then everyone did it with full contact. Nothing changed, even though it was a Cup final.'

The squad assembled again at 11 a.m. for a 50-minute training run. At the end, Lam reminded the players they would invariably come under pressure against Leinster.

'If we're under pressure, what do we do, boys? Trust our system, trust our system.'

Afterwards, he spoke to Ellis. Lam was worried that there was maybe a little too much laughter, that it could have been more intense and focused.

'Pat, I'll tell you what, I just see real confidence,' said Ellis.

'Good,' said Lam, reassured. That's the sort of feedback he wants from his coaches. They watch, they observe.

The squad broke up for weights and lunch, before re-assembling to take a bus from the Sportsground to Knock airport at 1 p.m.

'There were schoolkids on the side of the road cheering and applauding as our bus drove past,' says Loughney. 'I don't know how they all knew we'd be driving past or how long they'd been waiting there. Maybe they put it up on Facebook or something. But all along our route schoolkids were waving as we went past Claregalway, Ballyhaunis and Claremorris to Knock airport.'

More so than at any time during the previous 11 seasons, Loughney had the feeling that Connacht were representing their province. As part of his degree at the University of Limerick, he had completed a thesis on merchandizing in Connacht Rugby in the offices of the Sportsground. 'We had focus groups and one thing that came out of them was how much Connacht was identified with Galway. The other counties had felt left out. But now there's a big effort to provide buses on match days, which is easier for Saturday games. Friday-night games are a big obstacle to that. It's also down to Pat, and bringing us to, say, Leitrim and Roscommon, where we would never have trained before.'

With no other flights scheduled from Knock at that time, they had the airport to themselves.

Lam: 'That's one of the things I love about this squad: the way they travel. The relationships are so good and, especially since Krasnoyarsk, sitting in airports is no problem. You've got a group that play cards, a group that play this dice game, but no one is sitting by themselves. It's just interaction, interaction.'

However, to their pleasant surprise, around 50 schoolchildren from Claremorris Rugby Club dressed in Connacht gear and waving Connacht flags formed a guard of honour as they made their way on to the plane, exchanging high-fives and taking photographs along the way.

'It was a nice little preview of what would come,' recalls Lam.

Lam had decided they should travel on the Thursday to give the squad more time to settle in and relax. 'Our travel is different from everyone else's, with the bus trip to Knock, so I thought let's get all of that out of the way, and it was a really good move. We had a nice meal that night, guys just mingled and played their games and hung around. So come Friday we'd had a really good sleep and instead of a travel day we were already there.'

Yet some of Connacht's longer-serving players had reservations. 'Going over there on the Thursday, a lot of things were running through my mind,' says Loughney. 'Leinster were used to playing finals. We'd be in a hotel for two days. A few years before, we couldn't win an away game. I remember us setting a goal of winning two away games – in a season.'

Indeed, in Loughney's first six seasons as a Connacht player, from 2005–06 to 2010–11, even that modest target had been out of reach. Connacht played 58 away League games, winning four and losing 54. Some of the losing margins were of that ilk too. Connacht were not particularly good travellers.

In the 2008–09 and 2009–10 seasons, Connacht lost all 18 away games in the League. In the 2011–12 season, they finally won two in the same season for the first time, their opening trek to Treviso in September and their penultimate away game against the Dragons in March.

'There were pats on the back all round,' says Loughney. 'They'd tried loads of things. Eric, who was in charge at the time, kept asking, "What are we doing wrong?" We were doing well at home at the time. Was it the hotels? They changed the scheduling. They tried pool warm-ups during the day, because match-days were long.

'So these things all came back to me. "Is two days too long in a hotel before a game?" But because the Glasgow semi-final had been so tough, it was nice to relax and get time in the pool. We had the two physios over. We stayed in Leinster's hotel on the Thursday night before their arrival the next day, when we moved to our hotel.'

Muldoon also admits to being fearful when Lam informed him

they'd travel on the Thursday. 'I thought, "Oh God! A night in a hotel and a whole day's build-up? This could be a long week and put lads over the edge." But the week actually went quite quickly. The fact that Edinburgh was so busy with the marathon and the final, and we had to change hotels on the Friday morning, probably helped in a way, because we never really got settled in on that first night.

'During the week I spoke very little,' he adds. 'I talked to lads individually as opposed to "ra-ra-ra-ing it" during the week. Pat usually lets me sign off a session with a few words. It was always just small little details. "Let's make sure we know our detail. Let's not let the emotion get to us. They're used to this. We've got to make sure that we don't let the whole thing get to us." The big one I was hammering home all week was: "Don't play the game early in the week. Don't let it get to you early in the week." And then backing up what Pat had said for the last few weeks: "Let's play our game. Let's not be afraid to go out there and chuck the ball around." Ultimately, this is what got us here. Why would we deviate from the plan now?'

That Thursday night in the Village Hotel, Duffy held a forwards meeting. 'Jimmy had retired at 21, when he was a seriously promising player,' says Loughney. 'He talked about his career and recalled the things he regrets not doing, the things he didn't do to prepare for games better. "Just make sure you don't leave anything out that you might regret, anything that might make a difference." He added, "You're not going to hear much from me after tonight. You shouldn't have to hear much more from any of the coaches." He said he was there for anyone who wanted to chat with him between then and the final, how proud he was of what we'd achieved all season and reiterated his belief in our ability to beat them. He added that he wouldn't swap any of our pack for theirs.

'Jimmy doesn't like having long meetings. He'll go through one or two things to get his points across. In fact, he doesn't normally have meetings, so when he called it I was a bit surprised. But he was very relaxed and spoke from the heart. Everybody felt better coming out of that meeting.'

Dan McFarland had been Loughney's forwards coach from 2006

before moving on to Glasgow at the end of the 2014–15 season, and he sent Loughney an email after the semi-final wishing him the best in the final.

'Jimmy has a very different style from Dan, just as Pat is very different from Eric. There's never been a more passionate man about Connacht than Eric, and Dan was probably as passionate, even though he is an adopted Galwayman from England. When Dan gave a "psych-up" talk, it did the job for me every time. It would get the hairs on my neck up. And apart from working with Gert Smal on that Irish tour to New Zealand in 2012, Dan was all I had really known as a forwards coach until this season.

'Jimmy is a great guy for instilling positivity and confidence. There's no bullshit with him either. I wouldn't like to cross him. Many of the younger guys would have huge faith in him from his work with the academy. I see the way he reacts with them, and he gives them a bit more grief than the older lads, but at the same time they really respect him and feed off him.

'He really knows his plays. He sees everything and knows it inside out. He'd have watched every single Leinster scrum before that final. And he covers all facets of the forward play, line-outs and rucks or whatever.'

Loughney never sleeps that well for a few nights after a game, and the nights after that bruising semi-final were no different. He'd been around to his parents' house on the Saturday night for a few glasses of wine and a pizza, and they'd stayed up late. On the Monday and Tuesday evenings, he and Finn had been busy making plans for their wedding.

By Thursday in Edinburgh, he was looking forward to two nights of sound sleep.

25

The Final Week – Friday

Tiernan O'Halloran's parents, Aidan and Máire, have been following their son's career all the way through his Irish Schools and Under-18s, -19s and -20s days, and also with Connacht through the academy and since making his debut in 2009–10. But come the semi-final against Glasgow, they had no plans to attend the final in Edinburgh. 'We didn't want to tempt fate by booking anything,' says Aidan.

Once Connacht secured their place, however, plans were made and they decided to bring their two eldest, Cian and Evanne, and also meet up with two fellow travellers from Clifden, Eugene Casey, and Cyril Joyce. Given the extortionate prices of hotels in Edinburgh, they opted to take the Friday ferry from Belfast, stay in Glasgow for two nights, commuting by train to and from Edinburgh on match-day.

The O'Halloran roots are steeped in Connacht, and Aidan was president of the Connemara club in 2009, becoming the club's first president of the Connacht Branch in 2010–11. Tiernan, their youngest after Cian and Evanne, attended Garbally College for his Junior cycle, before switching to Roscrea College for his last three years, and played on their Senior Cup team for three seasons.

'There were times when he was difficult, like all children,' says his father. 'He's our youngest and was a bit of a rebel. He liked to have fun, but he also had the single-mindedness to push himself to get where he is today.'

That was now taking him and them to new territory – a first car ferry to a first final.

Meanwhile, earlier that Friday morning, the squad transferred to the Marriott Hotel, unpacking and checking into their rooms before lunch, and met at 1.30 for a review of the Thursday training session. Lam was ultra-positive about the 'understanding' and 'shape', just tweaking one or two things.

'Matty, I need you to hold your line here. A. J., just look out first, so Ringrose sees you, and then put the pass back on the inside.'

From the Marriott, they took the bus to Murrayfield for their Captain's Run at 2 p.m.

Having won the toss, Connacht had the home dressing-room, which is designed with the Scottish team in mind. 'I'd never been there, and it's pretty cool,' says Loughney. 'The lads brought their suits, so we could leave them there for after the game. Each cubicle has its own number, with a list of some of those players who have played in that position before. I meant to take a picture of it, but forgot. They're going to be upgrading our changing-rooms in the Sportsground and, like that, Pat wants the names of some of those who have worn the Connacht jersey over the years below each number.

'Unlike our pitch, which by now was like concrete, Murrayfield's is half 4G and half normal grass. That was good for me at scrum time. The week before against Glasgow, both my calves had started cramping. The pitch [at Murrayfield] was beautiful. Pat kept saying the venue and the pitch and the weather would suit us. Pitches may only differ by a metre or two, but this one was also wider. 'Edinburgh traditionally like to play a wide game, and I remember a lot of tough nights there as well. Five or six years ago, we lost to them by 40 or 50 points,' says Loughney, in reference to the 62–13 defeat in September 2009.

What's more, Connacht had won there with a bonus point the preceding March, whereas they had a dismal record against Leinster in both the RDS and the Aviva. 'I knew it would suit the boys,' says Loughney.

Normally, Connacht would not show much in a Captain's Run, especially away from the Sportsground. But Lam said, 'I don't think there'll be any Leinster people here, let's go for it.'

Loughney says it was 'a relaxed run-out', adding, 'We didn't show anything they wouldn't have seen in their analysis; we didn't do any of our new variations. But we went through our line-outs, and got all the subs in for a run.'

Normally, too, Lam would wear jeans and shoes to the Captain's Run and sit in the stands as a signal to the players that it's their turn now. His coaching is done. But as there was a pre-match media briefing, he wore his 'work clothes' – Connacht training gear.

Being back in the hotel by 3.30 p.m. made for a long evening. Loughney and J. P. Cooney walked down to a nearby shopping centre for a coffee. 'I get on really well with J. P. and props generally form a close bond. You'd go for a coffee with anybody in the squad. I have to get out of a hotel. Some lads like Browney never leave the hotel, either the day before or on match-day.'

Back in the hotel, as usual on the night before a game, Loughney went through all the line-outs and starter plays. Then he started to think of the final. 'I thought of all the internationals they have, and then I tried to stop thinking about it. I started to watch movies. I was rooming with Dave Heffernan. He's a good guy. A quiet guy. We chatted about different things but nothing major about the game.'

After dinner, Lam, Allnutt and McPhillips were the only ones amongst the management who took up an option to go to the movies. McPhillips was more in the mood for a comedy but was outvoted by Lam and Allnutt, who opted for X-Men. 'We wanted to see some action,' explains Lam. 'I wanted to zone out. So I was able to relax, have some popcorn and enjoy the movie.'

A few hours killed. Lam went back to his room, chilled out and slept well.

26

The Final Week – Saturday

When Pat Lam signed a new, two-year contract extension with Connacht in January 2015, Tim Allnutt's first comment to him was, 'Ah bugger, that means more running.'

Under Lam's watch, away match-days always start with a 7.30 a.m. management run, and the final was no different. Not 8 a.m. but 7.30 a.m. Lam is a cruel taskmaster, no doubt about it.

This practice dates back to his initial foray into coaching at the age of 35 with Auckland in the ITM Cup in 2004. He'd noticed that most of the management team went out drinking the night before away games.

'I didn't want to be the spoilsport and say, "Look, fellas, stop the drinking." So after that first season [with Auckland], one of the recommendations in my review was that on match-day we prepare as a management team and start the day off together. So at 7.30 you can run, walk, whatever you want to do, but basically the principle is you go out for fifteen minutes, everyone on the watch, and then you come back in.

'It's good team bonding. It's a good way to start the day, and straight away in Auckland I noticed that the management started going to bed earlier the night before games. And in Super Rugby you run in some great places, although in somewhere like Jo'burg we went to the gym.'

And so it has continued with Connacht. 'It's half an hour. You go out for fifteen, back in fifteen, so those who can't run, like Jimmy Duffy who has got a bad knee, can walk out fifteen, come back fifteen.'

On an overcast morning in Edinburgh, after the run, as normal, each member of the backroom team goes through their duties for the day. After returning to their rooms for a shower they meet up for breakfast. That's been Lam's match-day ritual since 2005.

Breakfast is from 8 a.m. until 10 a.m. For home games, Loughney likes to sleep through to 10 or 10.30 a.m., so as to make the day shorter. He has his 'little support team' of his brother and his dad, who cooks him breakfast, usually porridge followed by grilled bacon and eggs. On this day, he can't sleep any later than 9.45 before replicating his match-day breakfast.

At 11.30, the forwards go through a few line-outs, and the backs walk through a few plays in the grounds of the Marriott Hotel. This is followed by another match-day ritual: a passing game of forwards v backs, whereby they stand in two lines opposite each other and pass the ball back and forth. If a player drops the ball, or alternatively Lam deems the pass didn't allow for a fair catch, one or other player is out of the game. If a second player brings his hands forward to catch the ball, he is eliminated, and retreats to shout abuse at the opposition. The same if the receiver doesn't catch the ball. And if two go for it and neither catches the ball, they're both out of the game. And so on until one side is completely eliminated. 'There are loads of other rules,' says Loughney. 'You can't dummy.'

'I want to put it on record that the forwards beat the backs this season,' states Lam, scarcely concealing his bias as a former number 8. 'The backs maintain they let the forwards win that game while they score the tries.'

The forwards had also won the semi-final, meaning the backs have to win on the final morning to force a play-off. This they do, so Lam decrees that the backs nominate three forwards and the forwards vice versa for the play-off. The forwards pick Peter Robb, Niyi Adeolokun and Robbie Henshaw, and the backs choose J. P. Cooney, Jason Harris-Wright and Dave Heffernan.

Adeolokun was getting a tough time of it, recalls Loughney. 'Niyi is never particularly good at it, for whatever reason. He jumped in behind a bush so the lads wouldn't see him, but they dragged him out. It's funny, some guys you wouldn't expect to be good at it are unreal, and others you'd think would be good are not. No offence to Finlay Bealham, he wouldn't have the same skills set as Robbie, but he's really good at that game. Aly Muldowney is also very good at it.'

The backs celebrate loud and hard when they think they've won, only for Lam to judge that Henshaw's final pass was too high. The forwards are duly declared winners again.

'We've never roared so much,' says Loughney. 'I was thinking the lads were getting too worked up beforehand, but there was a nice relaxed mood throughout the day.'

Bringing their focus back to the game, as always Lam speaks about the referee, in this case Nigel Owens. He mentions Owens' status and how they can have total trust in the number-one referee.

'Leinster might have a go at him, but we'll stay off him and accept his decisions,' said Lam, adding, 'Look, fellas, we talk about distractions, so make sure you get all your ticketing and stuff done early and then stay out of the lobby. Get up to the team room or into your rooms. You still have your social time, but stay out of the lobby; there's a lot of supporters congregating there. If needs be, put your tickets in reception and get your families to pick them up from there.'

Music blares in the team room at the hotel as players drift in and out for strapping and massages. 'Everybody was keeping it fairly light-hearted. It wasn't too intense,' according to Loughney.

Of all the familiar messages on the board in the team room, one has particular resonance for Loughney. 'One of Pat's team talks during the season that really stood out for me was about having "no fear". I'm 11 years playing, but I don't know if you ever fully learn how to quell the nerves and not have little doubts and fears going into a game. But because Pat reminds us that we know everything we're doing, I've less fear nowadays.'

After lunch, Loughney goes to his room for an hour's sleep before taking a shower, turning the tap to cold for 20 seconds to waken up properly and then have a coffee in readiness for the team meeting. For his part, Lam goes back to his room to watch some Super Rugby and a player he is eyeing up as a possible signing.

The Marriott Hotel
3.50 p.m. – Connacht's team meeting

Lam doesn't like to read from notes at this meeting, preferring to speak from his heart on a particular theme. Before the semi-final, Ruane had shown Lam the video which accompanied Connacht's Strategic Plan, 'From Grassroots to Green Shirts'.

'My eyes started to water, and I said, "Willie, can I have that for the semi-final?" It was perfect for our last home game of the season.'

On this occasion, he talks about the specifics of their work on and off the ball. That's the secret to Connacht's game. Their work on the ball means nothing if they're not working off the ball. This applies to attack and defence, where the quality of their tackling is predicated by the speed with which they get back into shape.

Then he says, 'We know the outcome we want. We know the support that's going to be there. Just channel whatever it is that's going on around this game for each of you, put it in there. Put it in there. That will determine how fast we run, how quickly we get up off the ground, how hard we hit, how hard we run back to scramble. Fellas, this is a celebration of who we are. Let's go and show the world what we're about.'

The meeting is short and sharp. No more than five minutes. After that, they are given a police escort to Murrayfield.

The journey is quiet, most players tuning into their own musical choices. 'I'd usually listen to Arcade Fire or someone like that,' says Loughney, 'not your average psych-up songs. You can see Murrayfield from the main road just past the zoo, and there were already hundreds and hundreds of Connacht fans outside the pubs cheering our bus along. All the pubs had put up special Guinness tents. You realized a little more how big a deal this was going to be.'

The Connacht bus pulls up at the main entrance to the East Stand. All on board are taken aback by the volume of green assembled on each layer of the outside staircase.

'It was all green with a scattering of blue,' recalls Lam, astonished by what he was seeing, and then hearing an impassioned rendition of 'The Fields'.

'I could feel the water in my eyes,' says Lam, who was the first to step off the bus. 'It was like being in a coliseum. The fans were around us and above us, and we were hit by this wall of noise. My arm was shaking as I picked up my bag. I looked around and waved to people. I went in to the changing-room and put my bag down. I was really watery.'

Lam sits down, takes a deep breath and watches the rest of the squad coming through the door one by one. Like him, they all have their heads down and are saying nothing.

'The videos don't do it justice,' recalls Muldoon. 'It was phenomenal, the shiver that everyone got. I walked straight into the toilet, and it just so happened that Ronan Loughney and Andrew Browne followed me in, so it was the three long-serving Galway lads in there. It may have hit home more to us than some of the other lads. I could have walked straight out on the pitch for the kick-off without warming up or doing anything.'

Tiernan O'Halloran hadn't even been expecting the police escort to Murrayfield, much less the awaiting thousands. 'I had my headphones on, and I was listening to music full blast, but I could actually hear "The Fields Of Athenry" over the headphones, and I thought, "I have to experience this." I took the headphones off and let myself enjoy it for a couple of minutes. It made the hairs stand up on the back of my neck, and I was close to tears.

'It's a hard feeling to describe. It felt like this was going to be our day. I had to put the headphones back on and get back into game mode. I wish I'd videoed it. It made me cry before the biggest game of my life so far, and that was not ideal. When we got into the dressing-room, we all kind of looked at each other. No one really said anything, probably because nobody could talk. Now you could sense the nerves.'

Loughney's fiancée, Finn, asked him later that night what the highlight of his day had been. 'Obviously winning and meeting my parents afterwards were all highlights, but in all my time playing rugby I never experienced anything like that!

'As you got off the bus, it just seemed to be all Connacht supporters. I saw a video of it, but I don't think the video does it justice at all. I started welling up straight away. I was half looking for my bag, half trying to take it in. I quickly realized I'd better get inside. I remember talking to Andrew Browne afterwards, and he was the same. His eyes welled up.

'Inside the changing-room, I had to sit down for a second. Everybody was looking around as if to say, "Oh my God! That was nuts!" It was quiet. I was thinking that every Connacht supporter must be at this game. I had said to Browney, "I bet you there won't be that many people over. There's been a lot of hype about it, but it's so awkward and so expensive." It was only afterwards when you talked to people that you realized the lengths they went to. Never mind about us never forgetting it, they never will either. That weekend will live with them for ever too.'

Lam gives them two or three minutes to put their bags down before pulling them into a circle.

'Fellas, what we've just seen is what we were talking about. Channel it. Put it all into your game. That's what we're about. Look, the last thing I forgot to mention to you, boys, and this is what I said to my teams at Northampton and Newcastle, this is the last time we will all play together. Some of you will move on after this game, but in 20 years' time, when any two of you meet, you will be able to look each other in the eye, and you won't have to say anything. You'll smile, and all the memories will come flashing back.'

Lam had been reminded of this on a return visit to Newcastle in March to celebrate their 1998 Premiership win with a squad reunion, most of whom he hadn't seen in the intervening 18 years. 'Give me the look' was the catchphrase of the night. He tells the Connacht players of this and says, 'Get ready and do your stuff.'

They go through their normal pre-match routine. Lam chews the fat with Leo Cullen and his former Auckland player, Isa Nacewa, on the sidelines.

'You could sense lads were a bit nervous in the first couple of minutes of the warm-up,' recalls O'Halloran. 'There were one or two dropped balls, and lads were a bit quiet as well.'

Muldoon stops everything and calls them into a circle. He says, 'Lads, let's just keep doing what we've been doing all season. Keep the chat up. Keep the skills going. We're well able to pass!'

That worked, according to O'Halloran. 'Thankfully, within another couple of minutes, everybody got into a rhythm. It was a beautiful day. Perfect surface as well, which suited us.'

Loughney had his own distractions. 'I had forgotten my gumshield, which is serious enough. I was so annoyed with myself. For years I'd never worn one, but then I got used to it. When you go into contact, you virtually bite down on it. I thought, "This is a nightmare." Marty [Joyce], our bag man, had these €10 gumshields, which I was trying to make fit. It wasn't working. I tried to mould it a few times, but it didn't stick at all. I wore it for the warm-up, but after about five minutes I put it in my shorts. Then I was thinking, "If I get my two front teeth knocked out a week before my wedding, I'll be killed!" But I couldn't breathe properly with it. It kept falling on to my tongue. I ended up playing without it.'

Back in the dressing-room, Lam's final message is, 'Let's be alert. We don't get caught by quick taps. We don't get caught by quick throw-ins. Don't get caught by anything. Just be alert.' He steps outside the dressing-room a few minutes ahead of the players, leaving the final words to Muldoon. 'That's John's time, not my time.'

As the players go out on to the pitch, Lam hugs each of them individually, wishing them well, before calling the back three – O'Halloran, Adeolokun and Healy – aside.

He says, 'Lads, just let loose, have a go. The pitch is there for you. The weather is there for you. This is it. This is your day.'

Part of their game plan was that they knew Leinster were going to kick deep.

In Lam's first season, they had famously beaten Toulouse away, but the defeat at home a week later had been a bigger benchmark for him. 'All week for the return match we showed the videos. We trained all week on the basis that they weren't going to kick. We got to the game and they didn't do as we had trained; they kicked and they scored two tries through Maxime Médard in the first 25 minutes. It killed me.

'Everybody talks about the first Toulouse game, which we won. I often talk about the "second Toulouse". Our wingers, Niyi and Matty, now stand a lot deeper initially.

'So now I told them, "Just back your speed to move up to the line, but first keep an eye on Johnny [Sexton]. Because Johnny is very good. He's constantly looking. So if he's looking, wave to him. That will force him to play along the line." Bundee and Robbie then did a very good job in closing down the space.'

O'Halloran also recalls Lam name-checking the Leinster back three of the Kearney brothers and Luke Fitzgerald. 'Prove a point. Go out there and do what you do.'

This was true to form, according to O'Halloran. 'All season he's given us licence to have a go.'

For once, Muldoon's final words had passed Loughney by. 'Mul had a few more words. Don't ask me what he said. It's all a blur now. I went on to the pitch with tears in my eyes.

'We knew we had a minute's silence beforehand for Dev Toner's dad. It was so sad for Dev. I've known Dev a long time, ever since I played Irish Under-21s with him. I played Irish As and Ireland with him too. He's a really nice guy. I can't imagine how hard that was to deal with and then to miss out on the final as well.'

Loughney looks up into the crowd. He spots some of the wives and partners of teammates and knows that must be the area where Finn, his brothers and his parents are situated, but he can't locate them.

The O'Halloran gang, now numbering eight, including Tiernan's girlfriend Dana, have passes for a corporate box in the Connacht hospitality area, where they meet Eric Elwood, Willie Ruane, Robbie Henshaw's Uncle Dave, a former Buccaneers and Connacht prop, and former number 8 Noel Mannion. But the nerves are still beginning to kick in.

'I get nervous, but Máire gets more nervous,' says Aidan.

'I'm desperate,' she admits. 'I get nervous for all of them, particularly Tiernan, that he gets a knock or something like that. Oh my God, even at the Glasgow game I was so apprehensive about it all towards the end. At one point, I just sat down and started praying. Someone asked me, "Are you OK?" And I said, "I am, because I'm praying."'

Their worries date back to O'Halloran's promotion to a development contract and his senior debut at 19, when still quite slight in build. 'At that stage,' explains O'Halloran senior, 'he was rather skinny, and we were a bit worried about him getting hurt, but physically he developed very quickly, and I no longer worry as much. I still worry that he'll get a bad injury but less about his getting hurt. You watch every move he makes, and you know that Joe and his team are watching him as well, so you worry about him not doing what he should be doing!'

They have good seats, adjacent to the committee box and above the players' entrance.

The kick-off

Leinster reclaim the kick-off and come at Connacht in waves.

Lam was still climbing up to the coaches' box with the rest of the staff at that moment, 'But that's when we showed composure,' he recalls. 'We always stress that when we don't have the ball we don't panic. It's get into shape, get the ball back as quick as we can, and once we get it back, let's go. And that's what unfolded.'

Whereupon, Muldoon, of all people, knocks on.

'The one person you wouldn't expect to drop the ball, and he does,' says Lam. 'He had a wry smile on his face as if to say, "I don't drop these."'

Muldoon admits, 'We didn't start that great, and Leinster had the ball for seven or eight minutes, but then we worked it to Matt, and he found space in the right-hand side of their backfield.

'Everybody thinks we're not allowed to kick the ball. That's not true. A big turning point in the first half was that kick by Matt, and

Matt is consistently one of our best kickers, because he gets up the wing, and he's got a good left peg and just boots it down the field. By moving it wide, we draw up their winger and then it's a foot race, and we all know how quick Matt is.'

Covering across field, Luke Fitzgerald has no option but to concede an attacking line-out to Connacht. Healy's kick and chase also introduce the Connacht crowd into the game.

Running downfield, Muldoon is taken aback at the roar. 'I was running along with Tom, trying to get the line-out call. We all had to cuddle in to Aly to get the line-out call because of the explosion of noise. That had been their first chance to get in behind us. It's amazing how little moments like that can lift a team emotionally. It was pretty cool.'

Loughney, though, feels like he is watching much of that first half. It doesn't help that in the first few minutes he is hit in the head with what he thinks is a teammate's knee when clearing out a ruck. Loughney rejoins the defensive line, but in the next break of play the team doctor, Dr John O'Donnell, comes on to check him.

'I wasn't concussed, and I answered all the concussion questions, but I was dizzy, and the pace was frenetic. My dad is always honest with me, and afterwards I said to him, "Dad, I must have been walking at different points in that first 20 minutes?" He said, "You looked like you were rattled for the first ten minutes all right. I don't know whether it was that bang or the pace of the game."'

The Connacht skills coach Dave Ellis then shouts at Loughney during a break in play, 'Loughs, you're walking. You're walking.'

Loughney thinks, '"Ah, fuck you." That's the worst thing that anybody could say to you. But I mentioned that to a few of the other lads, and apparently he was saying it to some of the backs as well. I think everybody was out on their feet because it was just so fast.'

The scrums go pretty well for Connacht, although it is the one area that provides Leinster with some succour.

Loughney recalls, 'Myself and Tom had discussed what Mike Ross might try. We had a couple of dodgy ones, but to be fair to Nigel Owens he's not the best ref in the world for no reason. As a front-rower, I would have to look at a scrum from both sides before I could tell you what might have happened, and even then I wouldn't be 100 per cent sure sometimes. For a referee to make a decision from looking at one side is a ridiculous expectation, so I have sympathy for a ref trying to referee a scrum, and I don't think there are too many refs who are ex-props either. But Nigel re-set a couple, or if the ball was at the back he said, "Use it", as opposed to penalizing one team when it wasn't very clear. I remember talking to Tom, and we tried a few things and it got a little bit better.'

13 minutes
Tiernan O'Halloran try
Connacht 7 Leinster 0

True to Lam's licence to thrill and their own inclinations to run from deep, Healy instigates the counter-attack when gathering Eoin Reddan's box-kick on his own 22, running infield, cutting between Ben Te'o and Garry Ringrose, eluding Richardt Strauss before eventually being hauled down by Dave Kearney on Leinster's 10-metre line.

O'Halloran himself recalls, 'Heals did well to cover at the back and catch Reddser's kick on the full. We know how dangerous Heals can be on the counter-attack, and Bundee, Robbie and Mul worked back to help create a little space for him. He saw the space and took it, and beat a couple of defenders. Dave Kearney was straight over the ball in a jackal, and Mul made a brilliant clear-out.

'At the same time, Robbie reloaded from the middle to the wing. I was about to hit the ruck but thought, "Just stay out here and hope Mul will clear out that ruck", which he did, brilliantly. A one-man clear-out! Finlay Bealham threw the scrum-half pass to Bundee, and his quick hands gave me and Robbie a two-on-one against Rob Kearney, and it was just a simple dummy and go after that.'

When O'Halloran goes past Kearney on the inside, it is clear from 25 metres out that Fitzgerald cannot cover the space this time. Unless he falls over himself, O'Halloran knows he is going to score.

'After I threw the dummy and just about handed him off, I realized, "I'm in for a try here. Don't drop the ball." Robbie and Bundee were there to celebrate straight away. It was a special feeling.'

'Tiernan had struggled all week with his hamstring,' reveals Muldoon. 'If it was a regular season game, they probably wouldn't have played him. He's had a really good season, but he's been unlucky with injuries. He's matured an awful lot too this season. He was wild enough in the first couple of years, but he's seen the error of his ways. He has matured a lot.'

Aidan O'Halloran watched his son's try unfold in what seemed like slow motion. 'An incredible moment. It wasn't quite a two on one until he got away from Jamie, and then he had the ball in one hand initially and a small little bit of acceleration to take him away from Rob and through the gap. You could actually enjoy the last couple of seconds, whereas normally it all happens so quickly.'

'It was the most extraordinary feeling of elation and surprise,' admits O'Halloran's mother Máire. 'I suppose there was always the hope that he would score, but I didn't expect it so early or so powerfully. I just screeched.'

They were surrounded by fellow Connacht families and friends, O'Halloran's brother and sister Cian and Evanne, his girlfriend Dana, Robbie Henshaw's parents, Tony and Audrey, Peter Robb's parents, David and Maureen, Matt Healy's parents, Niyi Adeolokun's brother Laurence, as well as non-playing Connacht players – hugs, high-fives and thumbs up from everyone!

For 15 minutes or so, Connacht are breathtakingly good, like an amalgam of the All Blacks and Harlem Globetrotters.

Lam looks on contentedly. 'Watching the boys play in that first half, I could see them getting more and more confident, and it was like we were just on a training run. It really was.'

As A. J. MacGinty lines up his conversion of O'Halloran's try, Muldoon calls the players in and says, 'Let's score again straight off the kick-off. Let's kill them.'

He explains, 'For the last few months, it's been a motto of ours to go again after scoring. We'd learned, from earlier in the season, when we'd scored and then tried to play conservatively. In the last few months, after scoring a try we'd said, "Let's go for it" and tagged on another score within a minute or two. That can really deflate a team.

'We just ripped them apart, but I wasn't surprised. We genuinely hadn't put together a 40-minute performance yet this season, never mind 80 minutes. We always made little mistakes.'

Connacht are rampant now. Using the full width of the pitch, they make it look small as they stretch Leinster's defence to breaking point repeatedly. Leinster miss ten tackles in the first 20 minutes.

22 minutes
Niyi Adeolokun try
Connacht 12 Leinster 0

Reddan box-kicks again off a Leinster line-out on their 22. Again, Healy catches and counters by linking infield to O'Halloran, who runs crossfield, is tackled by Ben Te'o but offloads to Henshaw. Henshaw then steps back inside Ross Molony and Jordi Murphy before being tackled by Rhys Ruddock, but offloads back to O'Halloran, who was quick to his feet in support.

'Maybe in the past,' says O'Halloran, 'we didn't read off each other too well, but I always know with Bundee and Robbie they're going to look for the offload. So I tried to get up as quick as I could, because I knew Robbie would break a tackle as he always does.'

O'Halloran feints to kick. 'I was about to put the kick in, because I knew if Niyi was outside he's going to get there before anyone else, but then I heard Bundee calling for it, so I kinda did a basketball pass to Bundee over the top.'

Aki passes behind him when checking Garry Ringrose. Kieran Marmion gathers off one bounce and scoops the ball to Adeolokun.

'And then it was all down to Niyi really,' says O'Halloran.

Faced by Fitzgerald, Adeolokun chips him and runs past him. Adeolokun and Reddan are then running side by side as the ball comes down. Recalling his old football days on the streets of Ibadan in Nigeria, Adeolokun cushions a first-time volley before the ball hits the ground, catches it on the bounce and dives over the line in one smooth movement.

'Unbelievable piece of skill,' O'Halloran says. 'But that goes back to Pat in the build-up saying, "Have a go." And we'd been practising our offloading all year, every week in training, often out in the rain and hail on the back pitch at the Sportsground. But this was the perfect day, and it suited us.'

Adeolokun's game flowered in the second half of the season, a run of tries seeing his confidence grow by the week. 'He won't mind me saying this, but 12 months ago he would have been fourth or fifth choice and pushing for a contract,' says O'Halloran, 'but he worked hard, put on a lot of weight and did a lot of work on his "high ball". He asked a few of us to stay on after training and help him with that, and you could see him taking a few great high balls in the last few games of the season.

'The thing with Niyi is his confidence. He knew he had the pace, but most of the time he wouldn't have a go on the outside. He'd be a bit scared to go, and instead cut back in. Pat would say to him, "Niyi, you're faster than anyone here. Just run. Just run when you get the ball." And you can see that he has the confidence now after scoring a few tries. It's oozing out of him, and it's great to see. He's got stronger too. His tackling is incredible. Himself and A. J. have been unbelievable in defence.'

In the East Stand, Laurence Adeolokun is sitting a couple of seats away from the O'Hallorans. More high-fives all round. 'It was like a dream,' is how Máire O'Halloran describes it. 'That's what it was like.'

'You felt, when that happened, that "this is going to be our day",' says Aidan O'Halloran.

Half-time
Connacht 15 Leinster 0

'I've never been as glad to have a half-time break,' admits Loughney. 'I pride myself on my fitness, but in that first half I just couldn't get a second wind. I was absolutely exhausted. Normally at half-time you'd think, "That was tough, but there's plenty more in the tank here." But I was wrecked. So I drank energy gels and Powerades, and got as much water into me as I could, and changed my jersey.'

After letting them take on fluids, catch their breath and sit down, Lam has prepared video clips from his iPad. 'The beauty about Murrayfield is that they have a massive screen in the changing-room and a projector,' Lam recalls. 'This is where technology has really come on so much, because I found as a player, when you're tired sometimes you're not listening. But the pictures make everyone focus. And everything is around either confirming that we're on the right track or just [pointing out] a couple of little opportunities that we were missing.

'One message was about space, and highlighting the edges and where Leinster were when we went wide, and more importantly when we ran from our own half that they didn't have enough width because they had guys back. So we were hitting tight with Aly or Bundee, when actually what was on was a pass out the back door to then go wide. So, in our own half, keep expanding.

'The other [message] was [about] our chase at the breakdown. In general, it was really good, except one time, so that's one too many, when Ultan went on his own and no one was with him. The overall message was that Leinster were under severe pressure. "They can't live with the tempo, so let's ramp it up in the second half."'

But both Lam and the players say the key message at half-time came from Muldoon.

'They are talking in their changing-room about Northampton,' says the captain, in reference to Leinster recovering from a 22–6 half-time deficit in the 2011 Heineken Cup final against Northampton to win 33–22. 'That's what they're talking about. They believe they can come back. We need to take it to another level, raise the tempo up again.

'We've got 40 minutes to make history here. Whatever you have to do, just put it on the line. Put your body on the line. It will be worth it. If you're prepared to put your body on the line and get this win, there'll be nothing sweeter. Just don't give them the ball.'

Lam reaffirms this message by adding, 'Don't kick the ball away aimlessly.'

Upping the tempo further struck a chord with O'Halloran. 'We were very tired. After 25 to 30 minutes, I couldn't believe the tempo of the game. I thought it must be half-time. I was ready to go off. But we knew that if we were tired and attacking this much, they must be even worse.'

Away from the pitch, the O'Hallorans encounter only good will. Máire goes outside and meets two Glasgow men. 'They said, "We're here for Connacht. All the Scottish fans here are supporting Connacht."'

Likewise, her husband recalls, 'One of my best memories is of Leinster people, even at half-time, saying, "Your lead is well deserved." And I think most of the Leinster supporters would have been happy to see Connacht winning on the day.'

Second half
Straight away, Tiernan O'Halloran detects a change in Leinster's defensive line speed. In their pre-match analysis, they had identified that Leinster didn't push up that hard, allowing Connacht to carry to the gain line and get their passes away. But from the start of the second half, Leinster push up quicker to stop Connacht behind the gain line.

43 minutes
Sexton penalty
Connacht 15 Leinster 3
'At the start of the second half, Bundee tried to carry through the middle,' says Lam. 'He came out of the system. It went to Aly, and Bundee must have seen a gap and went for it, whereas it was actually on to go out the back and get it wide and away we go. Instead, he knocked the ball on. Scrum. And they got three points.'

Within two minutes of the restart, Leinster replenish their front row by bringing on Sean Cronin and Tadhg Furlong for Strauss and Ross. 'We knew Furlong would attack more aggressively from having watched him when he'd come on against Ulster a week before,' recalls Loughney.

'So first scrum, a penalty to them. That made it 15–3. "Fuck, I don't want to be the reason they get back into the game." We'd even

314

said at half-time, "Let's not allow their scrum to get them back into the game." We really needed to pin down the next one. We were definitely under pressure after that. Although we launched pretty successfully off our own ball, they had a serious pop off us on theirs. Another ref might have been a lot harsher against us.'

Now it's game on. Leinster come calling again, through multiple phases. Muldoon lines up a tackle on Hayden Triggs.

'I came around the corner and shouted, "Axe". I was going to go low. But he led with the ball and [Sean] Cronin was beside him. It's a risk, because it's near the 22, and if you miss he could be finding good leg drive. So I went low and at the last second rose up to have a go at the ball, and I managed to lift it out of his hands. It just happens.'

Marmion scoops up the loose ball and counters with a daring 40-metre break off the turnover. A week before, in the semi-final, Connacht had forced a turnover in the same position inside their 22 and the same player, Marmion, had kicked downfield. Lam had shown that clip to Monday morning's Alignment Group and asked, 'What's on?'

'Maybe it was to move it,' admitted Marmion.

'So it was fantastic that Marmo, one week later, recognized the same situation and, bang, had a go, backed himself and broke out. That broke their momentum in the second half,' says Lam.

Off the recycle, Tom McCartney sidesteps first Jack McGrath to break through the blue defensive line and then, astonishingly, does the same to Fitzgerald.

Later, Loughney and co. would slag McCartney that he must have torn his hamstring, as he had done when scoring his first try for Connacht in the home win over Treviso in November. He'd torn the hamstring five metres from the line but carried on to score and was then sidelined for two months.

This time, Loughney is on his inside and tries to keep up with him. 'But it was like he went up three gears. Everybody was out on their feet, because it was a long passage of play beforehand. I was sure he'd get there before the lads piled in for the clear-out.'

57 minutes
Matt Healy try
Connacht 20 Leinster 3

From the ensuing scrum and a few rucks later, MacGinty chips deftly into an unguarded Leinster backfield for the predator Healy to score his 13th try of the season.

'Matt called that,' reveals Lam, 'and I've got plenty of footage from training. Matty calls that all the time on A. J. or Jack Carty. It's something that Andre [Bell] brought in too. He has a game in which you have to kick at certain times, that the backs play where it's pass, pass, pass and then you have to kick, but you have to kick to get it back. That's why you see so many of those little grubbers or chip-kicks through, as well as the long ones.

'After Bundee's chip through for Niyi's try in the semi-final against Glasgow, I told Andre that he could take a lot of the credit for that. "Show me any footage at all of Bundee in Super Rugby putting through a grubber? It's only since he's been here." And that's the confidence and the skill that come from training.'

Muldoon looks at the clock after the try, thinking, 'These next seven or eight minutes are huge. We can't concede.' And for the next seven or eight minutes, all Connacht can do is tackle as Leinster own the ball. When Muldoon casts a glance at the match clock again, it has only reached 60 minutes. Only three minutes have elapsed.

'Don't kick the ball away if we have it,' he tells his teammates during a break in play. 'Look after the ball.'

But then Connacht go off script and start kicking the ball away.

Watching from the coaches' box, Lam becomes more annoyed. He has an innate dislike of chip-kicks inside his own team's half. When he sees MacGinty chip from his own 22, he looks at his teammates' body language. It is all wrong. Only Sean O'Brien, on for Eoin McKeon at half-time, chases.

'Because there weren't three or four chasing it, someone didn't call that properly or someone called it selfishly. But ultimately it was the wrong choice. Leinster got the ball back. So they were getting back into the game when I truly believe we could have put another 14 points on them by keeping the ball, because they were under severe pressure and we lost that opportunity.

'I remember at the post-match press conference someone asked me, "Are you happy?" I said, "Oh, yeah, I'm happy that we won and all that." But my "review side" was thinking, "Jeeze, we could have nailed them."

'I got really frustrated. I hit the bench a few times and I don't normally lose my cool, but I did there because at 20–3 we really should have rammed it home. I always like to place myself in their [the opposition's] shoes. If I'm down by 20 points to three with 20 minutes to go, "Then give us the ball. At least we've got nothing to lose, so we have to go for it." But if they have to tackle and defend, it breaks their spirit. And that's what I wanted.

'When we got a penalty, I sent down the message, "Get it into the corner." I don't normally interrupt those [on-field] decisions, but I knew A. J. MacGinty didn't have the distance into that breeze. I thought the message would reach them because there was an injury break, and then I saw the signal for the shot [at goal], and I thought, "No!" Because all we're going to do is take the tempo out of it. We needed to keep the ball and go again.'

68 minutes
Sean Cronin try, Johnny Sexton conversion
Connacht 20 Leinster 10

With O'Halloran flat out on the ground receiving treatment, and Connacht effectively playing with 14 men, Leinster stretch them continuously before Cronin runs in the try.

Loughney recalls, 'Watching the highlights, I actually thought I'd been moving slower. I felt like I was watching it unfold and couldn't do anything about it, and we were short with Tiernan down as well. But they moved it well and scored. As Johnny Sexton was lining up the conversion and we were behind the goal, both my calves had started to cramp.'

Loughney ultimately put in a 68-minute shift before being

replaced by Rodney Ah You. 'My energy levels were a little depleted at that stage!'

As he trudges off, Loughney is pessimistic. 'I had a really bad feeling. Maybe it was because of stuff that had happened to us over the years, more so last season and the year before. We lost a load of games from being in front with five or ten minutes to go. For four or five minutes, as they had possession and came at us, I couldn't watch. "If they score again here now, this is going to be the worst last five minutes ever!"'

Back on the pitch, O'Halloran has clashed heads with Te'o and is being treated for suspected concussion while play continues to a cacophony of boos from the Connacht supporters.

Máire O'Halloran says, 'I was stricken, and because of the way people were milling around Tiernan I couldn't see anything. So I thought, "He's not moving." It was like the previous game when the two Glasgow lads clashed heads. I was just so apprehensive, wondering, "What's taking so long?" It looked awful, the wallop he got. I felt it in my insides.'

'I think in fairness to Nigel [Owens] he saw a bit of movement,' says Aidan. 'He obviously got some indication from the medical staff that Tiernan was going to be OK.'

O'Halloran completes his pitchside concussion assessment and is back on the field within three minutes. His father admits, 'I was amazed, and relieved, to see him coming on as quickly as that. Talking to him afterwards, he said it was nothing and that the bang was mostly to the cheekbone. He knew he was going to be OK.'

As Sexton lines up his conversion, Muldoon calls in his players. 'Lads, if we want to win this game, we've got to score again. If we try and defend for 12 minutes, we're dead. We're dead.'

From the kick-off, Luke McGrath box-kicks, and Dave Kearney wins the ball in the air.

Muldoon thinks, 'Uh-oh, this could be trouble.'

By this stage, John Cooney has replaced Marmion at scrum-half but lasts only five minutes, meaning Healy goes to scrum-half, his formative position until his early 20s.

'We ended up defending for a while,' says Muldoon. 'I won a turn-over and I was lying at the bottom of a ruck and I could see Matt shaping to kick. "Noooooooo, don't kick it." Tom was close to me and he shouted, "Don't fucking kick it." Ahh. Too late. We had to defend for another two or three minutes.'

On the pitch, straight after the game, Healy comes up to Lam and says, 'I should have run that, shouldn't I?'

'Too right, buddy,' says Lam. 'Too right. You were probably think-ing more as a winger than a half-back.'

Entering the last six minutes, Leinster attack through a few phases off a line-out. Furlong makes a half-break but, in offloading out of a tackle by MacGinty, he's also tackled by the flying Rodney Ah You, deflecting the ball on to the foot of Jordi Murphy for a turnover. This time Connacht keep the ball, and Nigel Owens penalizes Fitzgerald at a ruck inside halfway for kicking the ball from an offside position.

Muldoon recalls, 'The second we got the penalty, I looked at A. J. and said, "We're mauling this." The thought process was: "We have the ball. They want the ball. Let's try and slow the game down, make them angry." Lo and behold, we've a penalty within three seconds, let's play out the advantage, but then we knock the ball on at the back, and Nigel comes back for the penalty. You look at the clock and the maul had started at around 75 minutes, and it's now 76 minutes.

'I looked at Aly and said, "Game over." He looked back at me and said, "Huh?" He hadn't heard me. "What's the call?" he said. I said, "We're mauling it again. We want another penalty just to piss them off." I've been in that position where Leinster were, and you get frus-trated and give away a penalty. So we mauled it and ended up with a scrum under the posts.

'I remember looking up and it was 78 minutes something. Sean O'Brien high-fived me and said, "We've fucking won it!" I said the same back to him. "We've fucking won it." And apparently at the same time Aly and Browney had slapped each other and said the same. They saw us celebrating. They'd had their moment, we'd had ours, and then one of them said, "C'mon, we haven't fucking won it yet."'

Loughney is standing alongside Dillane on the sidelines. Sitting has long since ceased to be an option. 'When we went to the corner, I was thinking, "Jeeze, it's going to be very hard for them to come back from here." I knew we had it. It was nearly too much. I was overwhelmed.'

Lam feels they have it won with about five minutes to go. 'But I didn't like to show it because things can happen.' He comes down to the sidelines around the 77-minute mark. 'I could sense the guys celebrating, but I said, "No, wait. Remember Gloucester." I didn't want to get carried away yet. The box can become very claustrophobic, and near the end I realized I had no more control over this; no more messages were going to be worth it. I wanted to get down there and get my own space.'

Full time
Connacht 20 Leinster 10

Loughney admits he didn't know what to do. 'I got a hug off Ultan straight away. And then, as I was trying to go on to the pitch, both my calves and my leg were giving way. It's all a bit of a blur then. I remember meeting Mul, though. He was hugging everyone, and that felt special. I'd soldiered with him for 11 years.'

Standing on the pitch, trading hugs with teammates, looking up into the crowd and seeing his family and then climbing on to the podium for the trophy presentation were the best moments Loughney ever experienced on a rugby field. Better even than facing the All Blacks and the haka with Ireland.

'No doubt. Being a part of it for so long with Connacht and then the way fortune favoured me with selection and Denis getting injured, and feeling that I'd had an influence or played my part. It's the people that you're representing as well, and looking at friends and family in the crowd, you do feel as if you're actually representing them.

'I saw J. P. Cooney with his granny, and she's in her seventies. I saw Sean O'Brien with his family. Sean's dad was very heavily involved with Galwegians and passed away about four years ago. Sean was with his two sisters and his mum, and all four of them were crying.

'Playing for Ireland and going over to New Zealand was an amazing experience, and I would still love to have more caps, but it was just fleeting, and I was a very small part of that squad. I was there off the back of Mike Ross being injured and got an opportunity and played 30 to 35 minutes maybe. But there's been nothing like winning that trophy with Connacht.'

On the sidelines, Lam is lifted from behind into the air. It is 'Big Jimmy Duffy'. He walks on to the pitch, hugging anyone and everyone in green and saying well done. 'Then I saw Mul,' says Lam. 'That was a longer hug! He's an inspirational captain. He plays in the position I played in. A captain like myself. I was just thinking how far this guy has travelled and how much he has grown and developed as well. This was so massive for him. I tried to get the boys into a huddle, but then I got pulled away for Sky TV.'

As well as his girlfriend and mum, and brothers Ivan and Conor, Muldoon's sister Olivia also travelled to Edinburgh for the final, as did plenty of friends.

'I recognized a lot of faces in the crowd, and my phone literally didn't stop for the next couple of days with people saying they'd travelled over. I just had to send a generic message thanking everyone. I just couldn't get back to everybody individually.'

Cue the trophy presentation.

Lam, standing to the side of the podium, notices all the suited, non-playing members of the squad were there as well and thinks, 'What's going on here?'

'I tried to go around to the back of the stage, and the pyrotechnical boys said, "Don't go there, you'll get blown up." So I asked the boys in suits, "Fellas, what's happening?" One of them said, "Oh, they told us to stay over here."'

As the players climb on to the podium, a lady who is seemingly running this part of the day explains to Lam, 'Oh, we just want to do the [match-day] 23. The other boys can go up after the initial trophy presentation.'

Lam says, 'Ah no, that's not what it's about.'

He turns to the players in suits. 'Just get up on the stage.'

As he says this, he sees Muldoon waving them over.

'I wanted everyone in there,' explains Lam. 'There's no point in just putting up the 23. That doesn't represent who we are.'

'Lifting the cup was very special,' says Muldoon, 'and you see the emotion and happiness of everyone there. But it doesn't hit home until you see it back once or twice.'

As the fireworks go off, Lam looks into the crowd, searching for his wife, Stephanie, and kids. She sees him and blows him a kiss. 'The kids were there with her, and that was special for me.'

The squad step off the podium to pose for group photographs. Lam declines to join in. This is their moment, and he prefers to watch.

The entire squad and most of the backroom staff conduct their lap of honour. 'Going around the field, you start seeing so many people you know in the crowd,' says Lam. 'Watching everything, taking in the fans and the players, was like an out-of-body experience. Just so proud.

'The TG4 Rugby presenter Máire Treasa Ní Dhubhghaill gave me a hug and said she wanted a photo with me and the rest of the TG4 crew because my Irish was so good!'

Lam also stops to speak with Nacewa, whom he had coached at the Auckland Blues. 'Jeeze,' says Nacewa, 'a lot of that stuff looks like what we were doing at Auckland.'

Lam smiles and nods in agreement.

'He had seen some of the same plays, and I said to him, "It's not just the plays, it's the brotherhood." And he knew exactly what I meant.'

Tiernan O'Halloran struggles to describe his feelings. 'I got emotional straight away, just seeing the supporters there, and what it meant to so many people. Mul as well. It was brilliant for Mul. I was delighted for him. For him to have that moment, and someone like Ronan Loughney, and Browney as well.

'When I saw my dad, I got a bit choked up. It was great to have my family there to experience it with them as well. It was my first time winning any silverware in rugby and to do it with my home province, on an occasion like that, was just extra special.

'Half of Galway seemed to be there. As well as my mum, dad, brother, sister and my girlfriend, Dana, so was my auntie and a lot of friends. I saw one of my best friends, Padraig Cuddy, in the crowd.'

Alex Payne, who is chatting pitchside with Gregor Townsend and Shane Horgan, pulls Henshaw over for a quick post-match interview.

Lam watched it over the next couple of days and says, 'That is the real Robbie Henshaw. That is straight from the heart. That is the country boy, the family boy.'

Henshaw subsequently threw his boots into the crowd, and two supporters wore a boot apiece while celebrating in the Grassmarket area of Edinburgh that night. One of them got Henshaw to sign them for a charity auction.

During the endgame, there is the same realization in the stands that this is to be Connacht's day. Aidan O'Halloran says, 'With two minutes to go, I said, "There is no way Leinster are going to get two scores." We were attacking anyway.'

By now the O'Halloran gang and all around them are standing up.

'The hugging started just before full-time,' Aidan O'Halloran admits.

'And the tears,' adds Máire.

'So then it was down to pitchside,' recalls Aidan. 'We reached where the security guys were and explained, "Our son is playing." But no way could I get on the field. Eventually Barry McCann, one of the Connacht staff, had an access badge which he kindly gave to me. I'll be forever grateful to him.

'The guys were on their lap of honour, and I know most of them from going to matches over the years and from being president for a few years as well. I was looking around to see where Tiernan was. He was last, of course, as he normally is. He was having selfies taken.

'But he is very good, especially with the kids, after any game in the Sportsground. He's always the last in because he'll stop for anyone. We have one photograph with him, in which he has his medal in his mouth!

'I just said to him, "You were outstanding. What a day." What more can you say? He was euphoric. I don't think I've ever seen him happier. It was a special, special day, and he's come a long way in his journey. The last couple of years have been really, really tough for him.' Indeed, the previous season Tiernan had only started seven League games, and nine the season before.

But all that was forgotten in the celebrations of the win. 'Nothing to touch it,' admits Aidan O'Halloran.

'Yeah,' agrees Máire. 'Incredible. Yeah.'

Máire, Evanne, Cian and Dana had climbed down a few rows, and after the squad had completed their lap of honour Tiernan looked towards the stand. 'Then, finally, he saw us,' recalls Máire, 'and the excitement from him in those moments was lovely. That meant everything.' Máire and Dana managed to work their way through the crowd for a quick hug.

Lam tries to keep the post-match dressing-room 'really tight' for only management and players. The 23 players in the match-day squad have received their medals, and everybody involved would eventually have one, but they have another 17 to dispense there and then. So those who were leaving Connacht at the end of the season are presented with their medals: Jason Harris-Wright, Fionn Carr, Conor Finn, Ian Porter, George Naoupu and Api Pewhairangi, as well as their doctor, Donal 'Ginger' O'Beirne, who is retiring.

'Then I just said my words,' adds Lam. 'How proud I was and how we had talked about it being a celebration, and I said they had done that and everyone had contributed. I thanked everyone and passed it over to John. He was very emotional, again expressing how proud he was and thanking everybody. And, as we'd won, we got into our circle and sang "The Fields Of Athenry". That was a big version. After that, it was off to do media.'

His media duties fulfilled, Lam turns on his phone. Plenty of missed calls, notably from Stephanie. He goes on to the main pitch but can't find them, eventually making contact by phone. His wife and kids are amongst the thousands of Connacht fans outside waiting to serenade the players. Lam sees them and brings them through. He hugs each of them and leads them into the changing-room for a photo with the trophy.

Bethany has photos taken with Aki and Henshaw, before the five Lams pose with the trophy. One for the house. 'Then I said goodbye to them, because I wasn't going to see them until around midnight on Monday. They were staying with Dan McFarland and his family.

'There were only a few of us there, so I had a chance to shower, and by then it was time to get on the bus. The boys were starting to sing, and I thought, "This is going to be interesting", because Tim Allnutt was beginning to stress a little as we'd been trying to find all the boys and the gear.'

Muldoon emerges from the dressing-room to go outside and look for Loran and his family, as he couldn't reach her on his phone. The team bus is surrounded still by hordes of celebrating Connacht fans, including family and friends. The first person he sees coming towards him, head down, is Elwood, trying to hold back his emotions but not succeeding. And when he embraces Muldoon, the captain's emotions give way too. 'I don't think we said anything to each other for a minute or two.'

Muldoon invites Elwood and his son Callum into the dressing-room. Elwood at first declines.

'"You put as much into this as anyone else. Come on inside,"' Muldoon insists. With Callum also cajoling his father to do so, Elwood relents and comes into the dressing-room.

O'Halloran was one of the first to give Elwood another big bear hug.

'"That's for you as well. You've put so much work into this province."

'You could see how emotional he was, and it was great to see him and Mul embrace. It's guys like that who have given this province so much. The same is true of Gavin Duffy. I met him in the airport. Gav looked after me and mentored me for a long time at both wing and full-back.'

Elwood, for one, was never in doubt. 'I knew we were going to win! I had a couple of beers before the match with people, and they were saying, "What do you think?" I was like, "Lads, enjoy it! We're going to win today." Because I knew once we got there we'd win. I'd seen these guys play all year. They had had bad starts; they had had good starts – it doesn't bother them. And they grow and grow and get stronger and stronger in every single game.

'We had a dream start, and even after the first try I just felt good. So that was one pleasing thing. Once we were there, I was going to enjoy the day, and if I'm going to enjoy the day, everybody was coming with me. Hence the five of us went.

'Getting there was the hard bit. I was so confident on the day just out of how the lads played all year, and then for my own family to be there and to see their faces was amazing! And then to see and meet people I hadn't seen in years who I know are true Connacht supporters was brilliant. And then the crowd! Oh my God! For our first final, there was always going to be a lot of Connacht people there, but the noise and the singing and the colour was special.

'What a season! What a journey! Callum has seen it at ten. Other boys and girls have seen it at five or six. Some of us had to wait a bit longer! But it's always worth the wait.'

Back at Murrayfield, the supporters sing as the Connacht bus drives away for their flight home, while on board Aki does his chant.

Thousands of Connacht and Leinster fans alike are already in Edinburgh airport, bound for flights home to Ireland. The Connacht fans are ecstatic, Leinster's generous in defeat, shaking the players' hands and saying, 'Well done, we're delighted for you and the way you've been playing.'

'That was pretty cool,' recalls Muldoon. 'A lot of the lads were finally meeting their partners and families for the first time that day. It was only then that I really got to chat with Lorna.'

There, Allnutt hands the trophy to Loughney and says, 'You look after that.' His pride in being the guardian of the trophy through the airport almost literally weighs him down.

'My arms started cramping up. It weighs a ton, and I was swapping it over and back between each arm.'

In Edinburgh duty-free, he meets Finn for the first time that day. So he places the trophy beside Muldoon for anyone who wants to pose for a photograph with the captain.

'Finn had been as nervous as I was all week. I think she wanted to get it over with, whether we won or lost, but now the win had set the week up perfectly.'

The O'Hallorans have passes for the post-match reception inside Murrayfield, where they meet fellow parents Tim and Jackie, Craig Ronaldson's parents, and James and Linda, James Connolly's parents. From there, they have access to a room set aside for the players and briefly meet Tiernan.

'Evanne got a photograph taken with Bundee before they headed for the airport and we got the last train out of Edinburgh, at 11.30,' says Aidan O'Halloran. 'So we didn't lose out on the occasion by staying in Glasgow. We had the entire day in Edinburgh from 10.30 in the morning until 11.30 at night.'

Their carriage is full of singing Connacht fans making the same journey, along with a few Scots. 'Of course yer man was leading them,' Máire says of her husband. '"The Galway Girl". "The Fields Of Athenry". "The West's Awake". The entire carriage was singing.'

Aidan adds, 'So many Connacht people ended up staying in Glasgow because of the [Edinburgh] marathon, which was a bit of a disaster, but the atmosphere was incredible.

'It's funny, we were speaking with Mike O'Grady from Kirwan's Lane [restaurant] in Galway, and he had watched the match from home and come into town on Saturday evening. He said the pubs were pretty quiet, that it was actually subdued enough, and he reckoned it was because most of the people who would normally be out celebrating had found their way to Scotland by hook or by crook.'

The squad's flight home to Knock

'I hate flying,' admits Loughney, 'and the plane journey was crazy. Bundee was doing his thing, and the lads were banging everything. That was erupting every few minutes. We had the trophy strapped in on a seat near the front, and there was a serious queue for the toilets for the entire flight; it was only 40 minutes! Then, as we were coming in to land, someone fainted, so we had to circle Knock for an additional few minutes.'

Consequently, Connacht's charter flight, a Titan Airways flight 122, a Boeing 737–300 jet, lands late at 12.51 a.m.

Lam: 'We were tired now, but everyone was happy. Someone jumped on the plane to say, "There are thousands here. We're going to let all the passengers off and the team stay on board. TV cameras are here, so then we want John and Pat to lead the team off the plane with the trophy. We will escort you to a stage and then to a bus that will take you back down to Galway."

'They led us to a back door, and as soon as it opened you could hear the crowd. We were brought to a half-open truck that was the stage.'

Blinded by the lights, Lam reckons there were at least a couple of thousand there. In thanking everyone, Lam name-checks the five counties of Connacht: 'Sligo, Leitrim, Roscommon, Galway and . . . MAY-O!' That goes down well. Muldoon speaks too, before Lam introduces each player individually.

Then Muldoon leads the team in 'The Fields Of Athenry'. The crowd respond with wild cheering and chant 'Conn-acht, Conn-acht.'

After an unscheduled hour in Knock, two buses take the squad back to Galway: the players on one bus, and management and partners on the other.

Lam: 'As soon as we came out of Knock airport, at the first roundabout, there was a huge fire.

'What the heck is that?'

'Oh, they're bonfires, to celebrate weddings and occasions like that,' he was told.

'Seriously? OK, cool.'

The main road is lined with cars and people tooting horns and cheering, and more bonfires. Going through Milltown, someone on the bus shouts, 'Look, it's a wedding party.'

'It was about 3 a.m.,' says Lam, 'and there was a bride in her dress, and men in their suits, all cheering "Conn-acht, Conn-acht". It was awesome.'

It completes a particularly emotional week for Jimmy Duffy. Tim Allnutt had given him a couple of pitchside passes that he was able to then pass on to Orla and Joseph. This meant they could join the lap of honour. 'I was in bits when he ran out; that kind of set me off. Of course, all Joseph wanted was to see Bundee and then the fireworks.

'Then there were the bonfires on the way home from Knock. The young fella was asleep in my arms on the bus. It was lovely, and when I sat down at home that night and looked at the phone there were 100 and something texts, and 40 something WhatsApp messages, and I don't know how many emails. It was just bizarre, because I mightn't get that in a year to be honest! Fellas I was in school or college with, friends and family. Certain things would set you off again, a text from a cousin or something. So I spent about two days crying. There were more tears than at a One Direction concert!'

Muldoon could appreciate the fans' arduous travel itineraries as well as anyone. 'My mum's sister had to go to Belfast to get a flight. My brother flew to Newcastle. My missus, Lorna, was in America doing a course with Failte Ireland as part of her work in sales and commercial in the Salthill Hotel, and she had to change her flight in order to meet up with my brothers in Newcastle. They had hired a car to go from Newcastle. Allowing for whatever sleep she could grab on the plane, she was basically up for over 40 hours! She had to do her course in the morning from 8 a.m. New York time [which is five hours behind], drag her bag to her course, leave the course just before it finished, go to JFK, take a flight from JFK at lunchtime in New York, to land in Dublin at around 5 a.m., then fly from Dublin to Newcastle, and then drive from Newcastle to Edinburgh.

'When we came back to our hotel after our little walk around in the morning, she and my brothers had just arrived. So when we got back to Galway, Lorna said, "Ah, I'm going to go home." I was like, "No, you're not going home anywhere. You're coming with us into town for an hour or two." I think we got home at around seven o'clock in the morning, and we took that photo of us with the trophy just as we were going to sleep. It was quite funny. It had been a long old day or two for her.'

Indeed, the night isn't done for most of them.

On reaching the Sportsground, they drop off their gear. Simon Heaslip, a member of Connacht's Professional Games Board, has opened up the Blue Note for those who want to continue celebrating.

'It's a small bar, and it was perfect,' says Lam, 'just the players, wives, girlfriends, management and all the staff. Nice and intimate. I was sitting there, soaking it all in. Some guys decided to go home but most came in. There must have been around 50 of us.

'At one point I was looking up thinking, "This is a very bright pub," and it was the sun beaming through the windows. So myself, Tim, John Muldoon and Lorna jumped in a taxi. We dropped John and Lorna off first, then Tim. Approaching home, I saw all these signs saying, "Well done, Pat, well done Connacht". All my neighbours had put up signs. I got home and crashed.'

Reflecting on the reception at Knock, Tiernan O'Halloran says, 'It was unbelievable. You'd have thought a lot of the kids would be in bed, or should be in bed. We had a rendition of "The Fields Of Athenry". It was emotional seeing what it meant to so many people. I had to pinch myself when I went to bed. "Did all of that really happen?" This was living the dream.

'There were bonfires the whole way back to Galway. When we got there at about 3.30 in the morning, there were still people singing and cheering. We had a good lock-in. It was good to have a few pints with the lads, to enjoy it with the people we won it with, and our loved ones.'

'I was nearly too tired to even drink,' admits Loughney. 'I didn't need alcohol, really, but the Blue Note was where I got to talk to my parents, because they had to leave straight after the game. I got to bring in the trophy, I don't know how. When I came in, my parents and my brother were just inside. My dad started crying straight away, and then I started crying. It was just mad. We got a few nice photos of the four of us and the trophy. After that, there was just too much to take in. We were there until around 4 o'clock. Then Finn and I strolled home, as we just live up the road on the Crescent in town. Actually, it was starting to get bright, so it might have been later than four!'

27

The Sunday Homecoming

Pat Lam set his alarm for midday in order to be in good time for the triumphant Homecoming and open-top bus parade through the streets of Galway. The squad were to be in the Sportsground by 3.30, but he wanted time to watch a recording of the final. In his rush out the door for Thursday's travel day, he'd forgotten to press the 'record' button at home.

Some of his neighbours – 'good neighbours, good people' is how he describes them – were outside, and he chatted for a while as photographs were taken with the victorious coach.

Loughney's day had already started, and a pretty nice start it was too. At 11 a.m., his buddy and groomsman, Henry Daly, called over with his girlfriend, Gail, holding a bottle of champagne. Along with Finn, the four of them sat on the balcony and sipped their bubbly as they went through photos from the day before.

Loughney's mum, Ann, arrived to give him a lift into town for the reception. Some Gardaí were manning a barrier blocking access to the Sportsground, whereupon Loughney held up his medal which he had draped around his neck. That worked.

At the Sportsground, there were, he says, 'a few ropey heads', adding, 'I drank about five bottles of water before they brought us out to the bus.'

In a post-match interview, Loughney had described the final week as the best of his life. At the Sportsground, Lam spoke privately to

Loughney. 'You can be proud of what you've done, and for the next week you can call it the best week of your life. But after next Saturday, you can say that will be the best week of your life.'

Another reason for Lam's early arrival in the Sportsground was to see which players arrived in good shape. They began drifting in, in various degrees of hangovers and even sobriety, some wearing hats and/or sunglasses. When they were all there, he addressed them briefly.

'Here's the deal, boys. All the alcohol stays here and all the hats come off. There are heaps of children, heaps of kids. Enjoy yourselves, but we'll all come back later on.'

They duly sharpened themselves up and filed on to the bus. Initially they had to sit down, as the bus travelled quite quickly up the Headford Road towards the starting point at the Town Hall Theatre in Courthouse Square.

Car horns tooted and people waved. As they approached the town centre, the bus had to slow down, such was the crowd congestion. Coming around the corner from the top of Headford Road, they could hear the increasing din. The streets were thick with people, thousands upon thousands of them. They stood up for a better view.

'Oh my gosh! Wowwww. Look at the crowd,' exclaimed Lam.

'We knew there would be a lot of people, but I never expected that many. As we started to go up Shop Street, they were waving, singing and shouting; the boys are singing, "Champion-es, Champion-es!" and "The Fields Of Athenry". And from Shop Street down to the town centre, the entire road was crowded. Then you looked towards Eyre Square, where we were going. It was phenomenal. The boys were loving it, absolutely lapping it up.'

On the Friday, Muldoon had asked Allnutt if any reception was planned should Connacht win the final.

'Oh yeah, we will have something on Sunday at three or four o'clock,' Allnutt answered.

Muldoon said, 'Tim, if we win, yeah, of course we'll do something, but if we lose I wouldn't really want to be doing something. The last thing I want to do is go around in an open-top bus with no trophy or have a reception. No, f*** that.'

Some Gardaí on duty reckoned there may have been 10,000 to 15,000 lining the streets of Galway for the 45-minute bus ride from the Town Hall Theatre, via St Francis Street, Eglinton Street, Williamsgate Street and on to Eyre Square North, Eyre Square East, turning on to Forster Street and then via College Road to the Sportsground.

Muldoon admits, 'It really only hit home when we hopped up on the bus in Galway and went the long way around to the Sportsground. You could see how everyone was so proud and happy, all our families and all those who made such an effort to get to Edinburgh. On the Wednesday, my sister asked me, "Oh, will there be anything if you win?" and I was like, "Jesus, none of you will be back for it if we win." And I said to one or two of the lads that if we won, there will be no one in Galway on the Sunday.

'When we got on to the bus and started through town, the next thing thousands began following behind. I didn't think there were enough rugby supporters for that size of crowd the next day, but evidently there were. In the meantime, we were all getting texts from friends. "We're sorry we're missing it. We're only leaving Edinburgh now." And some supporters only got back on the Monday or Tuesday, so it was quite surreal to see so many rugby fans around.'

At the exact time the bus parade officially began, the O'Halloran gang of six had taken the 3.30 p.m. ferry back to Belfast, having stopped in Girvan for some lunch. Hence, like so many thousands more heading back by planes, trains and automobiles, they missed the victory parade in Galway.

On the ferry, they met a couple of supporters from Athlone who showed them photos from their mobiles of the scenes in Galway with the caption 'Wish You Were Here'.

On the open-top bus, while most had converged towards the front and were singing lustily, Muldoon and a few of the more experienced players – Loughney, O'Halloran, Browne, Muldowney, Bealham, McCartney and George Naoupu – drifted towards the back. These were players Muldoon had soldiered with for years, the exception being Bealham. 'Finlay is only 24, but he's part of our lunch crew,' explains Muldoon.

For Muldoon, the previous day had been too much of an emotional whirlpool, too intense altogether, to really consider the scale of their achievement. Now he could do so.

'I was at the back of the bus thinking, "This is pretty fucking cool." I was beside Browney and Loughs, who are probably the two longest serving along with me and Georgey. It got me thinking about this whole journey. Of course part of me always thought we could do this, but now that we were actually here, having done it, I was thinking, "I never thought this day would come." Looking down at the thousands walking behind the bus chanting, it felt unreal.

'I had admitted in the post-match press conference that I had been very jealous of Leinster and Munster. I'd been happy for them and happy for Irish rugby, but there's always that egotistical part of you which thinks, "When is my day going to come?" Or, "When is our day going to come?" It was nice to finally have our day.'

Lorna had been slagging him the night before and that day.

'Are you going to stand in every photo with everyone?' she asked him.

He answered, 'Probably!'

'Growing up, I watched rugby, but I wasn't an avid supporter of rugby, and I think it's going to do an awful lot for the province and inspire an awful lot of young lads. Connacht have been crying out for a bit of success in something, and I'm sure a lot of kids will be picking up rugby balls, which is great, because while the game has grown massively, nothing helps it grow like success. Ireland's successes have been brilliant for the last few years, but I think Connacht's winning the League will have a bigger effect on kids. I hope it does.'

Though only 25, O'Halloran is also a relative veteran, having first trained with the academy when he was 16 and having made a try-scoring debut in the Challenge Cup in October 2009.

O'Halloran turned to his long-standing teammates. 'Lads, this is unbelievable. Let's enjoy this. Let's never forget this.'

Looking back, he adds, 'As a kid, I'd always dreamed of playing for Connacht, but to win a trophy with Connacht and have that homecoming was beyond belief. All the shops' staff were on the streets. Thousands walked behind the bus and clapped and cheered and sang all the way to the Sportsground. I had photos; I was tweeting it. Then, to have the whole of the back pitch packed with fans. Incredible. Incredible.'

Photographing those moments was too much of an effort for Loughney. 'I was trying to take photos, but then I thought, "I just want to take it in and not worry about photos." Up by Forster Street, there were people as far as you could see.'

The bus snaked slowly through the crowds already assembled in the Sportsground, followed by the thousands behind, for the players to alight and assemble again in the gym. From there they walked behind the barriers to the stage, set up at the far end of the back pitch, to face the supporters.

Lam addressed the crowd. 'We've seen many times on the field when the going has got tough, and it has got tough this year. What makes the boys dig deep is the people whom we represent. We understand what we play for. We understand what we represent, and I think for the guys it is quite emotional to see everyone here today, as well as all those who can't be here because they're still making their way, by planes, trains and ferries, to get back home again. But this is for everybody, and again we'd just thank you so much for coming out. *Go raibh maith agaibh*!'

Then it was over to 'Mr Connacht himself, John Muldoon'.

'I'm stuck for words, for two days in a row! When we left Edinburgh last night, we thought every man, woman and child in Connacht were left over there, and to come out today to see the amount of people that are here, to see the amount of people that had bonfires last night, everything is just absolutely phenomenal.

'I speak for myself and everyone on the stage tonight, the amount of messages of support, from family members and supporters, everyone that's supported us and come up in the wind and rain and everything over the years, this makes it all worthwhile. This is absolutely phenomenal. It's very humbling to be here, in front of so many, the people who've worn the jersey before us and familiar faces in the crowd and last night. The amount of young people here that will go on to wear Connacht jerseys, and there's a lot of those behind me who will wear Irish and Connacht jerseys in years to come. I've said it before and I'll say it again: we've got to start looking forward at Connacht Rugby. It's not about what we've done in the past. It's what's going to come, and with the people that are up here what's coming is a bright, bright future, and I'm just going to say one very last thing: thanks to everyone for coming out today, last night, throughout the year. We will see you all in September. We . . . have a title to defend!'

Cue the day's biggest roar.

Lam again introduced every single member of the playing squad and backroom team, mentioning their positions or role and where they came from. Well, all bar one or two who hadn't lasted this particular pace. Bundee Aki was still in An Púcán, and so, despite the crowd's imploring chants of 'Bun-dee, Bun-dee', there was to be no Bun-dee.

'All right – Bundee,' said Lam, calming them down. 'As you know, last night we played pretty hard. As you also know, Bundee plays pretty hard, and then, when we got home to Galway at about 3.30, the boys were taken to a place where they had some time together, and some of us have made it here and there's a couple that haven't! So let's make a big shout out for Bundee Aki!' He also excused the injured duo of Denis Buckley and Nathan White, who were at home.

Lam then asked a slightly hoarse Loughney to kick-start yet another rendition of 'The Fields' as an encore of sorts. The players filed away slowly, signing autographs and posing for photographs as they made their way back to the gym. Eventually, Muldoon, Loughney and O'Halloran were the last three left. The security guard said 'I'll drive ye into town' and dropped them into the Dáil Bar.

Connacht's second most-capped player, Michael Swift, was there, having driven from Dublin to be part of the celebrations. This win was also for players like him, Johnny O'Connor and many, many others who had soldiered through the tough years. For Loughney, it brought to mind Lam's pre-match talk about 'that look' in 20 years' time.

'I remember our underage coach, Joe Gorham, saying the same to me about our Connacht Youths team,' recalls Loughney. 'And I still meet guys from that team, who were a really tight-knit squad as well. I actually got texts off a few of them in the past week. The hooker on that Youths team was one of my groomsmen. I was the number 8. So I can only imagine what it will be like for us.

'Even then, that Youths team lost to Ulster after beating Leinster and Munster, and I was part of a Galwegians team that won a Connacht final, but apart from that I hadn't won anything in rugby. I don't think I still could have believed it until we had actually lifted the trophy.

'I didn't allow myself to think about it, because I didn't want to curse it or allow myself to think about something that might never happen. Now that it has, I think it might lead to us having a different level of confidence. Not arrogance, but confidence, because there'll always be a modesty within this squad. But as you saw with Leinster, when you win one trophy it can change the mindset within a club or province. As Mul said, we've a trophy to defend. For the first time ever.

'When others left, like Mike McCarthy or Mick Kearney, I appreciated that they had an ambition to win something. "What's in it for me?" My thought process was that I'd love to win something but realistically I probably wouldn't win something with Connacht. That is the way I would have been thinking up until this season. Even at the end of last season, I thought it would take four or five years of that kind of improvement each year to actually win a final; it's such a huge thing to win a final. For us, getting up to mid table or even making top five would have been like winning something. Yeah, I'm just unbelievably grateful to be part of it.'

And for him and the other Connacht stalwarts especially, it simply could never have been as meaningful to win the Pro12, or any trophy, with anyone else.

Whereas most of the squad rejoined Aki in An Púcán, Loughney, O'Halloran and Muldoon hooked up with Muldowney, McCartney and all the management in the Dáil Bar. Lam wanted all those players in An Púcán to enjoy themselves without seeing him.

The Dáil's owner, John Mannion, had a table upstairs for Lam, Ruane, Allnutt, McPhillips, Duffy, masseur Robbie Fox and Marty Joyce, their logistics manager. They had dinner, steaks all round, before joining everyone else downstairs for a few drinks with the senior players, wives, parents, girlfriends and supporters.

For Lam, it was a pleasantly relaxed finale to the weekend. 'I got to talk to people. It wasn't shouting or loud. Then myself and Tim agreed that we were in the same boat. If we stayed any longer, we were going to stay there all night. So myself, Tim, Willie and Conor shared a taxi home at around 11ish.'

As for the Elwood clan, they were home in bed by 11 p.m. on the Sunday night. Missing the homecoming was a relatively minor inconvenience for their former out-half and coach. 'I was fortunate enough in that I've done a lot of good things in rugby. I've had great experiences. I've played for my country and played in World Cups, but Connacht winning the Pro12 is right up there.

'You can couple that with getting married, and the birth of three kids, but, genuinely, for all I've done in rugby, to be there as a Connacht person and supporter, to experience the journey, the road trip, the ferry, meeting old and new friends, and old faces and people who are a lot longer in the tooth than I, and to see Connacht win on that day against Leinster, and even the journey of having it in a different country, and even the weather was special. It was conducive to how Connacht wanted to play all season! Things happen for a reason!'

Meanwhile, having arrived in Belfast at 6 p.m., the O'Halloran gang of six drove as far as Newry for a bite to eat, and then on to Dublin to drop off Cian and Evanne. Aidan and Máire then called into his mum's house in Moate. She had stopped watching the game when Tiernan had gone down injured, before learning, to her relief, he had returned to the pitch and that Connacht had won.

The O'Hallorans eventually reached home in Clifden at about 1 a.m. Some odyssey. Some weekend. Some memories.

Epilogue

Monday, 30 May

Allnutt picked Lam up at his house at 9 a.m. and drove them into town. En route, they listened to playbacks from the weekend on Galway Bay FM.

'I started to get a little emotional,' admits Lam.

Walking into the Huntsman Inn for breakfast, they were greeted with a standing ovation. Supporters insisted on vacating Lam and Allnutt's normal table.

'That was a good start to the day,' says Lam.

They drove up the road to their offices in the Sportsground 'to do a few bits and pieces', which entailed Lam sitting down and watching the final again properly. 'Instead of watching it as a fan, I thought, "Ooh, we could have done this better or we could have done that better." Or, "That was good. Loved that." And when you know that you've raised an awareness in a player – you've seen a player do something not quite right, you have a plan to fix it, he works on it and when you see it come to fruition – it's just so satisfying. That's why I say there are no mistakes; there's only learnings. And that's why we coach.'

He went out to his car, which had been there overnight, and drove home. The sun was shining. He tidied up the detached five-bedroom house in readiness for his family arriving late that night.

'Then I just chilled out in the back garden with a glass of wine.'

He looked across at the green farmland facing his garden. No radio. No video. No TV. Nobody around. Not a sound, except for the birds singing. 'Yeah,' he thought, reflecting on a whirl of memories from the weekend. 'That was awesome. Just letting it all sink in and realizing that was special.

'Even when I won the Heineken Cup with Northampton, or the championship with Newcastle, we were full of international players. Newcastle had never won the League before and Northampton hadn't won a major trophy in 120 years. We were both under-achievers, but we had plenty of internationals.

'Winning the ITM Cup with Auckland in 2005 and 2007 was big, but they were like Leinster. They were expected to win. This one here, when I look back and reflect, we had the smallest squad, with the smallest budget, the lowest number of international players, and seventh had been our best finish – never in the top six. That's unbelievable. And it just shows you that when there's a vision and real clarity in what you're doing, and people are willing to work and there's a belief, you can do anything in a team sport and in a great sport like rugby. And it's not only given the players real belief, it's given me real belief as a coach.'

Yet he knows there also has to be a legacy. This cannot be a one-off.

The previous day, Lam had been struck by all the young kids who had turned out at the Sportsground. He had shaken hands and chatted with kid after kid, pretty much all wearing replica Connacht jerseys.

'Do you play rugby?'

'Yeah, I play rugby.' Or, 'No, but I'm going to play rugby.'

'Who are you going to play for?'

'I'm going to play for Connacht.'

'And are you going to play for Ireland?'

'Yeah, I'm going to play for Ireland.'

When Lam returned to the Sportsground on Monday, he knocked on Elwood's office door. Connacht, Lam told him, had to tap into this feel-good factor. If Elwood needed anything from the professional team, he was to tell Lam, and vice versa. This well of goodwill had to be used and fostered. Otherwise it can just as easily fade away. Lam has seen it before.

When Auckland first won the Ranfurly Shield under Lam's watch, he immediately sought to take the trophy into schools and clubs, and this Pro12 success will intensify his efforts to take Connacht around their province. A first trek to Clifden and a return visit to Belmullet are uppermost in his plans, albeit visits to clubs and schools cannot be done in the flush of this triumph due to the summer holidays.

Working in tandem with Elwood is key. Wherever and whenever Elwood wants the squad to call into a school or club in the province, Lam will do his best to make that happen. Inspiring more kids in Connacht to take up the game will be the legacy. Then it's down to the underage coaching, which is another major focus for Elwood.

'I know the coach has a massive responsibility,' says Lam. 'I can improve or kill things real fast by what I do. The bottom line is that the experience has to be an enjoyable one for young kids.

'All we've done, with our coaching group at Connacht, is help to ensure we've all had a wonderful experience. The boys have come to me and said, "That was one of the most enjoyable experiences I've had." That should be the same for the Under-6s and Under-8s, that they come away from a season saying, "Oh, I loved that! I loved that! I want to go back!" Because if a coach is shouting at them, the kid will say, "I don't want to go back." And that's the key responsibility for anyone coaching rugby in the west of Ireland and rugby in general.'

Another coach was cleaning up his desk in the Sportsground that Monday. The three-year journey and tumultuous finale had left an indelible imprint on Dave Ellis, in every sense.

'This ranks right up with forming that Pirates club in Darwin, because at Connacht we've progressed to a totally different level. We have something of a zero-to-hero type complex. We've helped bring a lot of new history to a club who really wanted to improve. We've done so well, but we're still pretty much the same people, and I'll never forget what we've done here. I've even got it tattooed on my leg, for God's sake.'

Indeed, there it is, above his ankle: 'Pro12 winners!'

'It meant that much. I did it the day after the game. I don't cele-brate like the other guys any more. I'm older now. I don't drink the booze I used to drink. I don't need to be noisy or go to a nightclub. But it still means a bloody lot to me. I've never had a feeling to compare with winning that final. When the crowd went nuts in the stadium, you felt like you'd actually done something. You'd made a lot of other people happy.'

Within 48 hours of the final, the squad had broken up, some already heading away on their travels. The non-internationals had a five-week break before returning for the first day of pre-season on 27 June, whereas the seven players who would be part of Ireland's tour to South Africa would return on 25 July, affording them four weeks' holidays.

Lam would allow himself all of ten days away with Steph and the kids, spending seven days just outside of Cambrils in Spain and a fur-ther three days in Barcelona.

That gave him two more weeks to make plans for the 2016–17 season. On the Tuesday after the final, Lam drove into the Sports-ground and knocked on Elwood's door one more time, poked his head in and went inside. Another handshake. Another embrace.

Elwood had been up and in the gym at 6.30 a.m. for a run. He still, as he puts it, 'does a bit'.

'That was special, kid,' Elwood said to him, and they chatted for a while, again looking ahead to next season.

'Look, enjoy June,' said Elwood by way of conclusion, 'because it's going to fly by, and then the real work starts.'

'I know,' said Lam. 'I know.'

Acknowledgements

This book wouldn't have been even remotely possible without the help of a host of people.

Firstly, many thanks to everyone in the entire Connacht Rugby organization, not least for first doing what they did so memorably on the pitch and then for trusting me with this project.

In particular, thanks to Willie Ruane for his loyalty, and then, in no particular order, to Pat Lam, Tim Allnutt, Eric Elwood, John Muldoon, Louise Creedon, Jimmy Duffy, Ronan Loughney, Dave Ellis, Jake Heenan, Bundee Aki, Tiernan, Aidan and Máire O'Halloran, Nigel Carolan, Matt Healy, Niyi Adeolokun and all the others who gave of their time so freely and could not have been more cooperative.

Ditto Warren Gatland, Michael Bradley and Billy Glynn.

To Eoin McHugh of Transworld Ireland, for his unstinting support and advice, and to Ailsa Bathgate for her thorough editing. It was a pleasure working with you both.

A huge thanks to Shay Livingstone for his friendship, hospitality and help, as well as Sarah and all the staff in the Connacht Hotel, and also to Ian and all the staff in the Huntsman Inn, an alternative interview room and office to the Sportsground.

To the many places where I was allowed to work on this book, not least to Patrick, Lisa, Peppe, Andy, Eric and Conor in Patrick's Café in Ballsbridge. To Gerry, Ian, Ciara, Paul, Danny, Haixia, Matt and Raj in Mulligans of Sandymount. To Jim, Louise, Carolina, Andre, Lochlann, Stella and Shona in the Gables in Foxrock. To Alan, Martin, the two Darrens, Owen, Martin and John in the Hairy Lemon, and to Ronan in Counter Culture, and to Dave and Lisa in Griffin's of Clifden. Thanks for the hours and hours of desk space, Wi-Fi, good coffee, food and occasional libation.

Thanks to the great AK, to Ciaran Smyth, Steve Ryan and Billy Stickland. To the Leinster press officer Marcus Ó'Buachalla, and also to Adam Redmond, Pro12 press officer, and Murray Kinsella for sorting out my web problems, and to David Carroll and everyone at the *Irish Times* – with a special word of thanks to Kevin O'Sullivan, Malachy Logan, Noel O'Reilly and Keith Duggan.

Most of all, sincerest thanks again to the team: Petria, Yseult, Evan and Marian, without whom this definitely wouldn't have been possible.

Picture Acknowledgements

With the exception of two photos kindly supplied by Connacht Rugby, all other photos in the picture sections have been sourced from Inpho Photography.

Section one

Page 1: Connacht squad of the late 1990s: courtesy of Connacht Rugby; Warren Gatland, Connacht coach © Patrick Bolger / INPHO 00007579.

Page 2: Conor McGuinness. Connacht v Northampton 11/10/1997 © Lorraine O'Sullivan / INPHO 00008413; (L–R) Brian O'Byrne, Gerry Thornley, Billy Mulcahy and Willie Ruane. A break in the south of France during the 1997 EPCR campaign: courtesy of Connacht Rugby; Nigel Carolan. Connacht v Racing Club 7/11/1998 © Lorraine O'Sullivan / INPHO 00806296.

Page 3: Friends of Connacht march on Baggot Street 23/01/2003 © Morgan Treacy / INPHO 00086310; Danno Heaslip (Friends of Connacht Rugby) leads Cassandra Deegan, Michael Farrell and Mark Rapple into IRFU headquarters to deliver a letter of protest. Also pictured is Tom Conlon (Joint President Buccaneers RFC) 23/01/20013 © Morgan Treacy / INPHO 00086311.

Page 4: Connacht coach Michael Bradley talks to the team ahead of a Celtic League game 28/11/2004 © Morgan Treacy / INPHO 00136903; Michael Bradley with Eric Elwood 4/9/2004 © Patrick Bolger / INPHO 00130517.

Page 5: Connacht's Michael Swift with Tani Fuga of Harlequins. Parker Pen Challenge Cup Semi-Final First Leg 11/4/2004 © Morgan Treacy / INPHO 00115899; Gavin Duffy with support from Brian Tuohy in Connacht's Magners League game on 4/3/2011 © Cathal Noonan / INPHO 00498158; Connacht's Fionn Carr gets away from Ray Ofisa of Rovigo. European Challenge Cup 12/12/2008 © James Crombie / INPHO 00314705.

Page 6: Eric Elwood. Connacht v Northampton 11/10/1997 © Lorraine O'Sullivan / INPHO 00008409; Eric Elwood. Connacht 13/11/1997 © Lorraine O'Sullivan / INPHO 00008450; Eric Elwood leaves the pitch after his last home game. Connacht v Neath-Swansea Ospreys, Celtic League 10/4/2005 © Andrew Paton / INPHO 00144513.

Page 7: Connacht CEO Gerry Kelly with newly appointed coach Eric Elwood at press conference on 3/3/2010 © Mike Shaughnessy / INPHO 00411451; Connacht coach Eric Elwood with Edinburgh coach Michael Bradley after the RaboDirect PRO12 game 24/2/2012 © Morgan Treacy / INPHO 00583947; Connacht's head coach Eric Elwood with family including children Laura, Rachel and Callum and wife Tara after the RaboDirect PRO12 match on 3/5/2013 © Billy Stickland / INPHO 00693526.

Page 8: Connacht coaches past and present Michael Bradley, Warren Gatland and Eric Elwood (with then CEO Gerry Kelly) at the Magners League Annual Awards Dinner 23/8/2010 © Billy Stickland / INPHO 00454111; IRFU president John Hussey hands over the seal of office to the new 125th president Billy Glynn of Connacht 20/7/2012 © Dan Sheridan / INPHO 00614969.

Section two

Page 1: Connacht's George Naoupu is tackled by Toulouse's Thierry Dusautoir. Heineken Cup 8/12/2013 © Billy Stickland / INPHO 00757391; Michael Swift and John Muldoon celebrate after the match. Toulouse v Connacht, Heineken Cup 8/12/2013 © Billy Stickland / INPHO 00757495; Connacht's head coach Pat Lam after the Toulouse v Connacht match 8/12/2013 © Billy Stickland / INPHO 00757507.

Page 2: Connacht players Aly Muldowney, Finlay Bealham, John Muldoon, George Naoupu and Ian Porter in Krasnoyarsk, Russia 12/11/2015 © James Crombie / INPHO 00983580; Connacht's Bundee Aki and Iurii Kushnarev of Enisei-STM. European Rugby Challenge Cup Round 1, Krasnoyarsk, Russia 14/11/2015 © James Crombie / INPHO 01026297; A. J. MacGinty cold after the Enisei-STM v Connacht game. Krasnoyarsk, Russia 14/11/2015 © James Crombie / INPHO 01026430; Connacht's Finlay Bealham, Bundee Aki, Shane Delahunt, Ian Porter, John Muldoon, Denis Buckley and Aly Muldowney trying to keep warm while looking on in the closing stages of the Enisei-STM v Connacht game. European Rugby Challenge Cup Round 1, Krasnoyarsk, Russia 14/11/2015 © James Crombie / INPHO 00993150.

Page 3: Connacht's and Ireland's Kieran Marmion, Nathan White, Finlay Bealham, Ultan Dillane and Robbie Henshaw. Ireland v Italy, RBS 6 Nations Championship Round 4, Aviva Stadium, Dublin 12/3/2016 © Dan Sheridan / INPHO 01020398; Launch of Connacht Rugby Vision & Strategy 2016–2020, Aviva Stadium, Dublin 18/5/2016. (L–R): Domestic Rugby Manager Eric Elwood, Connacht Rugby Academy Manager Nigel Carolan, CEO Willie Ruane and Head Coach Pat Lam © James Crombie / INPHO 01062638.

Page 4: Glasgow's forwards coach Dan McFarland and Connacht Skills coach Dave Ellis. Guinness PRO12, Sportsground, Galway 7/5/2016 © James Crombie / INPHO 01062318; Jake Heenan of Connacht is tackled by Glasgow's D'Arcy Rae. Guinness PRO12 Play-Off, the Sportsground, Galway 21/5/2016 © James Crombie / INPHO 01063663; Connacht's Niyi Adeolokun runs in for a try. Connacht v Glasgow Warriors, Guinness PRO12 Play-Off, the Sportsground, Galway 21/5/2016 © Billy Stickland / INPHO 01063615; Aly Muldowney celebrates with his son Arlan at the end of the match. Guinness PRO12 Play-Off, the Sportsground, Galway 21/5/2016 © Billy Stickland / INPHO 01063692.

Page 5: Connacht's Ultan Dillane with Dave Kearney and Richard Strauss of Leinster. Guinness PRO12 Final, BT Murrayfield, Edinburgh, Scotland 28/5/2016 © Dan Sheridan / INPHO 01066966; Connacht's Tiernan O'Halloran beats Rob Kearney of Leinster to score a try. Guinness PRO12 Final, BT Murrayfield, Edinburgh, Scotland 28/5/2016 © Dan Sheridan / INPHO 01066955; Connacht's Bundee Aki and Richard Strauss of Leinster. Guinness PRO12 Final, BT Murrayfield, Edinburgh, Scotland 28/5/2016 © James Crombie / INPHO 01067005.

Page 6: Connacht's Tom McCartney. Guinness PRO12 Final BT Murrayfield Edinburgh 28/5/2016 © Billy Stickland / INPHO 01067938; Niyi Adeolokun beats Eoin Reddan of Leinster to score a try. Guinness PRO12 Final, BT Murrayfield, Edinburgh, Scotland 28/5/2016 © Dan Sheridan / INPHO 01066953; Matt Healy celebrates scoring Connacht's third try. Guinness PRO12 Final, BT Murrayfield, Edinburgh, Scotland 28/5/2016 © James Crombie / INPHO 01067076.

PICTURE ACKNOWLEDGEMENTS

Page 7: Tiernan O'Halloran and Ronan Loughney after the game. Guinness PRO12 Final, BT Murrayfield, Edinburgh, Scotland 28/5/2016 © James Crombie / INPHO 01068160; Connacht's captain John Muldoon celebrates with Eric Elwood. Guinness PRO12 Final, BT Murrayfield, Edinburgh, Scotland 28/5/2016 © James Crombie / INPHO 01067188; The Connacht team celebrate. Guinness PRO12 Final, BT Murrayfield, Edinburgh, Scotland 28/5/2016 © James Crombie / INPHO 01067157.

Page 8: Connacht's Skills Coach Dave Ellis, Backs Coach Andre Bell, Head Coach Pat Lam, Team Manager Tim Allnutt, CEO Willie Ruane, Forwards Coach Jimmy Duffy and Head Performance Analyst Conor McPhillips in the dressing room after the Guinness PRO12 Final, BT Murrayfield, Edinburgh, Scotland 28/5/2016 ©INPHO/James Crombie / 01068271; Head Coach Pat Lam and John Muldoon. Connacht Rugby Team Homecoming, Galway 29/5/2016 © James Crombie / INPHO 01067466.

Index

INDEX

ABOUT THE AUTHOR

Gerry Thornley has been the rugby correspondent of the *Irish Times* since 1997 and is a regular contributor and rugby analyst on both television and radio. He is the award winning author of *Trevor Brennan: Heart and Soul*, which won the William Hill Irish Sports Book of the Year in 2007 and the Irish Book Awards Sports Book of the Year in 2008. His other books include the bestselling *Ronan O'Gara: Unguarded* (2013) and, with Peter Stringer, *Pulling the Strings* (2015) which was shortlisted for the Irish Book Awards Sports Book of the Year.